The Laws of Style

*Sartorial Excellence for the
Professional Gentleman*

DOUGLAS HAND

Illustrated by Rodrigo Saldaña

Cover design by Elmarie Jara/ABA Design.
Interior design by Betsy Kulak/ABA Design.

Printed in the United States of America.

22 21 20 19 18   5 4 3 2 1

ISBN 978-1-63425-896-8

Discounts are available for books ordered in bulk. Special consideration is given to state bars, CLE programs, and other bar-related organizations. Inquire at Book Publishing, ABA Publishing, American Bar Association, 321 N. Clark Street, Chicago, Illinois 60654-7598.

www.ShopABA.org

For Douglas, Sr. and Theodore
Handing knowledge down through generations of Hands

Contents

Foreword

The French artist Jean Cocteau once said, "Style is a simple way of saying complicated things." When I first met Douglas Hand, I knew he was someone important, someone sophisticated—a man of style and inner refinement. He had that air about him. It was decidedly so.

We were both leaving a menswear show at Lincoln Center. I was introduced to him by a fashion stylist I knew. Douglas shook my hand with a warm but serious smile, and I noticed that while his sleeve cuffs were a crisp half inch from his gray flannel suit, his tie knot was appealingly knotted somewhat imperfectly—perhaps even artfully. He also had an odd (somewhat morbid), cryptic copper hand peeking out from his trouser pocket (which I later came to know held his keys). He was running back to his office after the shows. I learned later through industry chatter he was a preeminent fashion lawyer, representing many of the menswear brands that have grown into American mainstays. And that made perfect sense to me. His presence communicated it all quite effectively and without a word.

Douglas is the consummate professional and a true gentleman. He's appropriately orderly and his appearance reflects that—neat but not annoyingly precise. Counselor Hand is no automaton; nor is he a fop. He is a true acolyte of the great Regency era cultural icon Beau Brummell in his ability and desire not to stand out for his clothes but to stand out for his intelligence, wit, and capability for action. As most of us know, Douglas' clothes are impeccable and discriminating, but they are just the frame for the man within. His statement is understatement.

As a consumer, writer, lawyer, and professor in the fashion industry, Douglas knows clothes. I mean he *really* knows them: not only how they are designed and constructed, the raw materials that comprise them, and the legacy of storied brands as well as up-and-comers, but he understands the power (or the lack of it) that apparel choices convey. The coded language of style.

To be sure—and he'll blush when he reads this—Douglas has been blessed with classic male physical proportions which neatly fill the lines of a suit. But through this book he'll teach you, without any disdain or conceit, that the great benefit of the suit as a garment to all types of men is that it brings most body types toward an agnostic mean rather than some hyper-proportioned one. In this book he'll make his case against over-casualizing a casual dress code. He'll teach you some laws (as any good law professor would), but he'll also encourage you to reach beyond your comfort zone (even—gasp—beyond the laws the book sets forth) to attain degrees of personal style.

Douglas is not only a man of style, not only my attorney, not only an engaging and droll writer, he's also my friend. He is that rare example of an actualized man in—readers, please forgive me here—the fairly homogenized army of legal and financial services providers. He's a wolf that runs his own way but still very much gets along with the rest of the pack. No *lobo solo* he, this attorney follows his own course with a subdued panache that is all his own but is still very much "lawyerly" (I don't really know what that means, but I know it when I see it). Douglas loves the law, academic discourse, old scotch, his late-model Saab, his kids, his dog, the perfection of an ocean wave at sunset, artists and their art, planting things and watching them grow, and, perhaps most of all, he loves being himself. As Whitney Houston tells us, that is the greatest gift of all.

This book is an achievement. Truly—there is nothing like it. You'll undoubtedly enjoy the anecdotes and the jocularity, but you'll come back to it for the guidance. It's what you'll earmark pages for. Designer Marc Jacobs once said, "To me, clothing is a form of self-expression—there are hints about who you are in what you wear." I believe that. So does Douglas. I'm pretty confident you will too after reading his insightful and compelling work. Now to it!

—Nick Wooster

Preface

Gentlemen of the readership—bankers, lawyers, consultants, accountants, educated service providers, my white-collar brethren (collectively, "Professional Gentlemen")—herein please find what I hope will be more than just serviceable guidelines of style on how to dress.[1] This book is my attempt to explore the topic of personal presentation through the very practical viewpoint of the Professional Gentleman's actual environment—your day-to-day office reality. The goal of this exploration is to encourage appropriate spheres of self-expression in your appearance and thereby enhance your career and enrich your life (hopefully more than just financially).

To put this in some perspective: if you are a young strutting peacock, fresh out of graduate school, the laws of style set forth herein (the "Laws") may rein in some of your more dandy impulses to a more subdued professional presentation.[2] Your innate sartorial curiosity, however, will be refined and encouraged by the Laws, giving you a subtle sophistication and mien all within your budget. Alternatively, if you are a grinding service partner at a large firm who couldn't care less about fashion, the Laws will escalate your style game to a level that could elevate your current standing. The Laws will also potentially expose you to a degree of sartorial appreciation that will allow you to actually begin to enjoy the self-expression your choice of dress affords you. Verily, you'll be a new man, man.

As Professional Gentlemen, we find ourselves in a period of distinct change—a cultural shift. More and more men are measuring success not just financially, but creatively in other spheres of their lives. I'd like you to be one of these men. We are also at a time when the general public takes a dim view of many of us. There is a common perception (not without some basis in fact) of bankers duping investors, accountants advising large corpo-

---

1. You'll indulge me, perhaps you'll even appreciate, the legal agreement formatting of certain text. I've been comfortable drafting agreements this way for 20 years, so I'm comfortable writing a book that way now. I assume you all know how the defined term works.
2. With so many choices available, often what we choose *not* to wear exhibits as much style as what we ultimately put on.

rations how to minimize their tax obligations, and lawyers suing for sport and the prospect of a fat payday. We are perceived as the 1% and, really, in the minds of many, perhaps the nastiest segment of it. Pitiless Trumpian henchmen. This collective opinion has many of us not wanting to actually look like Professional Gentlemen. I don't want you to be one of these men.

I truly believe that style is a form of self-respect. Respect yourself. Respect your profession. Respect your appearance. And by the transitive property of equality—respect the clothes. What you wear and how you wear it are, as one of my clients, menswear designer Robert Tagliapietra puts it, "the first and last defining thing you present to people when you meet them."[3] Do not underestimate the importance of a first impression. Your appearance speaks before you do. Let it have a dulcet tone.

There are no books focused on educating Professional Gentlemen on this subject. Moreover, we are living at a time—an aesthetic inflection point—where business norms in manners of dress are changing. Casual Friday has given way to the full-time casual workplace in many industries. This has thrown many men (not to mention many menswear brands) into a state of generalized confusion. Sadly, for many, the default reaction to this state of affairs is apathy.

The books for men that focus on how to dress like a British gentleman in a suit (and there are too many of such books to count) have become hopelessly outdated for today's Professional Gentleman. And yet interest in menswear has seemingly never been greater.[4] To many economists, men are the new women—and we want options, dammit! With options come choices, and choices are best made with advice. That's where this book comes in—offering good advice for your particular station.

I certainly hope this book will be fun for you, a good read, a decent catalog of apparel, accessories, and brands, as well as a source of some chuckles. But *I know* this book will offer very practical advice. At its most basic level, it is a guide to improve your ability to effectively interact with clients and other Professional Gentlemen and thereby advance your career. Yes, clothing and accessories and how you put yourself together are career tools. What we will consider herein is not frivolity but is indeed important stuff.

So I will attempt to treat this subject with the degree of gravity it requires from the perspective of a fellow Professional Gentleman, not a fashionista nor a fusty old snob. Which is to say, I'm prepared to be extremely serious about the subject of menswear, but not damned precious or snotty about

---

3. Council of Fashion Designers of America, *The Pursuit of Style: Advice and Musings from America's Top Fashion Designers* (New York: Harry N. Abrams, 2014).
4. The growth of the global market for men's clothing was up 24% in 2015 and will reportedly reach $40 billion by 2019, according to a January 2016 report from Barclays.

it. If you don't get your shoes made by hand with a cobbler your family has had a relationship with for generations, that's fine with me. Given my background, I am sincerely hoping I am able to commiserate and accept professional realities in your clothing and accessory choices rather than talk down to you from some stylistic ivory tower.

I've been representing clients in the fashion industry for 20 years as a corporate lawyer. I've done this in big law settings (Shearman & Sterling in New York and Paris offices) and boutique settings (HBA—one of the preeminent firms in fashion law). I've . . . well, I've been there friends: dealing with large public company clients in Asia, Europe, the Middle East, and South America; in late-night drafting sessions at the financial printers with lawyers, bankers, and information agents; in court with clients with a lot on the line; and in diligence sessions with lawyers and accountants of various stripes. In addition to maintaining my practice at HBA, I am the general counsel at the American brand Rag & Bone, as well as to the Council of Fashion Designers of America.

I am also an adjunct law professor, with a course on fashion law at my alma mater, New York University School of Law, as well as a practicum on fashion law at Cardozo Law School with law students working with students from the Fashion Institute of Technology, where I've been a long-time member of the school's Couture Council and sit on the FIT Foundation's Board of Directors.[5] For good measure, I am a member of the London-based Luxury Law Alliance and speak about cross-border issues facing the fashion industry. I received an MBA from NYU's Stern School of Business and focused on finance. I interviewed with a sharp-elbowed crew of investment banking hopefuls in the '90s and considered taking up banking as my occupation but ultimately felt my temperament and skills were better matched to legal practice.

My wife started one of the first new-media companies focused on fashion—*Daily Candy*. Despite her high level of credibility in the industry and her consideration of personal appearance, she does not dress me. Far from it. I revel in my clothing choices. I am my own man.[6] I challenge her for closet space (just ask her). I present myself the way I want to be seen and the way I feel most confident and comfortable. I look capable and elegant.

I've seen a few professionals dress very, very well. Of this group, they are all, without exception, wildly accomplished, confident men. I've seen many others do an adequate, safe job of it. Of this group, some have done very well, others not so well. And lastly, I've seen way too many men do it

---

5. No, this book is not the textbook for either course. Both courses address the actual legal regimes facing companies that operate in the fashion industry.

6. I am both a man of style and a man's man. I don't at all find these to be contradictory terms. In fact, they are complementary terms.

wrong—sometimes not only to their own shame, but to the general denigration of our professions.

So gentlemen, since we are a rule-based group and, to our credit, have logged the hours of study and practice to commit many of those rules to memory, I hereby offer up a few helpful rules of style. The Laws! With which, I hope and expect you will do great things.

Acknowledgments

Douglas Hand is grateful to Gina Guzzardo, Nick Wooster, Justin Perez, Dany Levy, Marc Reiner, Jon Malysiak, John Palmer, Ashley Valdes, Lara Cohen, Chana Ben-Zacharia, Tom Chung, and for the subtle flair of Rodrigo Saldaña

Introduction

WHEREAS, heretofore, the banker, the lawyer, the business consultant, and the accountant (each a "Professional Gentleman"), have not had any serviceable guidelines, specific to their professional circumstances, regarding how to dress, present themselves, nor with respect to any matters of style;

WHEREAS, while the various industries in which Professional Gentlemen operate are filled with both men and women, the author, being a man, is best equipped—and also personally inclined—to comment solely on male sartorial choices;

WHEREAS, personal presentation for the Professional Gentleman must, of necessity, be considered through the very practical perspectives of (i) the expectations of the Professional Gentleman's clients, (ii) the hierarchical realities that exist within the Professional Gentleman's firm culture, and (iii) the outlooks and expectations of other professionals outside of their firms with whom the Professional Gentleman interacts;

WHEREAS, these perspectives lead to certain advisable rules of style (the "Laws") which can, with skillful drafting and articulation, be elucidated and relied upon to set forth best practices for the Professional Gentleman's personal presentation and choice of apparel and accessories;

WHEREAS, the Laws are fluid constructs, taking into account professional realities and specific factual circumstances, and thereby result in different mandates for different Professional Gentlemen and different sartorial choices, all of which are correct;

WHEREAS, by following the Laws, the Professional Gentleman may always "look the part" and maintain and even advance his career;

WHEREAS, there is no "professional uniform" or sole ideal wardrobe, but many possibilities of items and brands that can be listed and categorized for the benefit of the Professional Gentleman as he endeavors, throughout his career, to expand his wardrobe;

WHEREAS, fashion is fleeting, and trends represent another party's choices for the wearer, which is distinct from *style*, which represents a personal choice;

WHEREAS, notwithstanding the Laws, it is right and good that the Professional Gentleman is recognized as a human being and, as such, should be afforded an appropriate sphere of individual panache and self-expression;

NOW, THEREFORE; for good and valuable consideration, the receipt and sufficiency of which is hereby acknowledged by the American Bar Association,[7] the following chapters shall set forth the Laws as a guide to stylistic choices in apparel and accessories for Professional Gentlemen focusing on those choices that will improve the Professional Gentleman's ability to interact with his clients, colleagues, and other Professional Gentlemen effectively and thereby advance his career positively.

---

7. My publisher.

—1—

The Importance
of Professional
Presentation

"Know, first, who you are, and then adorn yourself accordingly."
—Epictetus[1]

The old adage goes: he who is his own lawyer has a fool for a client.[2] The same can often be said for most Professional Gentlemen (as defined herein) and their sense of style. All you need to do to genuinely understand this unfortunate phenomenon is perform your civic duty spending an afternoon down at the New York Supreme Court on jury duty and bear witness to the endless parade of lawyers in rigid, ill-fitting suits, interrupted only briefly by a too-shiny pair of oxblood Berlutis or a wayward western tie.[3]

---

1. Born a slave in A.D. 50, Epictetus taught that philosophy is a way of life and not just theory. He was a stoic and lived a simple life, but clearly understood the basic concept of rules of dress.
2. This proverb is based on the opinion that self-representation in court is likely to end badly. As with many proverbs, it is difficult to determine a precise origin, but this expression first began appearing in print in the early nineteenth century.
3. Mandated by law no less, jury duty must be served in the state of New York, and the Service Professional has a legal right to be absent from work to serve—New York Judiciary Law § 519. But then I suspect you knew that already.

The other Professional Gentlemen are no exception. I've seen haughty junior investment bankers in printed suspenders that match their shiny ties and pocket squares. I've witnessed clueless accountants pairing boxy suits with stained white sneakers. I've worked with too-cool consultants in ripped jeans and flip flops. Oh, what horrors mine eyes have seen.

Yes, individuality is a glorious notion, and one that should be celebrated—just not at the expense of dignity, courtliness, or your job. Beyond just preserving your job, dressing well can actually advance your career. Academic and noted dandy Herbert Harold Vreeland once said, "Clothes don't make a man, but clothes have got many a man a good job."[4] Wise words.

What Is a "Professional," and What Do They Dress Like?

A common definition of a service industry professional is someone both qualified and employed in the areas of law, financial services, accounting,

---

4. Vreeland was no fashionista. He was a subtle dresser—a man of style and somewhat of a badass. He served in military intelligence as a member of the American Expeditionary Service and after World War I—rising to the reserve rank of brigadier general. He also served as assistant registrar at Yale and on the faculties of Philips Academy, Andover, Massachusetts, and Smith College.

or consulting (each a "Professional Gentleman").[5] Many of these positions require an advanced degree (e.g., JD, MBA) and professional licensing or accreditation (e.g., CPA, Series 7, admission to the bar).

Professional service industry organizations are usually referred to as "firms." These firms are typified by a hierarchical structure, a focus on traditionalism, and conservative practices. Firms function in the tertiary sector of the economy. A service industry professional almost uniformly performs his work in an office or other administrative setting based on the type of firm he is employed by.

An easy and apt (for purposes of our subject matter) synonym for the Professional Gentleman is *white collar*.[6] Let's pause here to recognize the subtle but clear level of formality in dress that white collar symbolizes—at least relative to the other collared professionals (e.g., blue collar, green collar, pink collar, etc.).[7] White shirts and collars have traditionally denoted a high level of affluence. Until the late nineteenth century, cleaning a white shirt was difficult and could only be accomplished at great expense. Moreover, any form of manual labor would obviously soil a white shirt. Consequently only "gentlemen"[8] wore them. In addition, traditional formal wear (white-tie or morning dress) is only worn with a white collar. Similarly the white-collar Professional Gentleman is typically expected to dress more formally than most professions.

---

5. I know, I know, I've defined "Professional Gentleman" three times now. This is because I view the Introduction, Preface, and body of the book as three distinct writings. A bit like a SEC Schedule TO, which is a wrapper to a tender offer statement, which itself also has a first page summary and multiple attachments that are separate documents. The same terms are defined on the wrapper, the first page, and in the body of the tender offer statement itself, as well as on many of the attachments. Junior associates tasked with reviewing such documents get into fits to make sure all three definitions are the same because there is a legal implication if these definitions are different. I'm under no such pressure, so you'll forgive any slight variations in defined terms. If you are reading this for yourself in your work, you are a Professional Gentleman to me, compadre.

6. The term was coined in the 1930s by American writer Upton Sinclair, who referenced the word in connection with clerical, administrative, and managerial functions. However, the term evolved and became rather elevated in the United States, where the term became more associated with the type of Professional Gentlemen I am referring to herein.

7. "Blue collar" designating jobs requiring manual labor; "green collar" for jobs in the environmental sector; and "pink collar" for jobs in the service industry dominated by women (like nursing or teaching). *Réka Benczes, Creative Compounding in English: The Semantics of Metaphorical and Metonymical Noun-Noun Combinations* (Amsterdam: John Benjamins, 2006), 144–146.

8. Notwithstanding appropriating the term *gentlemen* to bestow it upon all of you, I'm not going to go into any belabored definition of what a gentleman was in the eighteenth and nineteenth centuries (though other very self-important tomes on menswear from time to time treat this subject at length and with great reverence). The definition I like best is from Alice Cicolini's *The New English Dandy* (New York: Assouline, 2005), in which she describes the modern gentleman as being the "aristocracy of talent . . . The new Gentleman's most important quality is success and the power that success affords; second is the reflection of his power through discreet and coded means." Goals AF.

During the work week, the Professional Gentleman, in most classic firm environments, is found in a clean, crisp (if somewhat sober) suit, with a tie, dress shoes, and with the necessary business accessories around him (writing instrument, mobile phone, calculator, briefcase, or satchel, etc.). With the advent of casual Fridays, this work-week dress may only extend four days. Since the Professional Gentleman may often find himself working six- or even seven-day weeks, and certainly working on Fridays, there is a second mode of dress—that somewhat oxymoronic term *business casual* that may find the properly attired Professional Gentleman without his tie or without his suit, but typically always in clothing that looks smart and neat, if not overtly fashionable.[9] More recently casual Friday has extended, for some firms, into a full-time business casual environment where the Professional Gentleman is not required to wear a suit and tie unless there are scheduled client meetings. This is the case not only at my law firm HBA, but also at places like J.P. Morgan Chase & Co. and PricewaterhouseCoopers, LLP.

We'll deep dive into both of these modes of dress (suited/business and unsuited/business casual) through the course of this book, but the main point I want to make here is that the Professional Gentleman, in most environments, should be easily recognizable both by his colleagues and those outside of the professional ranks. There may be some degree of debate as to what stripe of profession a Professional Gentleman is in, but the sharp and business-like manner of his mode of dress should announce his station to the world without need of any particular uniform or superficial adornment (like an airline pilot's military inspired suit or a doctor's white lab coat). The Professional Gentleman's look should convey elegance and capability. Elegant and capable—it's a devastatingly powerful combination. The first (and certainly most general) of the laws of style for the Professional Gentleman (the "Laws") follows:

Law #1

~

The Professional Gentleman shall dress in a manner that is elegant and capable.

~

---

9. Of course, this applies only to "in office" settings; the Professional Gentleman certainly works remotely and often from home on "non-business" hours. During such deportment, he's typically free to wear what he wants. His home is his castle, and what goes on behind the gates is for him and his family to know and enjoy.

"Elegance is not standing out, but being remembered."

—Giorgio Armani[10]

"Capable goes beyond just having the ability or quality necessary to do or achieve a specified thing, it means being able to achieve that thing efficiently whatever it is; competence in abundance."

—Marcus Wainwright, of Rag & Bone

Now we all know that there are many varieties of Professional Gentlemen, and we charge all manner of fees for our services, but one constant in relation to our fees is that clients rarely, if ever, think we are inexpensive. As Professional Gentlemen, we know that our fees reflect not only the going rate for our services, but also years of post-graduate schooling and high-level experience in the field.[11] Therefore, it is very important for a Professional Gentleman to recognize that our clients often need to be reminded that they are dealing with a "professional." At the risk of stating the abundantly obvious, a very easy way to remind the client that they are dealing with a professional is to always look like one.[12]

Res Ipsa Loquitur—Casual Breeches and the Duty of Care

However, in the common practice of dressing for work, some Professional Gentlemen just don't take adequate care, arguably breaching a fundamental duty they have toward their dress and those they work for. Let me take the lawyers amongst you back to first-year torts. The doctrine of *res ipsa loqui-*

---

10. Another favorite one of mine is, "Elegance is defined by an ability to mix small gestures, wear clothes that are simple and not loud and that show respect for materials, texture and cut." From Guy Trebay, "A Return to Elegance," *New York Times*, January 21, 2016.

11. Granted, these rates usually also reflect an allocation of the overhead of our firms. So the Professional Gentleman who works at a global firm with lush offices in places like Budapest or Tegucigalpa that are not particularly productive and/or has offices in high-rent locales like Hong Kong, New York, and London, might have a higher rate than a better Professional Gentleman in a focused firm with offices outside of such high-rent districts. But I digress; this is a subject for another book—a much more boring one about firm economics.

12. See John Ortved, "Passing the Style Bar: Skadden Arps Updates the Image of the Staid Litigator," *New York Times*, December 4, 2015.

tur provides that the elements of duty of care and breach can be inferred from the very nature of the accident.[13] Let's consider this briefly in the context of pants.

Early in my career, I was on an overseas M&A due diligence assignment outside of Paris. *C'est vrai!* The target (we were representing the acquirer) was a French company, and the guy running our team was a capable and highly dedicated mid-level associate—let's just call him Tucker.[14] Now, as many of you may know, doing due diligence, even in the City of Lights, is a grueling and uncomfortable process. Even with your jacket off and tie loosened, it can be agonizing to be in suit trousers while rifling through heavy redwelds with a sizzling laptop on your thighs summarizing legal documents or financial disclosures . . . for days.

Having played on the UVA golf team[15] in college and having gone through this white-collar boot camp more than a few times, Tucker had developed a fondness for what he proudly named his "diligence slacks." These were, basically, an early version of what might now trendily be called athleisure wear. Ventilated rain pants with an elastic waistband that you'd wear for golf in foul weather, colored khaki or navy or black (he had several pairs), made out of some initial version of dri fit/climacool material. Efficient and seemingly inoffensive when paired with a proper dress shirt, tie, and sport coat (the latter of which would come off quickly). Tucker had worn his "diligence slacks" on high-pressured assignments in the Dulles Tech Corridor, late-night drafting sessions in Menlo Park, and even at the printers in New York. He truly (I'd even say "sweetly" if it wasn't so completely misguided) thought his resourceful comfort made him inherently more efficient. "And it's really hard to notice these are actually golf pants!" Tucker would brightly offer. *Fore!*

Enter the stately and impeccably dressed chief legal officer of our client—thin silver mustache, bespoke Cifonelli suit, bright Hermès tie, Breitling nicely just peeking out of his perfectly crisp half inch of shirt cuff—for an impromptu report and caught a glimpse of his lead lawyer's getup; he

---

13. Although modern formulations differ by jurisdiction, the common law originally stated that the accident must satisfy the following conditions: (i) it ordinarily would not occur without someone's negligence; (ii) it in this instance probably did not occur without someone's negligence; (iii) it was caused by an instrumentality that was under the exclusive control of the defendant; and (iv) it was not caused in any way by the plaintiff (i.e., no contributory negligence). Upon a proof of *res ipsa loquitur*, the plaintiff need only establish the remaining two elements of negligence—namely, that the plaintiff suffered damages, of which the accident was the legal cause.

14. Names have been changed to protect the innocent. Any resemblance to actual persons, living or dead, is purely coincidental.

15. The University of Virginia golf team in 1990 ranked 15th regionally, and featured Tim Dunlavey (who played with Tucker). Cavaliers!

quite perceptibly uttered a soft but potent "no"—holding the "o" for an inordinate amount of time as it slowly dissolved into a horrified whisper. The poor older man actually became visibly flustered, asked a few questions of some of the more properly attired but more junior lawyers, and walked confusedly out of the room muttering to himself gently in French. *C'est pas possible. C'est pas vrai.*[16] As comfortable as Tucker's pants may have been, as intelligent as he was, and as competent a job he may have done, he was very much undone by his negligent trouser choice.

Brands to Know

Cifonelli: Cifonelli is a bespoke tailoring company founded in Italy in 1880 that established roots in Paris beginning in 1926. The brand is famous for the Cifonelli cut, which combines the precision of English tailoring with the comfort of Italian style. Particularly notable about the style is the Cifonelli shoulder, which has become the worldwide signature of the brand due to the freedom of movement it permits while still appearing elegant and refined. While the Cifonelli name has become synonymous with luxury tailor-made clothing around the globe, in 2014 the brand launched a full ready-to-wear collection that remained loyal to the Cifonelli fit.

Hermès: What started in 1837 as a horse harness and leather workshop is now one of the world's most celebrated labels. Over the years, Hermès has delivered coveted men's style staples from their ubiquitous patterned ties and sleek briefcases to the H belt kit. Bespoke services are a key component of the Hermès Men's strategy. Under the design direction of Véronique Nichanian, the Hermès menswear line is full of non-ostentatious details that challenge more traditional menswear conventions. Hermès Men's silk neck ties have outsold its women's ornate silk scarves, accounting for approximately 10% of the company's revenue. Offering ready-to-wear, ties, pocket squares, scarves, and leather goods, Hermès menswear offerings are in abundance for any man seeking modern luxuries.

---

16. Basically, in French: "No way. This is not happening."

Breitling: A Swiss specialist in technical watches, Breitling was founded in 1884. The brand has played a crucial role in the development of the wrist chronograph and is a leader in the industry. Breitling offers 11 different lines of watches and produces sturdy, reliable, and high-performance instruments that feature Breitling's own mechanical chronograph movements. As a longstanding partner in aviation, Breitling's focus has been on quality and precision designs to withstand intensive use and the most trying conditions.

The same Professional Gentleman charges the same billable rate for the hour spent doing due diligence in a New Jersey storage facility for a client from 2:00 a.m. to 3:00 a.m. as he does appearing before the United States Supreme Court.[17] His client has a right to expect that he look like a Professional Gentleman in both instances and, in particular, that he wears proper seasonal suit trousers. So that's your duty of care. Sweat pants, track pants, golf gear, or shorts are a breach of that duty while on the job. But the Laws will lay this out much more clearly *infra*.

Smart Dress = Smart Performance?
Enclothed Cognition

Granted, one short anecdote from my career should not fully convince you. Educated, rational, and practical as you no doubt are; likely you need more objective data. Fair enough. Let us look at some scientific studies on the subject.

A group of very smart (and likely smartly dressed) psychology PhDs from Columbia University and Cal State Northridge published a study in 2015 that observed how our apparel choices may impact our abstract and concrete thoughts.[18] Seriously, this happened. The results found that wearing more

---

17. If, in fact, there were such a lawyer commissioned with two such dissimilar tasks.
18. Michael L. Slepian, Simon N. Ferber, Joshua M. Gold, Abraham M. Rutchick, "The Cognitive Consequences of Formal Clothing," *Social Psychological and Personality Science*, Vol. 6, Issue 6 (2015): 661–668.

formal clothes can liberate us from concrete thinking while enhancing our ability to think more abstractly.

As they elucidate in their paper, abstract thinking "facilitates the pursuit of long-term goals over short-term goals," while concrete thinking "often leads people to prefer smaller immediate gains relative to larger future gains." For example, when you deposit an expense reimbursement check, a concrete

thought would be, "I'm putting the check in the ATM" while an abstract thought might be "depositing directly into long-term savings may help me force saving and give me a better interest rate," or perhaps the more sophisticated abstract thought—"my firm should really give me a firm credit card so I don't have to, in effect, loan them money when paying expenses like these; do they not trust me? Should I return that headhunter's call and start looking around for a new firm? Do I really dress that poorly?" Concrete thought limits ideas to the basic—what's taking place in the here and now. Abstract thoughts take a broader view—they are more sophisticated, more cerebral, smarter.

So anyway, here is the most important part. These bicoastal scientists proved that more formal apparel *increased* abstract thoughts in a series of experiments. The experiments asked undergrads to wear a variety of clothing—some deemed "formal" (e.g., suits or a jacket and tie), some "informal" (e.g., the uber-casual wear these students typically wore to college classes)— rank how they felt in this clothing, and then perform a group of tasks. This must have been a bit of a trip for the college students, no doubt, and I've zero confidence that any of the deemed "formal" vestments were fit or tailored (I'd expect it was more like the ill-fitting jacket one might unfortunately receive at one of those holdover clubs or old school restaurants that still believe a gentleman must wear a jacket to be properly dressed).[19]

---

19. As you will learn, in most cases I happen to concur with this sentiment.

In any event, the results were striking. The students who self-ranked their clothing as more formal (i.e., the guys in suits) unanimously scored higher in abstract thinking than their casually dressed counterparts. BOOM! Cue well-dressed researcher dropping the mic at some psychology conference and walking off the stage in his Alden brogues, his fitted Canali suit sliding easily and luxuriously underneath his ubiquitous lab coat.

The researchers deduced that the notion of power and feeling more powerful through dress led to these results. According to the study, "power significantly mediated the relationship between clothing formality and the number of actions identified at a high level." Put another way, the subjects in suits felt more powerful. Their better clothes made them feel more potent, which allowed them to think more abstractly. And Christ Almighty, these boys were in "loaner" suits. Imagine if their "formal" clothes also fit them well and they were comfortable in them. Extrapolating from these findings, one could even rationally posit that if you're bright to begin with and you wear bespoke Huntsman everywhere, you can change the world!

Brands to Know

Alden: Founded in 1884, New England shoemaker Alden Shoes has retained its devotion to high-quality dress shoes despite the growing demand for low-cost, mass-produced footwear. A New England–style shoemaker, Alden Shoes maintains its production in Middleborough, Massachusetts, and is the only remaining original New England shoe and boot maker carrying forward a tradition of quality genuine-welted shoemaking. The shoemaker is known not only for its quality and class, but also for its devotion to making a comfortable shoe.

Canali: Since 1934, Canali has been one of the paradigms of tailor-made Italian luxury. Canali promotes the values of Made-in-Italy excellence, creating masterpieces of exceptional wearability and comfort that blend culture and history with style and taste. Canali's suits are known for their meticulous attention to detail and premium fabrics. Canali offers a personalized suiting experience, Su Misura, which combines the expertise of made-to-measure specialists and the artistry of their master tailors, creating distinctive and entirely unique suits for their customers. Premium stuff.

Huntsman: In 1849, Henry Huntsman set up a tailoring shop on Dover Street that became the start of bespoke tailor, Huntsman. Huntsman prides itself on its heritage and reputation as one of the finest and long-standing, yet innovative, bespoke houses on Savile Row. In 1866, the company earned its first Royal Warrant as Leather Breeches Maker to the Prince of Wales and established itself as the premier destination for riding and country attire. In 2016, the company opened its first American store in New York City to better serve its growing American market. I love Huntsman suits.

There's more. A study reported in December 2014 in the *Journal of Experimental Psychology: General* found that less formal clothing may hurt in negotiations, and more formal clothing may help in it.[20]

In this study, the male subjects: (i) wore their usual clothing (which, because they were all likely undergraduates, consisted of fairly casual fare), or (ii) were placed in a proper business suits (which, again, undoubtedly didn't fit well, but nevertheless upped the degree of formality considerably), or (iii) were allowed to wear sweats. Gray, hooded, "Rocky"-like sweats.

Then the subjects engaged in a mock investment banking negotiation that involved banging out the financial terms of a deal with a counterparty. This was done Gordon Gekko style with little facts to go on, just leverage, chutzpah, and a business suit. Not surprisingly, those who were suited obtained more profitable deals than the other two groups. Just for the record, the study also found that those who dressed down had, *ahem*, lower testosterone levels. Before I go on about the claims certain suit manufacturers might make subject to FDA approval, let's break it all down.[21]

The wise doctors here (and those in the Columbia/Cal State Northridge study as well) point out that social rank in humans is signaled by a variety of behaviors and phenotypes. In both studies, the sartorial manipulation of social class (a lovely phrase—I'll try to use it again) was found to engender class-consistent behavior and physiology during dyadic interactions. Scholarly and appropriately scientific sounding. What does that mean?

---

20. PsycINFO Database Record © 2014 APA.
21. The FDA (Food and Drug Administration) enforces the Federal Food, Drug, and Cosmetic Act and other regulations, most of which apply to ingested items as well as medical devices.

"It's not a question of enough, pal. It's a zero sum game, somebody wins, somebody loses. Money itself isn't lost or made, it's simply transferred from one perception to another."

—Gordon Gekko, *Wall Street*

"Yeah. I been out there walkin' around, thinkin'. I mean, who am I kiddin'? I ain't even in the guy's league."

—Rocky Balboa, *Rocky*

Wearing suits and looking like a Professional Gentleman compared to wearing sweats and looking like the "Italian Stallion" induced dominance—measured in terms of negotiation profits and concessions, and testosterone levels. "Upper-class" clothing also elicited increased vigilance in perceivers of these symbols. Relative to perceiving "lower-class" symbols, perceiving "upper-class" symbols reduced perceptions of social power and catalyzed physiological contagion such that perceivers' sympathetic nervous system activation followed that of the "upper-class" target. Enclothed cognition. Um, okay. It all points to: dress better, do better—particularly for the Professional Gentleman.

The Artistic Perspective— Style and Aesthetics

As Virginia Woolf—no scientist to be sure, but a pretty bright and creative genius—put it, "Vain trifles as they seem, clothes have, they say, more important offices than to merely keep us warm. They change our view of the world and the world's view of us."

Artists have always understood the objective pulls of certain deep, primary aesthetics to the human senses. The visual beauty of a sunset over the ocean. The melodic sound of chords of the minor scale played on the piano. The crisp smell of pine. That first bite of an "animal-style" double-double at In-N-Out. This understanding of the sensory has certainly informed how artists from all disciplines have presented themselves through sartorial choices.

"Your silhouette will charge the view
Of distance atmosphere"[22]

—Yes

The great musicians and writers have always respected looking resplendent. David Bowie was honored with a CFDA tribute in 2016 for his progressive tailored dress. Serge Gainsbourg, the French singer and songwriter, dressed like an investment banker on a bender. Ian Curtis of Joy Division was known as the angry man in the stylish utilitarian trench coat. Thelonious Monk, Bryan Ferry, Andre 3000, Elvis Costello, Miles Davis, David Byrne, Paul Weller, every member of Interpol—these musicians have always understood the power of tailored clothing. The suit as an avatar for communicating their art.

Oscar Wilde was always well turned out if a bit of a glamazon. He kept his hair tidy but long, wore bright colors in his impeccable suiting, and espoused the highest quality in all of his apparel. F. Scott Fitzgerald had a wardrobe of perfection and wrote glowingly about menswear (who can forget Daisy swimming in Gatsby's shirts in *The Great Gatsby*). Truman Capote made bowties and tortoise shell glasses a fashion staple with his attention to the fit and quality of his suits. Tom Wolfe is still a style icon strutting around New York in his white three-piece suits and impossibly high collars.

In the visual arts, Salvador Dali was a noted dandy as was Lucien Freud and David Hockney. Just have a look at how the young contemporary artists John Currin or Ryan McGinley put themselves together. Suited for most occasions, they look dapper and wear their clothes well. As the always decorous and natty Mark Twain once pithily put it, "Clothes make the man. Naked people have little or no influence on society."

So there you have it. Your appearance, the manner in which you present yourself, your choice of clothing—it all matters. Science is showing you this objectively. Arts and letters are encouraging you colorfully. More importantly, I'm telling you this. And I'm one of you.

Ignorantia juris non excusat.[23]

---

22. Yes, "Roundabout," on *Fragile* (Atlantic Records 1971).
23. Ignorance of the law is no excuse.

—2—

Dressing Relative to
Your Clients

"Bad laws are the worst sort of tyranny."
—Edmund Burke[1]

Before I conduct an overview of all the sartorial gorgeousness you can adorn yourselves with to look sharp, advance your career, and possibly even change the world, let's first get into the Laws themselves. To truly understand these mandates that should govern a professional's dress habits, we will consider a hierarchy of rules (with necessary provisos) that, like the common law itself, is not static, but active and evolving.[2] The Laws take factual circumstances into account. They are not a one-size-fits-all paradigm, but a usable scale that can contemplate multiple wardrobes, as well as multiple Professional Gentlemen and the unique circumstances of each of them.

---

1. An Irish statesman, Burke was born in 1729 and is remembered for his support of the American Revolutionaries as well as Catholic emancipation.
2. A common-law legal system is characterized by case law developed by judges, courts, and similar judicial tribunals. The decisions rendered in individual cases by such tribunals are recorded and have precedential effect on future cases. Hence the legal system evolves through rulings that contemplate different fact patterns. Common law originated during the Middle Ages in England (also where the modern men's business suit came from!) and from there was propagated to the colonies of the British Empire, including the United States.

One goal I have for you all is to express yourself without jeopardizing your career or client roster. To do that, a Professional Gentleman must understand the principles of relativity.[3] What I will develop here is that there are some basic laws of relativity in dress that depend on several factors. What factors? Namely upon the Professional Gentlemen's client base (the type of clients he has and the industry(ies) they are in) and upon the Professional Gentleman's level of seniority within his firm. I will advance a few rules here, setting minimums and maximums with respect to what you should put on and how you should present yourself.

Ceilings and Floors in the Laws

As those amongst you who went to law school will remember, laws are rarely bright-line rules. Our lives and the appropriate restrictions a cultured and organized society adopts for the harmonious interaction of its members are based on factual circumstances (at the risk of sounding like a law professor). But here's the rub—laws are usually not binary, right-or-wrong, yes-or-no mandates. This is why lawyers answer most questions—often to the great consternation of our clients—with "it depends."

But rather than being subjective only—if not black and white, then one flat shade of gray—the most useful laws go a step further and give us gradations of gray; a spectrum with "almost black" at one end and "almost white" at the other. Well-considered and constructed laws are relative and scaled so that persons can be guided by factual circumstances and more safely determine if they are operating within the law or outside of the law.

---

3. Not to be confused with Albert Einstein's theory of relativity, which as it's been explained to me really outlines two theories—special relativity and general relativity, and introduced the concepts of spacetime (as a unified entity of space and time), length contraction, and the relativity of simultaneity. I'll just stop right there.

On Good Laws

Take, for example, that learned articulation on what constitutes negligence in US tort law put forth by none other than Judge Learned Hand.[4] The calculus of negligence, or "Hand Rule" or "Hand Formula,"[5] as it is sometimes called, outlines a process for determining whether a legal duty of care has been breached. The original description of the calculus was set forth in *United States v. Carroll Towing Co.* in which an improperly secured barge had drifted away from a pier and caused damage to several other boats. Hand put it this way:

> [T]he owner's duty, as in other similar situations, to provide against resulting injuries is a function of three variables: (1) the probability that she will break away; (2) the gravity of the resulting injury, if she does; (3) the burden of adequate precautions.

So a useful law, yes? It is fluid in the way it can deal with multiple circumstances, and, by inputting factual components, members of society can attempt to reasonably evaluate whether they are breaking the law, as can potential plaintiffs and judges.

I will attempt to produce something similar for the Professional Gentleman here, but it will quite obviously not deal with barges or boats. I will set forth a set of rules on sartorial presentation that will guide you depending upon your career reality as well as all of the various factual circumstances you find yourself in. So let's get to it, amigos.

---

4. One of the greatest names of all time. Right up there with Ace Frehley, Sinjin Smith, and, of course, Wolfgang Amadeus Mozart. Learned and I have no direct relation that I am aware of, by the way. This, of course, did not stop all of my law school professors at NYU School of Law from calling on me each and every time a Learned Hand case was covered in our casebooks. And Hand was prolific—so I was on call a lot. What it cost me in having to brief many cases subject to sometimes brutal Socratic method was the certainty of knowing when I'd be called upon. This was good. When you know the fastball is coming, it is a lot easier to hit.

5. Not to be confused with the "Hand Formula" in my house, which is actually my personal recipe for the perfect Rusty Nail (not just Drambuie and Scotch whisky, my friends!).

The Formality Minimum

No matter what your specialty or practice area as a Professional Gentleman, we are all in client services, and our clients will always have dress codes as varied as the number of industries and occupations that exist. Some are more formal than others, some are more affluent than others, but all have their expected modes of dress. As advisors, we are wise to acknowledge these norms and dress accordingly.

Examples of Dress Codes Across Industries

Industry	Formality of Dress	Affluence of Dress	Usage of Professional Gentlemen
Media	High	High	High
Technology	Low	Low	Medium/High
Energy	Medium/High	Medium/Low	High
Food/Beverage	Low	Medium/Low	Medium
Sports	Medium	Medium/High	High
Fashion	Low	High	Medium
Pharmaceutical	Medium	Medium	Medium
Financial Services	High	High	High
Publishing	Medium	Medium/Low	Medium
Construction	Medium	High	Low
Transportation	Low	Low	Medium/Low

There are important constants when appearing in front of clients. Please observe, the immutable second Law follows:

Law #2

~

The Professional Gentleman shall always dress more formally than his clients.

~

This Law is driven by a number of factors. One is, quite simply, clients are paying a lot of money to your firm for you to do your Professional Gentlemanly work for them, and you want them to be assured of your competence and standing. Put in the simplest of terms, your clients expect you to look like a professional.

Ask yourself, "What are my client's expectations? What does my client think a Professional Gentleman looks like?" These are questions you should ask yourself a lot as you get dressed until you are confident you have it down—either because you have focused on servicing a particular industry, and thereby have become part of it, or you are just "dialed in" as a sartorial prognosticator.

Some of you reading this may rankle at the thought of so much deliberation going into how you present yourself to clients. "I am an exceptional Professional Gentleman," you may be saying to yourselves. "I went to Stanford. I've got an MBA from Wharton. I'm well trained and have a great reputation at a storied firm. My clients' evaluations of me will not be based on their impression of my appearance but on my performance and on the quality of my work."[6] You are partially right. Yes, your client's evaluation of you will be based on your performance and on the quality of your work. But before any of these important factors see the light of day, before performance and work product can even be evaluated, before your brilliance and exceptional talent can even be exhibited, you will make a first impression . . . and a second, and probably a third—all of which will mainly be based on how you look. According to research by Albert Mehrabian, professor at the University of California, Los Angeles, upon meeting someone for the first time, we form an opinion of them within the first 30 seconds. While some of that opinion is based on what the other person is saying, the majority of that evaluation is shaped by their appearance. And I can tell you without reservation that in under 30 seconds, no client on this planet is going to be able to determine the quality of your drafting, your knowledge of GAAP, or your ability to run a Black–Scholes calculation.

Now, you could be brilliant, and motivated, and tireless, and, despite dressing poorly and being an unmitigated slob, you could still have a great rapport with clients. You could be that special unicorn who struts even if he does so without the luxuriant white mane and tail. You could be that one-in-a-million Professional Gentleman. But most of us aren't.[7] Most of us can't be. Most of us won't be. I'm sorry, on multiple levels, if I'm the one breaking that to you.

---

6. Also, some of you may be thinking, "I've got enough to deal with just doing my job; now I have to worry this much about how I dress?"
7. 999,999 out of 1,000,000 of us to be exact.

Will dressing well cover flaws in your performance? Shoddy work product? Blown deadlines? Laziness? Of course not. *Vogue* editor Anna Wintour, that doyenne of style, once said, "If you can't be better than your competition, just dress better." While I don't think it's that simple, you certainly should not make your success harder to achieve by having to overcome preconceived notions of being flawed, sloppy, or lacking in attention to detail; in short, of not actually being a competent Professional Gentleman (which is tantamount to not being a professional at all).

A surefire way to look like a Professional Gentleman is to dress like one, and, as will be mentioned over and over again, a Professional Gentleman should look elegant and capable. Well-executed formality, generally, covers both of those traits pretty damn well.

Now, if you are representing a sporting goods startup in Southern California, some skateboard company, for instance, and the founders are hoodie and sneaker guys, you have some real leeway in terms of how casual you can go and not dip below the bar as it has been set. Honestly, you could choose not to wear a suit, perhaps not even a jacket, and be above this floor of informality. Safer and certainly more becoming for a Professional Gentleman might be the relaxed tailored offerings from brands like Todd Snyder, Billy Reid, or Steven Alan. American casual wear like this would be acceptable, dapper, and appealingly youthful looking. Well suited to the client.

But know this: you will likely never go wrong even if you dress quite a bit more formally. Remember—*ab initio*[8]—you are always out of harm's way in a conservative suit. Gray flannel is your safe zone; blue pinstripe is your warm blanket. We'll get to a detailed breakdown of these anodyne standards in due course.

---

8. Something being the case from the start or from the instant of the act, rather than from when the court declared it so.

Brands to Know

Todd Snyder: Inspired by Savile Row craftsmanship, military tailoring, and a New York sensibility, Todd Snyder launched his menswear line in fall 2011. After some time spent at Ralph Lauren, the Gap, and J. Crew, Snyder branched off to create his own line, which has since been sold to American Eagle Outfitters ("AEO") (NYSE: AEO) in 2015. At the helm of his own brand, Snyder delivers well-cut suits and twists on basics that are targeted at the discerning younger Professional Gentleman. Snyder's brand appeals to a young generation with easy, relaxed, but at the same time detailed, clothing. DISCLOSURE: my firm HBA represented Todd when he sold his business to AEO, and he is a drinking buddy of mine.

Billy Reid: Billy Reid began his career at Saks Fifth Avenue and then launched his own men's collection, Billy Reid. The first Billy Reid shops opened in Dallas, Houston, and, somewhat incongruously, Florence in 2004. There's a nice little store in the West Village I like to pop into from time to time to see what the brand is up to. Billy Reid emphasizes US manufacturing using proprietary textiles and high-quality construction. Offering outwear, jackets, suiting, sweaters, knits, denim, and bags, Billy Reid's penchant for traditional style with a twist shines through.

Steven Alan: Steven Alan is the son of jewelers. He launched his own line of ready-to-wear clothing back in 1999, catering to customers seeking better made traditional basics with a twist here and there, and a more modern fit. Discovery is a crucial element in Steven's philosophy, which plays out in his stores. The slightly out of the way locations, his merchandising, and his choice of designers (he offers other brands besides his own at his stores) are all made with this in mind. Steven's own collection incorporates handpicked fine-cotton fabrics and focuses on fit. The shirts are fitted, with subtle design elements that give them their individuality. Each shirt is washed and treated to create its own distinct worn-in, perfectly disheveled feel. The shirts are often seen as collectibles due to the fact that the fabrics change every few months. I have a couple of the original "inside-out" dress shirts that actually have the breast pocket on the inside. DISCLOSURE: my firm HBA has represented Steven for years.

The point is this: the safest path is to hover well above the baseline set by your client since they will rarely admonish you for looking *too* formal. Even if they do so, it will be in more of a joking, light-hearted way. Secretly, they will appreciate your business-like appearance. Your formal demeanor will lend gravity to the matters you are presiding over and give your client the comfort that the job is not only being done, but it's being done by a professional.[9]

Moreover, if your clients are all casually dressed by choice or industry norm out of some nod to comfort or, even more so, some statement against what they perceive as conformity, they will likely feel grateful that it is you, and not they, who "has to" wear the suit and tie. They will assume (since they don't regularly wear a suit) that you are stifled and uncomfortable (though as we will see, *infra*, your suit can be the furthest thing from stifling and uncomfortable). They may also feel that it is right and good that you be made to writhe in your conservative uniform, as it is you that is charging them—what they doubtless consider to be a lot—for services you are rendering. Services that, of course, are necessary but are, in most instances, still considered expensive by the clients who make use of them.

I'm reminded of an initial meeting I had with a father-and-son Italian accessories manufacturer—let's call them the Giacomettis—on a Saturday on the East end of Long Island at the lovely home of client designer Phillip Lim. The Giacomettis were in fairly typical Italian sprezzatura splendor. Head to toe in what was probably Brunello Cucinelli. Elegant and casual, with no ties and open linen shirts. J.P. Tod's loafers with no socks. Basically they were magnificent, but informal. When Mssrs. Giacometti came into our New York offices the next week to formalize the engagement of our firm, the head of our tax department, who had asked me previously if the Giacomettis had dressed casually when I met them, showed up in the conference room in his version of business casual: GH Bass saddle shoes, chinos, and a short-sleeved button-down shirt. While this was not an outright affront to office decorum, when compared to what the Giacomettis wore to a weekday meeting—namely Isaia and Kiton suits respectively, Etro ties, and shoes from a northern Italian craftsman their factory manager knows—my partner looked like a complete schlub. Honestly, my tax partner's entrance was a tense moment. The Giacomettis looked taken aback, and one could tell they felt disrespected or put-off (or both) by my partner's casual appear-

---

9. Sort of like the state-sealed stamp many corporate clients insist on getting for newly formed entities. Those things cost a lot and require that you stamp corporate documents as if it was the eighteenth century, but they look elegant and purposeful and professional; and so they remain—formal and permanent.

ance. It was as if I were introducing them to the fella who fixed the photocopier, not a Georgetown-educated, advanced-degreed Superlawyer (which is what my partner is). We kept the business, but even on sophisticated tax questions, the client never contacted my partner directly. They would put their questions to me, and I would retrieve the answers from my partner and pass them on. It was as if they wanted to forget meeting him, and it was all because he fell under the formality floor—trapped in the dank basement of a poor style choice.

Some within firms (the "Misguided") argue that by dressing more formally than certain clients (particularly creative and technology clients), the client becomes alienated. The client, the Misguided reason, does not trust a "suit" and prefers to deal with someone who dresses more like themselves. Ostensibly, this is explained as being so that the client can relate to their Professional Gentleman better. The Misguided presume that the client needs to feel like he or she is with someone who "gets" them and that for the Professional Gentleman to dress informally helps to achieve that perception.

The reasoning of the Misguided is, of course, misguided. The client is not hiring you to be their buddy. The client has not engaged your firm to hang out with you and your colleagues. The client does not want to think that the Professional Gentleman providing them with sophisticated banking, legal, accounting, or consulting wisdom, for which they are paying a lot, is actually a frustrated designer, artist, programmer, performer, or what-have-you.

No, no, no. The client wants to think that being a Professional Gentleman is what you were born to do, what you live to do, and what you are fully and totally committed to do. As A.D. Aliwat put it in *Alpha*, "Being a rocket scientist isn't all that smart when you could work in finance."[10] Your clients need to believe you feel that way, so it really behooves you to at least look like you feel that way (even if in fact you do not). Clients will appreciate your formal dress as it will lend seriousness to their business matters and give them the comfort that the job is being done properly. The creative clients will also appreciate how casual and insouciant *they* look when juxtaposed against your conservative uniform.

So, to reiterate this second Law, your clients set a floor in terms of formality in dress. Present yourself below this floor at your own peril, and when in doubt, or just as a prophylactic matter of course, always aim quite a bit higher. As the Giacomettis would surely tell you, undoubtedly with some hand gesturing thrown in for good measure, *puntare le stelle!*[11]

---

10. A.D. Aliwat, *Alpha: A Portrait of the Asshole as a Young Man* (Altair Press, 2015)
11. "Aim for the stars" in Italian.

Brands to Know

Isaia: Beginning in Italy in 1920, and expanding internationally to distribute its high-quality garments in Europe, Japan, China, and the United States, Isaia has become an international business model of high-end tailored menswear while maintaining its Neapolitan traditions. Putting an emphasis on uniqueness and individuality, the Isaia brand strives to express the personality of the man wearing the suit. Expanding into ready-to-wear men's clothing, Isaia has maintained its renown not only through its craftsmanship but also by its coral branch logo.

Kiton: Beginning as a small artisan workshop of 40 master tailors in Naples, Kiton expanded into the European market and later into the United States with the founding of the Kiton Corporation in 1988. Thereafter, they opened flagship stores in the Far East. Their international expansion was coupled with development of their finely crafted products as they moved from a concentration in tailored garments for men to handmade shirts and ties and further expanded into the shoe, knitwear, eyewear, and womenswear markets. The Kiton Tailoring School was established in 2001 in an effort to maintain the high quality of the brand by training young tailors in high-class tailoring. Kiton now employs over 750 people in over 40 stores across 15 countries, illuminating their prominent place in the high-end global garment market.

GH Bass: George Henry Bass started G.H. Bass & Co. in 1879 with the goal of making the very best shoe. G.H. Bass is credited with creating the world's very first penny loafer in 1936, a shoe that is still seen on industrious feet today. Worn by the likes of James Dean and JFK, the Bass penny loafer, the Weejun, became one of the most popular shoes of the time. In 2011, the company collaborated with Tommy Hilfiger to create an upscale, limited-edition loafer, "The Penny Loafer—Originals with a Twist." The GH Bass saddle shoes also cannot be beat for price-to-quality ratio, though they do look a touch professorial.

Affluence Ceiling

Formality is one parameter in your dress to be mindful of; it sets a baseline. Affluence is another parameter that often goes to set a convenient maximum ceiling on how profligate you should present yourself. Therefore, the third Law follows:

Law #3

〜

The Professional Gentleman shall not dress more affluently than his clients.

〜

Serving a paying client while looking like a billionaire (when the client is clearly not a billionaire) makes the client suspect that the professional is overpaid. Overpaid by whom? Oh yes, by the client. Nothing but bad work product tweaks a client more. "Who is working for whom?" the client might ask themselves when accosted by too rich a sartorial presentation. It might go something like this:

"How much does that lovely gold Rolex Submariner with the blue face cost? God, that thing is lovely, but how can he afford that? He almost certainly has a car waiting outside the building, and I'm paying of that, too! Is it, like a normal, Lincoln Town Car or something exotic? A Maybach? And that tan in February! Was he just in St. Barts? Ibiza? Somewhere I can't even name because I'm an impoverished rube, and he's a privileged worldly doyen? All on my company's dime? WTF?"

Such client ruminations on your splendor can go south or sideways fast. In most instances, whenever possible, it is wise to dress less affluently than your client.[12] A hard-working CFO or COO of a public company that is your

---

12. I recognize there are exceptions for those of you in criminal law, immigration, personal injury, and other fields. Please refer to the client inversion qualification *infra*.

firm's client, sitting, perhaps, in your firm's 58th floor conference room admiring not only the view but also the richness of your bespoke Gieves & Hawkes suit and gold Bulgari cufflinks, may be tallying how much of your hourly rate goes to cover these lavish effects, even putting aside the choice real estate. This may cause that client to reevaluate not only their company's legal, accounting, investment banking budget, but also their choice of firm.

Brands to Know

Rolex: The Swiss watchmaker is the single largest luxury watchmaker worldwide and has become world-renowned, evidenced from their ranking as 64th on the Forbes list of the world's most powerful brands. Founded in 1905, Rolex has been a pioneer in the watch industry, creating the first waterproof wristwatch and the first wristwatch with an automatically changing date and day on the dial. Rolex is also a sponsor of many prestigious sporting events in golf and tennis, as well as equestrian tournaments, illustrating the prominence of the brand. Rolex watches have become more than just a timekeeper, as their brand has achieved a profound level of fame and value globally, much of this due to the high quality of Rolex watches. Their watches are made from handmade gold and steel that is expensive and difficult to machine because of its aesthetic quality. Further, Rolex employs stringent quality controls and makes virtually all of its parts in-house to ensure the quality of Rolex watches lives up to the high expectations it has established in the world markets.

Gieves & Hawkes: Founded in 1771, this is one of the oldest continual bespoke tailoring companies in the world. The company provides ready-to-wear options, military tailoring, and bespoke services. A royal tailor since 1809, Gieves & Hawkes has continuously enjoyed the patronage of British Royalty, reinforcing its paralleled pedigree and international status. Quoting Oscar Wilde, Gieves & Hawkes states that, "One should either be a work of art, or wear a work of art." Offering both private tailoring and bespoke services, the company prides itself on provided a unique and expertly tailored suit engineered to meet the requirements of the customer. Their private tailoring provides a high level of customer care and attention to detail usually only afforded to bespoke services. Their combined tradition of excellence and craftsmanship has in modern times led them to supply not only royal houses in Europe and around the world but also many titans of industry and the Professional Gentlemen that represent them.

Bulgari: Founded in 1886, the Bulgari is emblematic of Italian excellence. In 1975, Bulgari delved into the world of watchmaking and introduced the now-iconic "Bvlgari-Bvlgari" watch. In 2011, Bulgari was acquired by the luxury group LVMH. Inspired by Rome's architectural history, Bulgari strives to reinterpret this beauty through watches and accessories. The brand's use of color is often one of its most identifiable traits.

This reality notwithstanding, affluence is a difficult concept with which to set an absolute. It has its subtle exceptions because, let's face it, fellas, some of the best well-made articles, some of the most stylish pieces of clothing—which I would never recommend you *not* wear or adorn yourself with—may well be some of the most expensive. What the ceiling is meant to capture are obvious, garish, and, at times, outright obnoxious displays of wealth through your personal dress. Accordingly, I'll set forth a qualification for non-obnoxious or hidden items (the "Subtle Hidden Proviso"):

Law #4

~

The Professional Gentleman may have certain articles of clothing and/or accessories that are expensive relative to his clients', provided, however, that these articles are subtle or hidden from view.

~

Many subtle forms of affluence are perfectly acceptable if kept understated and do not announce themselves. Even an expensive bespoke suit, assuming it is in a tasteful color choice (just don't unbutton the sleeves or go with flashy linings) passes muster here.[13] As we will discuss *infra*, well-made shoes in black or brown are subtle luxuries and don't offend. Many elegant watches of expert craftsmanship are mainly hidden and very often only known by watch aficionados, as will be explored *infra*. Moreover, there's something about that knowledge of the quality and provenance of an expensive item you own that allows you to cock your chin a few degrees higher, square your shoulders, and stand up against some of the Professional Gentleman's indignities with grace and charm.

It also needs to be said that inexpensive items do not necessarily equate with informality. There are several suit manufacturers that are quite modestly priced but still put forth a high-quality conservative garment. Certainly, Brooks Brothers has been doing this for almost two centuries, and more recently J. Crew and other affordable brands have provided many a junior analyst or associate with their first few suits and outfitted them nobly within a modest budget. Value propositions like Suitsupply and Frank & Oak, as well as various accessories manufacturers like Seiko and Shinola, are also examples of inexpensive and acceptable style. Even on a budget, capable and elegant is within reach.

Brands to Know

Suitsupply: Suitsupply, a recent entrant to the men's fashion market, was founded by Fokke de Jong in his Amsterdam dorm room in 2000. The European suit maker has become a "go-to" for many American men, as the brand has achieved the ideal combination of style, convenience, and affordability that many desire. Suitsupply is able to reduce costs while preserving style through their use of vertical integration and keeping many of the stores in lower-rent areas. The quality and aesthetic appeal are first rate. What one would expect from more expensive brands. The

---

13. Somewhat ironically, it is very likely that the more expensive bespoke suit is likely to be more refined and more understated than a less expensive version as the more traditional and expensive cutters on Savile Row pride themselves on subtlety.

brand's nonconformist ad campaigns are matched with innovative styles, including suits that are more tailored and cut slimmer than those found in traditional, similarly priced menswear brands.

Frank & Oak: Frank & Oak was founded in 2012 in Canada with the goal of helping men to dress with style while preserving affordability. Designing on-trend styles for both casual and more formal environments, the brand maintains modest prices through innovative design and the help of technology. Beginning solely as an online retailer, the brand provided 24/7 styling assistance on their e-commerce site. Now, with 14 retail stores that boast accoutrements like coffee bars and barber shops, the brand is taking the North American market by storm through what they believe is the future of retail shopping. DISCLOSURE: HBA represents Frank & Oak.

Shinola: Selling moderately priced watches, leather goods, and other accessories for men and women, this Detroit-based luxury lifestyle brand strives to provide high-quality, aesthetically appealing products at a feasible price point. Stressing the importance of value, the brand provides a lifetime guarantee on every watch it sells. Shinola has not only received notoriety for its on-trend products, but also for becoming what has been dubbed an "American success story," as the company does all of its manufacturing in Detroit, helping to revive business and provide jobs.

Seiko: Seiko is a Japanese watchmaker that manufactures men's and women's luxury and moderately priced watches. In Japanese, Seiko means "success" or "exquisite." A pioneer in the watch industry, Seiko produced the first-ever quartz watch, the Seiko Quartz Astron, in 1969, and also manufactured the first GPS solar watch. The brand's commitment to quality and innovation, coupled with its moderate price points, makes the watch an ideal choice for a man seeking a formal yet affordable timepiece.

Of course the opposite is also true (perhaps more so). Expensive items don't always equate to the most formal. There are a host of examples of "premium denim" brands that sell jeans at more than the price of a Brooks Brother's suit, but I'd never equate the two in terms of formality. Also, high-end fashion houses and designers like Raf Simons, John Paul Gaultier, Hedi

Slimane at Saint Laurent, Visvim, Ric Owens, Duckie Brown are expanding the boundaries of men's fashion and attempting to expand the way in which men and society view menswear from a cultural and artistic perspective. This is laudable. And perhaps these avant-garde items are appropriate to be worn for those creative professionals who are doing the same in their industries (or think they are and want to dress the part). For you, Mr. Professional Gentleman, these brands represent fashion that is best left alone and certainly not invested in as pieces of your business wardrobe. For a more fulsome treatment on fashion and why, by in large, the Professional Gentleman should avoid it, see Chapter 3 *infra*.

The Client Inversion Qualification

There is a small qualification that should be noted, however. In some professional situations, dressing to exhibit affluence is actually a benefit. When your client expects that, by engaging you and your firm, they have made it to the "big time" or expect to hit some sort of financial jackpot, then, and only then, is it advisable to out-dress them in terms of affluence. Hence what we'll define herein as the "Client Inversion Qualification":

Law #5

~

The Professional Gentleman shall dress less affluently than his clients, provided, however, that if his clients lack sophistication, he may dress more affluently.

~

Personal injury attorneys are a good example. They typically do not charge an hourly rate but rather a success fee, taking the most egregious cases on contingency. In this branch of the legal field, the client often wants to see evidence of the professional's success. They may reason crudely that the more bling, the bigger the damage award. So, looking like a vulgarian actually makes the personal injury lawyer look good at his job.

Investment bankers, entertainment lawyers, and agents are other good examples of this phenomenon. Again, this is due to the economics of the relationship. The common practice in investment banking, as well as the entertainment industry, is a success fee, taking a percentage of deals where the client only pays if and when they actually make money or consummate a transaction.[14] Again, the grander the display of wealth, the greater the perceived success the magnificent Professional Gentleman will bring to the M&A deal, band, athlete, actor, etc. Or so the reasoning goes.

You may notice that some of the clients in these areas (personal injury, sports, and entertainment) are perhaps not the most sophisticated consumers of professional services. This is not to denigrate these spheres of the professional ranks (or these clients). Some of our finest examples of professional expertise can be found amongst these practitioners. However, while they are liberated from the affluence ceiling with respect to their clients, some of them seem to be in a sartorial arms race with their competitors to be more audacious and raise the bar on luxurious dress to the point of boorishness. I sympathize with Professional Gentlemen in these practice areas to a degree, as their careers have led them to a circumstance where they risk looking like hucksters rather than gentlemen.

The stylish and intelligent amongst these Professional Gentlemen recognize that not all individual clients are swayed by overt material displays (some actually are sophisticated consumers of both professional services *and* apparel). And the stylish and wise amongst these Professional Gentlemen recognize that trying to dress like a mogul is beneath them, as it is contrary to true style and is slavish only to looking wealthy. True style for a Professional Gentleman means dressing like a Professional Gentleman, which means looking elegant and capable.[15]

So, subject to the Subtle Hidden Proviso and the Client Inversion Qualification, think of these two Laws ((i) dressing more formally than your clients, and (ii) not dressing more affluently than your clients) as mandates of relativity. A covenant you should be bound by with a floor and a ceiling. Stay above the floor of casual dress set by your client, but be reminded of the ceiling they set with how much wealth can advisably be displayed in front of them.

Ignorantia juris non excusat.

---

14. Admittedly, the concepts are somewhat different in practice, and investment banks certainly charge an engagement fee on top of their percentage success fee, but the point is the client's perception of success for both practitioners is the same.
15. With apologies for the tautology, I want to underscore that dressing the part of the Professional Gentleman is the style the Professional Gentleman should aspire to.

—3—

Dressing Relative to Your Employer

"It is an interesting question how far men would retain their relative rank if they were divested of their clothes."
—Henry David Thoreau[1]

C lients—their needs, wants, and perceptions—obviously drive what many of us do, how we do it, and how we should want to look doing it. This is because we work for them. But more directly, we also work for our employers. Hence, another Law that should guide the Professional Gentleman's dress habits is one of relativity within his firm. Each firm has its own mores and norms driven largely by its clientele, but also by its geographic region, reputation, and overall culture. I know L.A. firms that are more formal than certain New York or London firms. Some firms in the South and D.C. have some of the most consistently formal Professional Gentlemen I've ever come across. Outside the United States, dress codes change drastically.

---

1. The famous nineteenth century American essayist, poet, and philosopher. Thoreau achieved the most notoriety for his book *Walden* and his essay "Civil Disobedience." He is also well known for his writings on natural history and his abolitionist activities.

The goal within your firm is to look generally sharp, exercise a degree of self-expression, and not jeopardize your career in the process.

Now, if you have a big book of business you feel secure about and you don't feel you need to gel with your colleagues, the Laws set forth in this chapter may be of limited usefulness to you. If, on the other hand, you are an associate, counsel, VP, a junior partner, or even a senior partner with more ambitious aspirations within your firm, in addition to the client relativity Laws, you should also adhere to the precepts that follow.

Dressing Like a Partner
Before You Are a Partner

Now the next law may be a hard one for you just starting out. I sympathize, but this mandate is necessary if not particularly just. But as Oliver Wendell Holmes[2] once said, "This is a court of law, young man, not a court of justice." While not fair, it is a fact that many of the older men who are in positions of authority at your firm (and let's face it, most of your firms are still dominated by older men—likely of a particular socio-economic background) envy those among you who still have your youth. This envy manifests itself in many ways, and one of them is for the old guard to reserve to themselves many of the more expressive and powerfully virile pieces that might otherwise be in your professional wardrobe. The old guard clings to these patriarchal vestiges out of an adherence to self-serving tradition and a sense of their own God-given right to them. My friend, the fashion photographer Dario Calmese, put it quite a bit more ominously this way: "In a racialized, patriarchal, and misogynist America, masculinity—or at least a convincing masculine performance—is a prized possession; highly gendered items like . . . suiting . . . serve as visual and cultural shorthand to intimate and reinforce male prowess."

For this reason, there are certain items of dress that are charged with legacy and entitlement. It has to do with the pecking order and—wait for it—the sartorial manipulation of social class.[3] The impact is that these articles come off as just a tad too showy to advisably wear before your business card has the right title under your name. The reason for this is that wearing these tokens suggest to the partners or the managing directors (not to men-

---

2. An esteemed poet, Holmes was acclaimed to be one of the best writers of the nineteenth century, famous for his "Breakfast-Table" series. He was also a well-known advocate for medical reform, writing an essay on physicians carrying perpetual fever, which was deemed innovative at the time it was written.
3. Yes, I got it in there!

tion the associates, analysts, and vice presidents) that you are enjoying the trappings of success before actually going through the rite of passage (i.e., the eight or more years of grinding slog) to rightfully attain them. Here is the Law:

Law #6

~

The Professional Gentleman shall dress according to rank and seniority within the firm.

~

Hopefully, this just serves as an added incentive for you to work hard, advance your trade, increase your knowledge, be dynamic, and get that brass ring. Think of it this way—in addition to prestige and larger income, once you reach this status, you can expand your wardrobe to afford you even greater self-expression.

To that end, some disparate but fairly well established principles around this Law follow.

Suspend Suspenders

No suspenders with prints (or, frankly, that are even noticeable at all). Suspenders are great for the line of a suit as will be explained *infra*. However, they have become a hallmark of partnership, allowing certain partners to not only hold their trousers up more properly (and, I think, comfortably) but also to explore sartorial expression through printed versions. This later practice I am generally against in any event, so I don't think you are giving up much to abandon printed suspenders until later. However, if the suit demands it, or if wearing a belt is troublesome given your shape or overall girth, wear muted versions of suspenders in black, navy, or tan so as not to draw undue attention to them lest you be taken for a parvenu.

Contrast Is the Same as Conflicting

Resist contrast-collar dress shirts. The contrast collar dress shirt is known at some firms as a "partner shirt." I've really no idea why, but given its name, really, truly, I implore you not to wear one until it's appropriate. Only a cowboy should wear a cowboy hat, only a basketball player should wear a tank top,[4] and only a partner should wear a partner shirt. It's a fairly natty garment, but the two classic versions are blue or blue and white stripes. Really, to me, these are only two acceptable versions. In any event, on any version of the partner shirt, the collar and cuffs should never be anything but white. In this format, the shirt is innocuous enough but can still punch up an otherwise staid suit-tie combination. Nevertheless, if you are not a partner, don't go there.

French Cuff—C'est Ouf[5]

Avoid French cuff shirts unless you have muted cufflinks (simple silk knots are good). Quite formal, the French cuff is also quite elaborate. Also, the cuff holes invite all manner of crazy cufflinks, which are often abused by partners/managing directors ("MDs") who are permitted to wear the French cuff. Again, but for different reasons, I am against regular use of the French cuff as it prevents one from easily rolling up one's sleeves, which, while informal in appearance, immediately communicates a seriousness about getting down to work. Think about it—literally rolling up your sleeves can be a great optic.

---

4. No, I honestly don't think a tank top is a good look, even as beach wear, even on a college student on spring break. It's not that a tank top is inappropriate in these circumstances; it is just that it doesn't look good on most men.
5. "That's craaaaaazy" in French.

But with French cuffs, it is a fussy procedure. There is the matter of the removal of cufflinks (where does one then store them?) and the inevitable challenge of putting them back on when the jacket needs to be donned. All of this outweighs the sharpness of the look in non-formal situations (i.e., at work).

No Water in the Pool

Don't dive into the splash hankie. We'll get into specific folds for pocket squares, but the splash hankie—where the ends of the handkerchief all show and often one or two ends collapse over the jacket's breast pocket like a tropical flower is reserved for senior Professional Gentlemen (and really only the most daring of them will go for this move). Think of this as the high dive. Not for beginners. Sporting a perfectly imperfect splash hankie as a junior associate—you'll look like an arrogant poseur.

Pee-Wee's Big Adventure

Forget the bowtie unless you are really, truly, from the South or have a teaching gig on the side. Don't get me wrong, bowties are great—communicating formality with a dash of bookishness (which most Professional Gentleman, given our years of schooling, incline toward). They can make a bold statement and are actually more comfortable and less of a physical annoyance than a tie in many work situations. But they remain a perplexing koan within firm culture for junior members. Bowties are the provenance of partners, MDs, and, of course, professors. If you are none of these, relegate them to your formal wear (by which I mean your tuxedo).

Advanced Suiting—Not Suitable

Think long and hard before you wear certain suit styles early in your career, like double breasted—although if you feel your body requires it, it is better to be comfortable and confident in your suits than adhere to this tenet.[6] Three-piece suits are also a challenge for a youngster, even though they are very dignified. In particular, one can look quite dashing and effective, even with the jacket off, when girdled in a slightly form-fitting vest. The vest structures an athletic and vital male silhouette—even on a Professional Gentleman who rarely sees the gym. The arms are featured and the rest of the torso and legs fade from primacy. This fact notwithstanding, the safest route is to wait until you've achieved senior Professional Gentleman status.[7]

Also, certain prints, like thick chalk stripe pins, windowpanes of any color, and multi-colored country tweeds, can be too jaunty at junior levels. You'll need to attain enough rank to suggest that you might arguably have ever been invited to someone's pastoral estate—to shoot small animals or jump hedges on horseback—in order to actually wear such traditionally English country garb (which will still look a bit outlandish in the city—but less so). So, young esquire, best to avoid.

Pipe Dreams

Smoking cigarettes and cigars is a vulgar habit. All smoking and tobacco should be avoided out of general health principles. Pipe smoking, however, can be sublime.

---

6. If you are thin and on the taller side, double-breasted suits give a fuller appearance to the figure. We will discuss suiting and sizing the suit and its cut to your shape in more detail in Chapter 7 *infra*.
7. I'm more on the fence about this one. I'd never fault a mid-level associate in good standing from having a solid-colored dark gray or navy version of a three-piece and wearing it judiciously. You can always drop the vest from time to time to suit the occasion.

"I believe that **pipe** smoking contributes to a somewhat calm and objective judgment in all human affairs."

—Albert Einstein

I am a partner and a law professor and immensely confident, and I still don't smoke a pipe in public despite my infatuation with it. This is because pipe smoking requires real silverback chops, good old-fashioned . . . age, to look right. But this is an activity, not a mode of dress or appearance, so I'm digressing. Like collecting vintage automobiles, like fly fishing with your grandkid, like knowing (and having a modest collection of) fine wines, pipe smoking is for studs of advancing age who relish life. You'll get there. And if you are there, enjoy, you old silver fox, you.

So until you are the boss man, don't act like the boss man or out-dress the boss man. Simple laws of the firm as savage jungle. The silverback rules and comes down hard on the fledgling upstart—ruining a youth's potential in order to maintain the precarious balance of the firm. It can get ugly, particularly when the juveniles attempt to adopt the trappings that their elders have claimed for themselves. No satirical manipulation of social class or firm hierarchy allowed, young buck. Adhere to this Law or you will find you get a lot of Friday calls from the staffing MD asking, "What is your schedule like this weekend?" Following this Law still allows you to go quite far in the direction of style—of appearing capable and elegant—without seeming insolent or giving offense.

Dress Better Than Your Peers

If you are reading this, and follow the Laws, chances are quite good that you will dress better than your colleagues. You will have more style. You will very likely be more confident. So there certainly can be sartorial manipulation of standing and rank within your peer group. For there is really no comparison between the Professional Gentleman who is well dressed and his colleague who is poorly dressed. It is *prima facie*.[8]

Now, it is often the case that when you are well dressed and appreciate the Laws, you may find it difficult to have complete respect for colleagues who, from laziness, ignorance, or both, are badly dressed. Partners and MDs prefer to (indeed—through economic necessity *must*) reward those Professional Gentlemen whom they think most redound to the firm's glory. This should be obvious. All else being equal, those Professional Gentlemen who look capable and elegant will be promoted over those who look defective or weak. There are "no weak men in the books at home."[9] So it is just and good that your poorly dressed colleague will not advance as swiftly (nor as stylishly) as you. A Law follows:

Law #7

~

The intelligent and wise Professional Gentleman
shall dress better than his peers.

~

However, in dressing with more style, the Professional Gentleman must maintain a degree of compliance (if not strict adherence) with all of the Laws. Given that your peers are, themselves, Professional Gentlemen, who care about promotion and advancement every bit as much as you, it is natural to suspect that a scrum might develop. A desire for one-upmanship in terms of sartorial presentation results, where to look "better" than your peers becomes interpreted by some unfortunate fellows as looking more fashionable—more current with what is in vogue or the mode of a current season or menswear fad. Brothers, this is not the path to go down.

---

8. Latin for "on its face." When referring to a lawsuit or criminal prosecution in which the evidence before trial is sufficient to prove the case unless there is substantial contradictory evidence presented at trial. A prima facie case presented to a Grand Jury by the prosecution will result in an indictment.
9. Gang of Four, "Not Great Men," *Entertainment* (EMI, 1979).

The Perils of Becoming
"That Fashionable Guy" at the Firm

"Fashions fade, style is eternal." The exceptional designer Yves Saint Laurent laid it out for us pretty succinctly. One could write a book on the subject of style and fashion (and many have),[10] but to me it basically boils down to fashion being what is current and offered by designers during any given season and style being, what you've selected, historically, from these fashions to dress yourself in.

Deep Thoughts on Fashion and Style from the Stylish:

"The difference between style and fashion is quality."
—*Giorgio Armani*

"Style is a way to say who you are without having to speak."
—*Rachel Zoe*

"Someone who is finding out who they are follows trends
and someone who knows who they are has style."
—*Norma Kamali*

"Fashion can be bought. Style one must possess."
—*Edna Woolman Chase*

"Style is a personal expression of who you are; trends
are the collective expression of others."
—*Blake Kuwahara*

"Style is when they're running you out of town, and
you make it look like you're leading the parade."
—*William Battie*

"Style is the visible manifestation of personality."
—*Glenn O'Brien*

---

10. Alicia Drake, *The Beautiful Fall* (London: Bloomsbury, 2007), Alex Newman and Zakee Shariff, *Fashion A to Z* (London: Laurence King Publishing, 2013), Diana Vreeland, *D.V.* (City: Sterling Publishing Company, 2003), Grace Coddington, *Grace: A Memoir* (New York: Random House Publishing Group, 2013), Scott Schuman, *Closer* (London: Penguin Books Ltd, 2012).

Law #8

~

*The Professional Gentleman shall not be
recognized as "fashionable."*

~

Given this Law, and given the general conservative nature of firms, fashion is something to be approached warily by the professional. I'm not saying don't be fashionable if it turns you on, but just don't do it in certain obvious ways that put you up for easy ridicule. The fop, the dandy, the coxcomb, the popinjay, "that fashionable guy"—he is the firm's *homo sacer.*[11]

This is a shame because, personally, I far prefer the bloke who's trying, who's taking care in his dress (even if it's too much care), who dreams of going to Pitti Uomo and being photographed by the latest blogger. Yes, I prefer this foppish swell over the lout who's not trying at all. But perhaps because most of the men at most firms are not trying at all, the dandy becomes the instant target. His thoughtfulness on matters of dress are viewed as rampant displays of preening. He appears too self-involved. He may even be regarded as purposefully conspicuous within the conservative firm culture rather than admired for his foiled attempts at creative elegance.

Early in my career I had a colleague in my class in the M&A group—Magnus. Tall, athletic-looking, fluent in a few languages, and up to snuff as an associate—he dressed well and nothing about him stood out in an offensive way. In short, Magnus was pretty impeccable and seemed destined for advancement. As we progressed at the firm, he started dating an editor at one of the seminal women's fashion publications. She was objectively gorgeous—a total fox.[12] Now this would typically be a development that would have others at the firm envying his good fortune, or looks, or both.

---

11. *Homo sacer* (Latin for "the sacred man" or "the accursed man") is an obscure figure of Roman law. He may be banned, even killed, by anyone in the populace, but, oddly, he may not be sacrificed in certain religious rituals.
12. Don't fault me for holding on to '70s slang. While the literal meaning of *fox* is, of course, a small, intelligent but still wild animal, the origin of the British word is *foxismonitism*, which means young and attractive.

But as his relationship with the beautiful fashionista progressed, he began wearing gray and even blue suede shoes into the office—I couldn't determine the brand, but it didn't matter: the shoes could evoke an Elvis song. This was followed by cravats (in seasonally appropriate fabrics and properly tied to be sure, but still, *cravats*), and some very fashionable but slim fitting suits. I think the last straw was when he wore Gianni Versace leather pants on a casual Friday. Really. Honest to Christ and the Ethics Committee. Yes, it was the '90s, but Magnus' leather trousers were, to say the least, fashion forward. Not magnificent. The quality of his work was forgotten amid the noise and flash of his fashionable moves. He left, perhaps for a more fashionable life, or at least that's what I've always assumed. But he was not long for the firm after these displays.

As Versace himself once noted, "Don't be into trends. Don't make fashion own you, but you decide what you are, what you want to express by the way you dress and the way you live."

Dressing Relative to Other Professional Gentlemen Outside of Your Firm

Not all Professional Gentlemen are in adversarial situations with opposing counsel. But for those who are, I say dress better than your opponent. You may win before either of you has even opened your mouths. Behold, a Law on this subject:

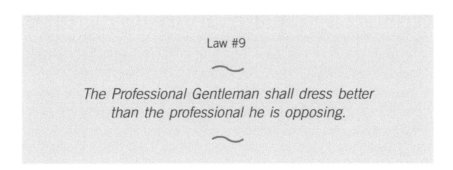

Law #9

~

The Professional Gentleman shall dress better than the professional he is opposing.

~

Of course, as we all well know, terms and their definitions are important. So, please note that "better" in this context does not necessarily mean more formal or more affluent, but does mean with more style—within a general adherence to the Laws.

There was a mediation I attended in Los Angeles on a hot early summer day. JAMs[13] in LA sits in a high-rise glass tower downtown. Row upon row of mediation rooms and breakout rooms punctuated by kitchenettes filled with caffeinated goodies and snacks. Sort of the litigator's version of the upscale financial printer's headquarters. Not at all uncomfortable like going into court—mediation represents a sometimes more expensive but, usually, less time-consuming path to dispute resolution. In any event, the client was represented by very adept and stylish counsel. A junior partner we'll call Mark Swift. Quick-witted and well-mannered, he sat in his crisp, light gray Oxxford pinstripe suit with a dark blue Charvet tie and discrete Allen Edmonds brown wing tips in the mediator's room.

Brands to Know

Oxxford: Committed to fine tailoring, Oxxford Clothes was founded in Chicago in 1916 and continues their strong tradition of commitment to precision and detail in the design and making of Oxxford suits. The remarkable quality of the garments produced by the clothier is evidenced by their cutting every piece from hand, matching all stripes at all seams, and hand stitching each buttonhole, taking the many hours necessary to produce an exceptional suit. Made from the finest fabrics and employing age-old techniques of the most talented tailors, Oxxford suits can be purchased only at specialty stops in America, the company's showroom in Chicago, and the Oxxford flagship store in New York.

Charvet: Charvet, a luxury French shirt maker and tailor, makes bespoke and ready-to-wear men's shirts, neckties, and suits that are sold across high-end markets internationally. Since its founding in 1838, the brand has developed acclaim for the fine quality of its goods and the array of color and style selections it offers, attracting the attention of royalty and celebrity purchasers. The brand offers its elite clientele the ability to custom order or customize any article he purchases. Charvet ties are handmade and are distinguished not only by their fine silk but also by the custom-made patterns and colors Charvet employs.

---

13. JAMs is a US-based, for-profit organization of alternative dispute resolution services, including mediation and arbitration.

Allen Edmonds: Maintaining the quality and precision employed for decades, Allen Edmonds continues to use the same 212 steps to manufacture its welded shoes as the American shoemaker used at its founding in 1922. The time and effort put into each pair of shoes is evident from their fine craftsmanship, beautiful style, and durability. The thin and high-quality leather allows for comfort and breathability. Allen Edmonds shoes also stand apart because of the manufacturer's attention to fit, evident from the 100 sizes the company offers that span from narrow AAA to wide EEE. While famous for their dress and casual footwear, Allen Edmonds has expanded its leather artistry into briefcases, belts, and leather bags as well.

He was opposite a couple of very turned-out plaintiff's counsel lawyers who were looking to settle a potential class action lawsuit before bringing the claim or having the class even certified. These are the kind of lawyers who advertise their services on bus stop benches and on midday television.[14] Even though no clients were in attendance, the plaintiff's counsel lawyers seemed to be under the impression that the Client Inversion Qualification was in full effect. They were from different firms with some arrangement to split the settlement award if one was granted, but with no agreement on how to dress. The younger one looked every bit the boy band member, with a black suit, fitted white shirt, and no tie, coupled with an aggressively jarring disconnected undercut hairstyle. He could have been a bouncer at a night club if he was not physically so small. His colleague, we'll call him Ralph Beckham, had on an (oxymoronic) light tweed suit in brown, which also had windowpane stripes. It got much worse. His silk pink tie and neatly folded silk pocket square matched, precisely matched, in hue and texture. They were made from the same fabric. The tie also had a neat tie clip on it. His dress boots laced up beyond where the eye could follow under his trousers. His heels were high.

As the initial conference in front of the mediator began, the plaintiff's lawyers came out guns blazing. Their claims were expressed with soap-opera emotion. There was some standing up. Some arm waving. And some

---

14. Attorney advertising is actually quite a regulated matter but does not prevent plaintiff's lawyers from throwing up advertisements, broadcasting television commercials, and web-based pop-up ads once people have searched terms like "my neck hurts" or "I was an unpaid intern."

less-than-businesslike, not to mention less-than-collegial comments made about Mark's client. When Mark protested to the mediator about the point of all this bluster, Ralph interrupted with a condescending air of mock sensitivity, telling Mark not to get emotional and that he did not want him to get offended by his remarks. Mark responded coolly that he was far less offended by Ralph's remarks than he was by his tie/pocket square combination. Ralph's diminutive colleague had no rejoinder—he likely agreed—and to the extent there actually was ever any wind in Ralph's sails, there was no longer. He looked down upon his wardrobe in self-doubt and was, for the rest of the day, cowed.

Ignorantia juris non excusat.

—4—

Insouciance and Breaches of the Laws

"A man must face the world with sprezzatura.
It literally means detachment, but a better way to
think of it is quiet confidence or low-key style. The most
forceful statement is understatement."
—Luciano Barbera[1]

Compliance with the Laws—Heuristics

How are you doing? Is your head spinning from too many rules? Feeling inhibited? Circumscribed by the limitations the Laws have put on you? I expect not. As Professional Gentlemen, we are educated and recognize the value of an orderly society. We are prone to a certain degree of innate compliance. Do you think much about assaulting or menacing other people?

---

1. Owner of the Luciano Barbera brand, as well as a textile mill that serves elite brands such as Ralph Lauren and Armani. He is known as a man of impeccable taste and idolized by many for his style.

Stealing other people's things? Committing securities fraud? Probably not. Crickey, I hope not.

Conservative by nature and driven by constant constraints on time, when something is mandated as a rule or law that, after some quick mental analysis, we find sensible (or so common to our station in life as Professional Gentlemen that there is no sense in rebelling against it), we typically adopt it. This heuristic technique allows us to free up mental space to deal with other issues—usually those of our clients.[2] There are certainly many benefits to this cognitive shortcut.

In most circumstances related to the Laws, this default should serve you well. Rules of thumb to get you properly dressed and prepared for your career. Continue to read this book, digest the Laws, understand and appreciate them. Once that is done, however, do me a favor. Don't stress about the Laws after you are dressed. Sir Hardy Amies, founder of the Savile Row brand of the same name, once said, "A man should look as if he has bought his clothes with intelligence, put them on with care, and then forgotten all about them." From this great sartorial knight's words, a Law takes shape:

Law #10

~

The Professional Gentleman shall appear confident about his clothing and personal appearance. Ideally, he shall actually be so.

~

I'm not saying be laid back or flippant. But honestly, if you've done as much as you can reasonably do, walk tall and be confident in your sartorial choices. You'll look better, believe me.

On a typical morning, after having my coffee, walking the dog, and showering, I'll be faced with the decision of what to wear that day. Say I'm meeting with designers in the morning, having lunch at the Princeton Club,

---

2. A heuristic technique is any approach to problem solving, learning, or discovery that employs a practical method not guaranteed to be optimal or perfect, but sufficient for the immediate goals. Where finding an optimal solution is impossible or impractical, heuristic methods can be used to speed up the process of finding a satisfactory solution.

and spending the afternoon in partner meetings. Later, I may have drinks with a client in the Village. So acknowledging who I'm seeing that day, the weather, and where the evening may take me, I might grab a dark blue Rag & Bone suit with a white dress shirt. A striped colorful knit Orley tie looks good with that. I'll opt for a simple white hankie, but perhaps match my Hook and Albert socks with one of the colors in the tie. Noah Waxman single monk strap suede shoes with a matching belt, and I'm good to go.

Brands to Know

Rag & Bone: British mates David Neville and Marcus Wainwright grew this edgy yet understated denim label from New York startup to a global brand. The menswear offering is fulsome with tailored clothing, knits, shirting, and accessories, as well as footwear. Rag & Bone melds classic British tailoring with a decidedly New York aesthetic. Quality, expert craftsmanship and attention to detail resonated deeply, informing the brand's core philosophy. DISCLOSURE: I am Rag & Bone's general counsel, and HBA has represented the brand since 2005. I love Rag & Bone suits, knits, and outerwear.

Orley: Best known for its Italian-made knitwear, the brand offers a full men's ready-to-wear collection. Orley combines elegant fabrics with youthful design, with a focus on luxury knitwear. The work of the Orley designers subverts classicism, using proprietary stitch techniques and an idiosyncratic color palette to create a unique product. DISCLOSURE: HBA represents the brand.

Hook & Albert: Designed with the aim of being a "go-to" for all men's accessories, this brand was formed by two friends who sought to incorporate fit, fun, and function into men's socks, bags, belts, neckwear, and other accoutrements. Selling dress socks that incorporate colors and patterns without being too loud, Hook & Albert sells the perfect socks for a man looking to add a little excitement into his everyday formal dress. The brand's other accessories, all moderately priced, help to add style to the Professional Gentleman's everyday dress without sacrificing function and durability.

Noah Waxman: Launched in 2013, the Noah Waxman line combines his love for all-American style with his classic European training. With a range of casual and formal styles, Noah Waxman shoes are brimming with character for the uncommon man. DISCLOSURE: my firm represents the company, and I personally own quite a few of Noah's creations. His offices are a stone's throw from my firm's offices in the Garment District of New York City, and I often walk in to see his new models.

I'm not looking back. Nor should I. I'm not questioning my choices, nor making corrections or edits during the day. Confident, I hit the streets.

> "So tall I take over the street with high-beams shining on my back. A wingspan unbelievable, I'm a festival, I'm a parade."
>
> —The National[3]

Few things are more contemptible than a fellow who's constantly primping, stealing glances of himself in mirrors, arranging his hair, touching his eyebrows, fiddling with his tie. Try to avoid this type of self-absorbed behavior at all costs. If you suspect something in your appearance is out of order, please find a private spot to investigate. Alone, you can correct any dressing glitches, wardrobe malfunctions, or odd events going on with your face or hair. But hey, slight dishevelment can be tolerated and, in certain circumstances, should even be encouraged. It makes you look real. Like you don't care *that* much about appearances, which of course suggests that you have powers in reserve.[4] It evinces the fact that you are, indeed, working, getting your hands dirty, etc. Don't be a peacock. Don't be a jackass. But don't be a prude either.

Once you are relatively confident that you are in fact quite well dressed, it will be an amazing feeling. You won't sweat the small stuff with your appearance. This confidence will further uptick your look, creating a posi-

---

3. The National, "All the Wine," *Cherry Tree* (Brassland Records, 2004).
4. This is actually the essence of sprezzatura, as a form of defensive irony: not showing you care about the very thing you care about because it makes you look like you'd be even better if you actually did care.

tive feedback loop. As Ralph Waldo Emerson[5] put it, "Being perfectly well dressed gives one a tranquility that no religion can bestow." Transcendental indeed! It is a wonderful sartorial Zen-like state to be in, allowing you to focus on other matters at hand—taking comfort and pride in the fact that the "looking great" box is checked.

Finding Freedom Within the Law

"The end of law is not to abolish or restrain, but to preserve and enlarge freedom. For in all the states of created beings capable of law, where there is no law, there is no freedom."

—John Locke[6]

So now that we've unpacked all these restrictions and before we get into a more general overview of their application to modes of dress and articles of clothing, it needs to be said that the ideal goal of following the Laws is not blind compliance but actually an acceptable form of self-actualization. What I want is for you not only to be able to dress in a suitable way that advances your career, but also for you to have a degree of uniqueness—a degree of you-ness that others (clients, bosses, colleagues, and friends), at best, respect, or, at worst, envy without rancor. As Coco Chanel knowingly put it, "In order to be irreplaceable, one must always be different." So while it may seem contradictory to the rest of what is set forth herein, be different!

After hearing all of the restrictions that the Laws set forth, this ambition of self-actualization through dress may seem a tall order. Let me assure you, there are areas of acceptable whimsy and broader areas of sartorial choices that allow you to both express yourself and look extremely fine doing so.

---

5. American author of the nineteenth century and leader of the transcendentalist movement. He is known for his philosophical writings on individuality, freedom, and the relationship between a soul and the world it exists in.

6. Known as the Father of the Liberalism, Locke was an English philosopher of the seventeenth century and one of the most famous Enlightenment thinkers. His work was instrumental in shaping political philosophy, and its impact is evident in the US Declaration of Independence.

In some sense, style is really merely understanding the rules and breaking them just enough to show confidence and a little bit of yourself. So if you are compelled, even after reading this book, to wear lux-trainers from A.P.C. or Lanvin with a sport coat, and you feel you can confidently pull that off within the Laws, more power to you, *mon ami.*

Brands to Know

A.P.C.: This French ready-to-wear brand was founded in 1987 by designer Jean Touitou. A.P.C. stands for "Atelier de Production et de Création." The brand is known for its innovative designs, which include some very sweet high-end sneakers. Its clothing features clean lines and simple patterns. Military-inspired minimalism. Logos are rarely visible, as well.

Lanvin: A French multinational high-fashion house founded by Jeanne Lanvin in 1889. Menswear for the brand has been headed by Lucas Ossendrijver since 2005. He launched the first Lanvin upscale urban sneakers with their iconic patent leather toe caps while presenting his AW 2006 collections. They have been a *succès fou.*

People, myself included, can easily label what you find visually appealing to be good, bad, or ugly. But absolutely NO ONE can question that your aesthetic judgement is uniquely yours. Please always recognize that.

So know these Laws. Know these Laws so that most of them you may follow to your benefit. But know these Laws also so that those you firmly do not agree with or find intolerant to your aesthetic judgment—those Laws you may break to your glory.

Listen, my brothers: caring about how you present yourself stems from a primary human impulse; a very natural and healthy place: pride. I wouldn't call it narcissism, conceit, or vanity. It's more about applying philosophy and aesthetics to yourself. It is both a noble project and a lifelong one. Dressing is a form of self-expression in which you provide clues about who you really are. I want you to have a way of dressing that, most importantly, allows you to express yourself, to feel true to yourself, and even (if you get into it, as I hope you will) explore other areas of real self-expression. It is my wish that your attire may become an external expression of your inner refinement.

All the tools to do this will be discussed in the chapters that follow. So let's dig in.

Ignorantia juris non excusat.

—5—

From the Ground Up: Shoes

"It is totally impossible to be well dressed in cheap shoes."
—Hardy Amies[1]

The aesthetic elements of what we choose to wear are inherently subjective, but craftsmanship is objective. Nowhere is this more evident than with shoes. Shoes are one of the easiest parts of your wardrobe to get right, and yet they are so often done wrong. In this chapter, we will consider proper footwear, as well as the modes of the dress shoe, and because business casual is a reality we likely all must deal with, the non-dress shoe.

Getting Obsessed Over Shoes

Most women who are contemporaries of Professional Gentlemen really, really love shoes.[2] Most men merely tolerate them. Given the inherent func-

---

1. An English fashion designer famous for his work as official dressmaker to Queen Elizabeth II from 1952 to 1989, Amies also created his own fashion label, Hardy.
2. As, to be sure, do many, many other types of women. As Marilyn Monroe famously said, "Give a girl the right shoes, and she can conquer the world."

tionality and literal groundedness of shoes, I find men's apathy over footwear to be odd. We should have some of the same obsessive, even lustful, impulses women do around truly fine footwear. Women's shoe designer Christian Louboutin put it reasonably well: "I would say that a good shoe is exactly like a good wine. These shoes are going to stay and last for a long time." Or to put it better (and in a parlance many men can refer to), fine shoes are exactly like fine cars. These shoes are an investment and will get you where you need to go in style and comfort.

Men's disaffection with shoes appears to be changing. With the huge proliferation in the athletic performance sneaker market over the last few decades and the more recent advent of "designer-casual" sneakers, there are growing pockets of "sneakerheads." These fellows, many of them Professional Gentlemen, wait on lines to visit stores like Flight Club or Union LA and love their shoes with a fetishism that exceeds that which many women have for their high-heels. Sneakers are not what we are permitted, or even advised, to wear most days, gentlemen. But this new interest in footwear is a step in the right direction (even if that step is an athletic cross-over step).

History and Construction of Shoes

Given the functional nature of shoes, it is perhaps surprising that so few of us actually understand how shoes are made and how much time, effort, and craftsmanship goes into the process. This is somewhat ironic with respect to Professional Gentlemen because, let's face it, many of our clients really have no idea what goes into the services we provide, either.

Many people believe Professional Gentlemen are performing dark arts: necessary evils of accounting diligence, obscure codification of legal regulation, or financial manipulation to fix markets. Our firms are viewed by many as awful Orwellian machines they would rather not understand. Sure, clients recognize the function and usually the objective results of most professional services, but often clients are not in a position to determine a truly excellent job from a job just proficiently done: an exquisitely crafted license agreement, say, from one drafted just acceptably; or an earn-out provision in an M&A deal that is negotiated elegantly and provides tax advantages acceptable to both sides rather than one that just provides for regular payments of a purchase price upon milestones hit. To the Professional Gentleman, these are beautiful and painstakingly made things, and we know the devil is in the details. So too with the well-made shoe.

Shoe Construction

Shoe construction is now largely done by machine, but as recently as the late nineteenth century, most dress shoes in England were still made by hand. One can still find handmade shoes, but they are absurdly priced for all but the most financially successful of Professional Gentlemen. The leather that goes into shoe construction is quite important and is typically calfskin but can also be cordovan (horsehide), pigskin, deer, or antelope, as well as certain reptiles, or even birds like the ostrich.[3]

A dress shoe is constructed around wooden lasts that represent the human foot. First, the inner sole of the shoe is cut or stamped out. This is then secured to the last, and a narrow strip of leather is stuck on or a portion is cut out so that there is a raised perimeter around the sole. This perimeter is called the feather. The feather is the part of the sole that the welt and the upper of the shoe connect to. This is done by stitching, but before that can be done, the leather needs to be punctured with holes so that the stitching may take place. This is an arduous process. Also, the upper must be cut from leather, and any of its components, like broguing[4] or back-stitched seams, must be prepared. The upper goes over the last, being stretched in the process. The feather, welt, and upper are then stitched together. The back part of the shoe where the heel will be is nailed to the last. The inner sole is then filled with cork and resin, which gets molded to the shape of the foot and becomes the base of the shoe. The outer sole may then be stitched to the welt. To provide the heel, a number of lifts (usually four or five) are placed at the back of the shoe. The lifts are all leather except for the next to last one, which is typically rubber to absorb the wear and tear of being worn.

Before you put them on tomorrow morning, take a look at your dress shoes. If they are well constructed versions, you'll recognize signs of the process above. Your shoes are feats of engineering and things of beauty. Often

---

3. Buckskin from deer and antelope, as well as pigskin (like peccary), is used in some of the nicer Italian loafers. But reptile and bird skin should really be avoided by the Professional Gentleman, as its odd appearance and high cost make most shoes made of it garish and flashy.

4. Broguing is not a forgettable dance from the '80s or a drinking game for frat boys but a form of decoration for dress shoes that comes from Scotland as will be detailed *infra*.

underappreciated, like some of your finer but less public or less understood accomplishments as a Professional Gentleman. Respect the shoes. Treat them well, and walk like a man.[5]

Dress Shoes: Form, Function, and Style

You may have heard that the best way to tell if a man is well dressed is to look not at his clothing but down at his shoes.[6] This statement is almost a mantra in most traditional books about dressing like a "gentleman."[7] I don't subscribe to this notion, as you will learn.[8] I believe all of our sartorial elements are important and relative. But, make no mistake, shoes are a fundamental component of your wardrobe. They are also critical to your personal comfort. Good shoes get you were you want to go and should be invested in accordingly.

There are several traditionally acceptable styles of dress shoe for the working professional.

---

5. The Four Seasons, "Walk Like a Man," *Big Girls Don't Cry and Twelve Others* (Vee Jay Records, 1963).

6. Judging a man by his shoes has too many sources to cite. Indeed, an enterprising "dating expert" and "shoe guru," Donna Sozio, combined both important disciplines in her seminal work on the subjects, *Never Trust a Man in Alligator Loafers* (New York: Kensington Publishing Corp., 2007), which purportedly helps guide women through judging a man by his shoes for mating potential. Rrright.

7. A term these tomes treat with great reverence and yet seems to require the man this term is bestowed upon is either landed gentry or part of the aristocracy.

8. At the risk of stating the obvious, I think the best way to tell if a man is well dressed is to look at his entire wardrobe, not just his shoes. Gorgeous shoes will not cover other obvious sartorial mistakes.

Oxfords

Oxfords[9] or Balmorals[10] are closed laced shoes. These are the most formal laced shoes a Professional Gentleman can wear, and you should have pairs in black and brown. Closed lacing means that the two sides of the part of the shoe that sits atop your upper foot that are pulled together by the laces (called, conveniently, the "upper") are sewn underneath the rest of the shoe. The tongue of the shoe is therefore also sewn on, underneath the lacing. The sleekness of this minimal presentation renders closed laced shoes dressy and apposite for reserved functions. But, please don't take this to mean oxfords can only be worn on formal occasions. Certainly, color—black—dictates the greatest amount of formality as well as the patina and clean lines of the shoe,[11] but oxfords can be worn in all manner of ways. Certainly, tan or suede versions of the oxford can be worn in casual settings and look spiffy.

Like other types of shoes, oxfords come in different breeds based on how much decoration and detailing with external perforations (known as "broguing") they come with.[12] The cleanest is the plain oxford with the seamless version (which must be, without any exception I can think of, custom made) representing the epitome of footwear elegance. Seamless oxfords, as the name implies, lack any seam.[13] Cap toe oxfords bring the formality down—but just a notch. Very business appropriate—still very clean, very classic, but with a bit of bolster at the toe where people can see it.

Black cap toes or plain oxfords are the first pair of dress shoes you should purchase. The Professional Gentleman is synonymous with these shoes. In many situations he *must* wear this shoe, and in all business situations he *can* wear this shoe. It represents the first of the Foundation of Five (as defined herein) shoes every Professional Gentleman must have.

From there, one can move to closed laced shoes that have more or less broguing. The more of this decoration the shoe features, the less formal and

---

9. Oxfords stem from a half-boot called the Oxonian, which was popular at Oxford University in 1800.

10. The name Balmoral derives from Balmoral Castle in Royal Deeside, Aberdeenshire, Scotland, which is one of the residences of the British Royal Family.

11. This is why many formal shoes are patent leather closed laced shoes or slippers. While slippers are certainly not appropriate for formal business settings, their clean lines (even when not in patent leather versions—some formal slippers come in grosgrain and velvet) have made them acceptable companions to the tuxedo.

12. It should be noted that brogues are said to originate in Scotland (purportedly to allow water to seep from shoes after a long highland hike), and broguing as a purely fashionable adornment was first popularized on women's shoes.

13. These models necessitate more leather, to say nothing of the expert craftsmanship required. Plain oxfords can also be wholecut, which refers to a shoe that features just a single visible seam at the heel. Plain oxfords of lesser quality will exhibit seams, but still are a very formal shoe.

the more rustic and "countrified" the shoe is considered. Hence, the half brogue with closed lacing is still a formal shoe, and even the full brogue is suitable for business (but not formal receptions if it can be helped). The full brogue also typically features a jauntily curved top cap and are known as "wing tips." Some wing tips—called "long wing tips"—even extend the cap all the way to the heel of the shoe. Most closed laced shoes have the traditional ten lace holes.

Color and texture of leather also determine level of formality, with the scale ranging from black leather being most formal to light tan suede being the least formal (setting aside for the moment white, blue, red, or other colorful versions that one could no doubt get their hands on in a sales bin). In addition, the more muted the leather, the less formal the shoes are, with patent leather being the most formal and suede being the least formal.

Brands to Know

Lottusse: Founded in 1877 in Mallorca, Spain, Lottusse is an artisanal shoe factory specialized in the Goodyear welted system. Each shoe is touched by over 60 artisans in a 120-step manufacturing process. Lottusse has an extraordinary relationship with leather. Quality has always been a pillar on which the business philosophy was built.

Tricker's: Once of the earliest established shoemakers in England, Tricker's was founded in 1829. Tricker's reputation for excellence established them as *the* maker for country boots for estate owners and the landed gentry. Built to the same exacting standards that established Tricker's reputation, the Tricker's boots and shoes today are known for comfort and quality. The irreproachable character of the brand comes through in the products.

Grenson: Founded in 1866 in the shoe making mecca of Northamptonshire, this is the first producer in the world to use the Goodyear welting construction method, which is now a hallmark of all well-made British shoes. Grenson shoes are divided into four categories of declining price: G:Lab (made to order), G:Zero, G:One, and G:Two. The first three categories are entirely made in the Grenson factory, with the difference between them being materials and finishing. G:Two is made in India.

Bluchers

Bluchers[14] and Derbys[15] are open laced shoes that have the sides of the upper sewn on (not underneath) the rest of the shoe. So instead of the tongue being sewn under the lacing, it comes up directly from the vamp (which is the part of the shoe that covers the toes and your foot's instep). Open laced shoes came about because they are easier to don and lace up. They are also, as you might guess, less formal. A good selection of open laced shoes should make up any self-respecting Professional Gentleman's closet in colors ranging from black to tan. Open laced versus closed laced is a personal choice, but your wardrobe should have a balanced offering of shoes ranging in formality. As a personal preference, I tend to prefer more brogued and brown and tan shoes to be open laced, as it seems to fit their folksy, less urban nature.

The difference between the Blucher and the Derby is that the Derby actually has lacing that joins two quarters (think, the sides of the shoe as they extend back from the lacing) of the shoe whereas the Blucher has lacing that merely joins two flaps across the top of the shoe. These flaps do not extend back the way the quarter of the shoes do. It's actually quite a pronounced difference, but many people still refer to all open laced shoes as either Bluchers or Derbys. Don't be one of these people because this is wrong, and the Professional Gentleman should avoid being wrong whenever possible.

Brands to Know

Alfred Sargent: Still a family-run business, Alfred Sargent was founded in 1899 in Northamptonshire, England, by the namesake and great-grandfather of the current owners, Paul and Andrew Sargent. These shoes are the fine leather, Goodyear welted, expensive real deals. For the Professional Gentleman of discerning taste and deep pockets.

---

14. The name "Bluchers" comes from a Prussian field marshal Blucher who, together with the Anglo-Irish Duke of Wellington, defeated Napoleon at Waterloo. The soldiers of field marshal Blucher are said to have worn open laced boots, hence the name. At least the Duke had the tasty beef dish named after him.

15. The name "Derby" likely refers back to an English Earl of Derby, who lived around the end of the nineteenth century. Reportedly, this particular Earl was a chubby man, may have even had gout, and therefore had difficulties putting on his boots. An enterprising shoemaker prepared for him shoes that were easier to put on and lace up (which open laced shoes are).

Meermin: Established in 2001 by members of the fourth generation of a renowned shoemaker's family from Mallorca, Spain, Meermin makes high-end Goodyear welted shoes at a reasonable price that are directly distributed from their factory to the final customer only through Meermin retail stores or www.meermin.es. This presents a value proposition for a quality-made shoe of high-end materials from world-renowned tanneries. *Rico suave.*[16]

Bowtie: Another Spanish *Zapatero*, Bowtie has three lines. Their "Causal" line features a cemented construction, "Goodyear Classic" is Goodyear welted, and "Premium Gold Series" is hand welted. These shoes are another value proposition as they are well made from quality materials in traditional Professional Gentleman models. Carmina is another Spanish brand to consider.

Another stylistic difference between open laced shoes relative to their closed laced cousins is that there are certain versions with only six or even just four lace holes. This can provide the desired optic (for certain men with small feet) of lengthening the appearance of the foot as a longer section of the front of the shoe is visible. It is also somewhat sportier than the more traditional ten lace holes.

Of course, open laced shoes also come with or without cap toes, as well as broguing of various degrees or none at all. The same rules on formality apply as well, meaning:

- the more decoration going on with your shoes, the less formal they are, with the plain Blucher or Derby being the most formal of the species and the full brogue (wing tip) Blucher or Derby being the least formal;
- the darker they are, the more formal they are, with black being the most formal and white or cream being the least formal (at least in a business setting); and
- the more muted the leather, the less formal they are, with patent leather being the most formal and suede being the least formal.

---

16. Gerardo, "Rico Suave," Gerardo, *Mo' Ritmo* (Interscope Records, 1991).

Loafers

These are not the dudes at your firm who delegate too much and seem to avoid all the short-term, high-stress assignments. The term *loafers* includes a number of types of shoes with no lacing at all. As a result, loafers are shoes you slip on and have a more casual and less formal character. These shoes sit low on your foot with the ankle exposed, and often the heel of the shoe is quite low.

Like derivatives markets, the capital asset pricing model, and the Sarbanes-Oxley Act, the introduction of the loafer as a shoe suitable for business attire is a uniquely American fashion invention. Eureka! As George Patton said, "Never tell people how to do things. Tell them what to do and they will surprise you with their ingenuity." The design of the loafer itself is related to the Native American moccasin but formalizes that casual design with the infrastructure of a heel, sole, and welting.[17]

The classic Bass Weejun loafer made its appearance in the 1930s, and the cross-strapped saddle loafer quickly became a staple shoe in the United States.[18] The "penny" loafer got its name from the predilection of Ivy League students in the 1950s inserting a penny under the diamond shaped cutout in the saddle of the Weejun.[19] Most Professional Gentlemen prefer to do this with Bitcoins, which is to say, we prefer nothing under the diamond shaped cutout in the saddle. We're not in college anymore. Many versions of the saddle loafer are not suitable for this practice in any event. While the traditional penny loafer is red-brown, it can be worn in versions ranging from black to tan. It is appropriate for wearing with a suit in darker versions with appropriately lustrous leather.

Another common loafer style is the tassel loafer, which purportedly originates from the lacing structure of boat shoes like the ubiquitous Sperry Top-Sider. The laces were passed through eyes around the perimeter of the shoe's opening and then tied in a bow on the top of the shoe's vamp. The ends of the laces were then decorated with leather pompoms.[20] While the

---

17. While related to the moccasin, most shoe historians (like four out of all five of them alive today) theorize that the loafer either (1) originated from an English royal commission in 1926 to the Wildsmith Shoe company of a new form of shoe to be worn by King George VI around his country houses (the Wildsmith Loafer), or (2) evolved from a Norwegian shoemaker who integrated moccasin and Norwegian shoes used for fishing into a loafer he introduced in 1930 (the Aurland loafer).
18. Named the Weejun for the shape of the loafer, which derives from shoes Norwegian fishermen used to make when not fishing.
19. Various theories for why they did this exist: (1) good luck, (2) two pennies were sufficient in 1930 to make a telephone call on a public phone, and (3) it made a moneyed fashion statement. I went to a Seven Sisters school. So I wouldn't know.
20. Today, not only the tassels but even the appearance of laces passing through the eyes of the shoe is purely ornamental in most cases.

traditional tassel loafer is brown, it can be worn in versions ranging from black to tan. Like the saddle loafer, it is appropriate for wearing with a suit in proper colors and patinas.

Other loafers appropriate for the Professional Gentleman are ones that offer tasteful metal decorations, like the classic Gucci loafer. The golden brass strap across the vamp of the shoe in the shape of a horse's snaffle bit is a nod to Gucci's history as a saddle maker, but in the right colors still has the provenance to be paired with a business suit. Of the loafers mentioned here, I'd lean against purchasing the Gucci loafer, as there are better-made loafer options for the same price. A good pair of loafers is a core purchase. One of the Foundation of Five shoes every Professional Gentleman needs. So purchasing the highest quality pair you can afford makes more sense than overspending for the most recognizable brand.

Brands to Know

Sebago: Founded in 1946, this American Michigan-based company produces a variety of affordable boating and deck shoes, as well as some dress shoes. It was the official supplier of yachting footwear for the American Sailing Team in the 1980s, during which time its "Docksides" shoe become a fashion trend at universities across the country. Most versions are not to be worn by the Professional Gentleman in a business setting.

Gucci: The largest Italian luxury brand was founded in Florence in 1921. It offers a full line of menswear, but its origins are rooted in leather goods as a saddle maker. Indeed, the classic Gucci loafer brass strap across the vamp is in the shape of a horse's snaffle bit.

Tod's: Owned by Italian fashion entrepreneur Diego Della Valle along with other footwear brands, the name J.P. Tod's (later shortened to Tod's) came from a Boston phone directory. But the Tod's driving moccasin became a staple from Portofino to East Hampton. Most versions are not to be worn by the Professional Gentleman in a business setting.

Monks

Monk strap shoes have no laces but are closed with a saddle buckle (or buckles) on the outside of the upper. The straps bring one of the three pieces of leather that constitute the upper across the tongue (which is wider to assist the securing of the wearer's ankle) from the instep edge and to the outside edge. The popular double monk has two straps and buckles, while the traditional single monk has one.[21]

Without the fussiness of lacing, the monk strap has an efficient, almost military bearing. If kept devoid of broguing, the monk strap can have a sleek, mod look. It can, of course, be tarted up with almost any amount of broguing one can imagine, but beware of these versions for business settings. While the black wing tip has a long tradition in the bank and the board room, the full brogue monk strap ends up looking overloaded. I believe this is because there are no laces to actually break up the brogue embellishments, and the one or two buckles themselves actually read to the eye as further embellishments. It's too much. The monk also comes in versions with three or even more straps, or with highly ornamental saddle buckles. Again, this is all just too much. The Professional Gentleman should avoid these versions.[22]

Brands to Know

Joseph Cheaney & Sons: Cheaney has been committed to making the finest footwear since 1886. Entirely made in England, Cheaney has been producing its footwear in the same factory in Northamptonshire since 1896. It takes eight weeks and 200 hand or hand-tooled operations to make a single pair of Cheaney shoes. Run by cousins Jonathan and William Church since 2009, Cheaney shoes was awarded the 2016 Queen's Award for Enterprise in International Trade, the company's third Queen's Award.

---

21. Shoe lore holds that this footwear is named after a monk from the Alps who created a special form of sandals in the fifteenth century. The design was brought to England (the great land of shoe-makers) and was first registered in 1901 (because Europe has a greater degree of design protection).
22. Note that bespoke monk straps can be the cleanest and least adorned of all versions. If the Professional Gentleman can afford such versions, they will come with a single buckle hole rather than the traditional four to five (since the wearer's feet will be measured perfectly)—a subtle way of signaling their bespoke nature while also maintaining the sleekest of lines.

Foster and Son: Foster and Son has been in the shoemaking business for 175 years. Often referred to as the "Shoemaker's shoemaker," Foster and Son's uncompromising quality is evident. Foster and Son creates refined "West End" style shoes in a workshop located just above their Jermyn Street shop. They've used the same techniques for two centuries and use their skills to offer both bespoke and ready-to-wear options for their clients.

John Lobb: Making the finest shoes and boots for Professional Gentleman since 1866. Mr. Lobb established himself as the premier bootmaker by providing bespoke service to the aristocracy, political, and business elite. The Paris atelier, the By Request service, and the ready-to-wear collection were acquired by Hermès in 1976. While the ultimate bespoke service is still available in the Paris atelier, the ready-to-wear collection still retains key bespoke qualities like John Lobb's 190-step manufacturing process.

A conservative monk strap is the last of the Foundation of Five shoes to get (and on the bubble with a light-colored wing tip, which could certainly substitute for it if the wearer is not into buckles). So, to be clear, the monk strap is not an absolute essential. But because it can easily be worn with great effect to convey a dash of the unusual and still be acceptable in business settings, I recommend you dabble with it. In more casual settings, these shoes can even be worn with buckles undone.[23] The double monk is the more popular of the two types as the buckles are usually smaller and less pronounced than on the single monk strap. A large single buckle monk strap can look rather seventeenth century. Remember, *mon frangin*,[24] you are a Professional Gentleman, not a musketeer or a pirate. *Un pour tous, tous pour un!*[25]

---

23. Believe me, this looks okay in more casual settings. Far less ridiculous and is far less dangerous than wearing one's laces undone.
24. "My brother" in French (sort of). *Mon frere* is a more literal translation. *Mon frangin* is slang.
25. "One for all, and all for one," the motto traditionally associated with the titular heroes of the novel *The Three Musketeers* written by Alexandre Dumas père, first published in 1844.

Dress Boots

When you think of boots, your mind may stray to functional, rugged versions appropriate for "work," but not necessarily the Professional Gentleman's place of work. Work boots mean construction boots, cowboy boots, hunting boots, hiking boots, snow boots, rain boots. All of these are sturdily made buggers and look like it. With their chunky soles and thick uppers, these boots do not coordinate with tailored clothing. They may be capable, but they are not elegant.

Dress boots, on the other hand, are permitted Professional Gentleman attire and can give you a leg up in colder climates when rain and snow are impediments to getting into the office looking sharp. Dress boots can be found in Balmoral, Derby, and even monk strap styles, and in heights ranging from ankle boots up to lower calf versions. The same rules of formality and informality apply to dress boots, assuming they have the same profile as the dress shoes they stem from. If they have a thicker sole or hint of less fine-grade leather, they are not dress boots and not appropriate to be worn with suiting (although likely fine to wear with certain business casual outfits).

A derivative of the dress boot, Chelsea boots have equestrian origins dating back to Queen Victoria, but they became objects of desire with the British Invasion bands in the 1960s including The Beatles, who wore them liberally. "Love, love me do!"[26] While the Chelsea boot may communicate bona fide rock'n'roll origins, they are quite subdued under a suit pant leg. Their classic lines and clean vamp allow them to be worn with suiting as well as with jeans. Comfortable and sleek, they are characterized by an elasticated gusset on the side (although many styles employ a side zipper—which, if you ask me, is even more groovy).

Brands to Know

Alden: Founded in 1884 by Charles H. Alden in Middleborough, Massachusetts, Alden specializes in handcrafted men's leather boots as well as dress shoes. Still a heritage, family-owned brand, many of the company's approximately 100 workers are second or third generation, and it sources its leathers mostly from small tanneries. I love Alden boots.

---

26. The Beatles, "Love Me Do," *Please Please Me* (Parlophone, 1963).

George Cleverly: An expensive English shoemaker gone perhaps a bit too Hollywood. This London-based brand certainly makes a fine shoe, but they also spend quite a bit of time making sure you know all the other famous men who have worn them and that they appeared with Huntsman suiting in the film, *The Kingsman*

Edward Green: This English shoemaker was founded in 1890 in Northampton, England. The brand is synonymous with excellence in craftsmanship, and only around 250 pairs of shoes are completed a week. During the 1930s, Edward Green was one of the largest manufacturers of officers' boots for the British Army. The brand's boots and shoes are available from their own shops on Jermyn Street in London and on the Boulevard Saint Germain in Paris.

The Foundational Five

There are certain fundamental shoes for the Professional Gentleman. These are: (1) plain or cap toe oxfords in black, (2) cap toe oxfords or half brogue Derbys in dark brown, (3) wing tips in black, (4) wing tips in tan or two strap monk shoes in brown, (5) cordovan penny loafers (the "Foundational Five"). The Foundational Five should be invested in accordingly.

Law #11

~

The Professional Gentleman shall allocate the bulk of his footwear budget on the purchase of the Foundational Five.

~

If well bought and preserved, they will last you forever. If not, you'll only end up spending more in the long run unless the Professional Gentleman life is not for you, and you plan on taking up an occupation that does not demand well-made and handsome coverings for your feet.

Black Wing Tip

Brown Cap Toe Oxford

Black Oxford

Tan Wing Tip

Cordovan Penny Loafer

Non-Dress Shoes

All right. Pay attention here because we've not yet discussed clothing, and we are already going into the deep end of the business casual pool. Trainers and sneakers are *not* dress shoes. Their origins are in sports and athletic pursuits, and the offerings we are discussing here are upscale hybrids. Models loosely based on tennis shoes, boat shoes, basketball high-tops, skate shoes, even running shoes are now offered in swank versions that arguably can be worn in a business casual setting. This has become a massive business with the growth of sales in "designer" trainers and sneakers significantly outpacing the growth in dress shoe sales.

These types of shoes come in all manner of color combinations. Some are wild, outlandish, and logo heavy while some are just sporty (which should tell you something). The best trainers to wear in the office are those that are simple, without adornment or contrasting color combinations. Look for leather, suede, or canvas variations in muted colors. Basically, you should only be wearing the most subdued versions of a trainer or sneaker into the office because, let me tell you, there will be an old guard at your firm who doesn't think you should be wearing them at all. Let's not give them a reason to get HR involved. In no way, shape, or form are any of the non-dress shoes dressy enough to be considered formal business attire (outside of very informal business settings, which most Professional Gentlemen do not enjoy). What Novak Djokovic or LeBron James wear to conduct their business on the court for their fans shall not be what you wear to conduct business in court for your clients.

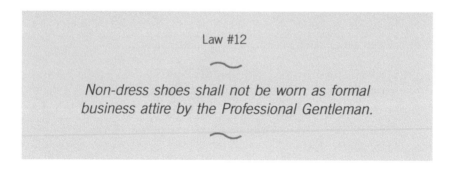

Law #12

~

Non-dress shoes shall not be worn as formal business attire by the Professional Gentleman.

~

Stick with one of three styles. Slip-ons, tennis shoe lace ups, and high-top lace ups.

Slip-Ons

You might think of slip-ons as the *most* casual of this trio, but surprisingly, slip-ons actually read to the viewer as the most formal since their lack of lacing makes them difficult to distinguish from dress loafers. Their construction is somewhat similar to a loafer construction, as well, other than the use of performance materials in the sole and, typically, two small sections of elastic on either side of the vamp to permit the foot to enter the shoe comfortably.

Slip-ons in an appropriate color and material are the easiest to pair with a suit and traditional tailored clothing as a result of this similarity with the loafer. So, the leather brown or black slip-ons are acceptable with suits. This color rule applies to slip-ons as it does to loafers, as well as the requirement that the leather match your belt if you are wearing one. Suede and canvas versions of the slip-on should not be worn with suits. Please note as well that while leather slip-ons may be worn with a suit, this should still be done recognizing that one is very firmly in "business casual" mode. You are dressing down the suit.

Brands to Know

Frye: This all-American brand has been nurtured by artisans since 1863. Frye began with boots but now includes a full line of shoes and bags. Frye makes a couple of chic leather slip-ons that work well for the Professional Gentleman outside of business formal settings.

Vans: Associated more with skateboards than board rooms, as a SoCal native I simply couldn't leave my beloved Vans off this list. Vans has been known since 1966 for cheap but sturdy athletic shoes, but they do make a leather version of their original slip-ons that are legit—if you happen to be skateboarding home after work.

Armani: The global Italian fashion house founded by Giorgio Armani offers everything from haute couture, ready-to-wear, leather goods, shoes, watches, jewelry, accessories, eyewear, cosmetics, and even home interiors. Armani also makes probably the highest-end leather slip-ons, which retail for about five times what the Vans versions do, but are pretty slick.

Low-Top Lace Ups

Tennis shoe lace ups in black or brown can also be easy to hide as well. However, there is a certain temptation to wear them in white or cream, particularly considering the many examples of finely made designer versions that come in these colors. You can choose to go with these—you bold Professional Gentleman, you—just be forewarned that you are inviting inspection as the shoes will, quite obviously, stand out with their whiteness and therefore also be noticed as non-dress shoes. You can counteract this with a strong selection of a well-made suede or leather model and pair it with appropriate clothing as we'll discuss *infra*. I do not think white tennis shoe lace ups are appropriate with any suit other than perhaps a seersucker. Treat me subject.[27] Even then, I find them just a bit ridiculous looking. But with deft selection of casual items, tennis shoe lace ups can be aces. Just keep them spotless.

Brands to Know

COS: Established in 2007, COS is a Swedish brand offering modern, functional, considered design in footwear. Their leather sneakers are understated and a great value.

The Last Conspiracy: The Last Conspiracy is another eclectic Swedish brand producing quality shoes imbued by history and a modernized twist. One of their marketing lines is "Evermore, humans remain solitary wanderers, comfortably equipped with sartorial anticipation." Okaaay . . . Not cheap, but certainly well made with a respect for the legacy of artisanal footwear.

---

27. For you non-financial advisory Professional Gentlemen, "treat me subject" is a phrase a trader may say to indicate that the client may have the order they want after the trader makes a phone call to double-check that it's all in the clear.

Superga: The "people's shoe of Italy" first appeared in 1911. These rubber-soled sneakers are low on design, but their simple construction and affordable price makes them worth recommending. I wear canvas Supergas all the time . . . when I'm on vacation.

Zespa: Crafted in France, Zespa makes expectation-defying shoes combining time-honored techniques with an irreverent spirit. Constructed from smooth leather with a tonal, rubber sole, the brand's slim ZSP4 sneaker is a good example of a Professional Gentleman–appropriate athletic-inspired shoe.

High-Top Lace Ups

High-top lace ups have obvious basketball shoe associations. The Air Jordan craze in the '90s led to Nike becoming a global juggernaut and billions of people to desire the latest drop from the big athletic shoe manufacturers. But I'm not talking about basketball shoes here. The high-top lace ups I'm referring to, and the *only* ones you should consider wearing into the office as a Professional Gentleman, look more like dress boots than basketball shoes. Russell Westbrook would likely break his own ankles attempting a crossover move in what I'm suggesting you are permitted to wear into the office.[28]

So think of the high-top lace up that you should wear into the office as a more comfortable version of a hard-soled dress boot. More like a chukka boot (see below) than a high-top for sports. No prominent logos (this applies across the board) or substantial striping that would obviously advertise their athletic origins.

---

28. But then again, smooth dresser that he is, while Russell wouldn't wear the kind of high-top lace ups that are Professional Gentleman–appropriate on the court, he might wear them into your firm if he's with his agents and lawyers, renegotiating an endorsement deal.

Brands to Know

Nike: Impossible to leave this massive American sportswear brand off the list. Nike started and still dominates the athletic shoe space. The problem with most of their offerings is the design is so logo driven, they don't suit a Professional Gentleman's office wardrobe. That said, there are a few designs devoid of logos; Air Jordan's since the logoless II's, Air Huaraches, and Flyknits all are minimal.

Santoni: Established in 1976, Santoni is renowned for expert Italian artistry. Often in opulent colors and contrast paneling to add a whimsical twist, they also offer more traditional colors. Masterful tailoring transforms durable leathers into lavishly comfortable pieces in classic shapes but at a high price. Santoni offers a full and exquisite line of men's dress shoes. Their leather high-tops, which approach $1,000, are the definition of luxury sneakers.

Adidas: This German brand is the largest sportswear manufacturer in Europe. The Adidas Yeezy Boost line was created by Kanye West for Adidas. Colorways vary but the "triple white," "triple black," and gray colorway releases look smart enough for the office. Yeezys in general are one of the hardest sneakers to buy for retail, and adidas.com is one of very few exclusive online retailers. The aftermarket is the only way you'll be able to get a pair. Great arbitrage opportunity.

Common Projects: Founded in 2004, these shoes are hand-stitched in Italy and often use Italian Nappa leather. The designs are simple and appealing. All of the shoes feature a line of numbers along the heel, displaying the style, the size, and color, respectively. This is a good branding element but could annoy some Professional Gentleman trying to wear them in the office.

Non-Dress Boots

Chukka boots are ankle high and constructed from two pieces of leather and have two or three high-lacing eyelets. This boot is related to the jodhpur boot in polo.[29] The chukka is a more casual shoe traditionally made from calfskin leather, but suede or black leather are dressier options. Crepe soles on desert boots were introduced by Mr. Nathan Clark after he saw what soldiers were wearing on their feet during a trip to Burma in 1941, hence the classic Clark chukka. The chukka is purely casual footwear and should certainly not be worn with a suit.

The only other acceptable non-dress boots for the office are foul weather versions like the Hunter Wellington boots, "wellies," or the LL Bean "duck" boot, which should be removed for a pair of loafers every Professional Gentleman should leave under his desk—for just such occasions. Biker boots, cowboy boots, construction boots are all verboten. Listen mates, those boots are all appropriate for other, much more physically taxing jobs. If you are dressing for the job you want, enjoy the demotion to manual labor.

Avoiding Attention-Grabbing Shoes

Many men tend to be suckers for shoes that "make a statement." Some of these specimens are quite lovely and well-made shoes: Berluti vermillion oxfords, the white Salvatore Ferragamo "Giordano" loafer, the Bally Plas oxford in python skin, right on down to the Florsheim red suede wing tips, done in collaboration with an LA-based designer I'm fond of, George Esquivel. All beautiful shoes, but all crazy footwear choices in most office settings in which the Professional Gentleman is likely to find himself.

Brands to Know

Berluti: Making artfully and expertly crafted men's footwear since 1895, Berluti tailors turn leather into both bespoke and ready-to-wear collections. Four generations of Berlutis have honed the techniques and expertise of footwear artistry once reserved just for bespoke shoes. Berluti's

---

29. A chukka is a period of seven and a half minutes.

Venezia leather, specially developed by and for the company, provides great depth and transparency in its patina. These shoes come in a variety of colors, which the company prides itself on developing.

George Esquivel: Los Angeles through and through, George Esquivel is the founder, president, and design director for Esquivel Designs. This Southern California company focuses on making handmade custom shoes and leather goods with the goal of creating a one-of-a-kind experience for each customer. Esquivel combines refined materials from tanneries around the world with progressive silhouettes and uncommon color combinations to create what I predict will be a new legacy brand.

Brands put these shoes out to help the general merchandizing of their black and brown best sellers. Admittedly, when separated from their wearer (and the other clothing the wearer dons), considered alone, arranged by deft merchandizers in captivating hues of green, blue, purple, and other nontraditional colors, these shoes can be compelling.[30] So some men purchase these ugly stepchildren. Some do this because they believe they are being fashionable or differentiating themselves (in a good way). Others jump on these odd shoes when they invariably go on sale. "I've bought some things that I sort of regret about now."[31] In any event, for the Professional Gentleman, these shoes are to be generally avoided. They have a time and place, which is usually someone's destination wedding (or bachelor party), but the payoff on the investment in shoes like this is flawed. Unless you are a man of unlimited budget (and closet space), I'd much rather have you spend all of your footwear allowance on the Foundational Five. This will not only save you closet space and upkeep time, and worry and cost (yes—shoes require maintenance), but it will also save you from the desire to actually put on some of these crazy, stunning, ridiculous shoes.

---

30. As with most purchases, unless one is absolutely certain and in a rush, trying on the article of clothing and considering it within the context of your wardrobe as a whole is essential. What best to pair red suede shoes with? A red suede belt? Now you are wearing a red suede belt too. What suit goes with that? What tie? And how on God's green Earth will you expect anyone to notice you (or any other element of your wardrobe) when they are accosted with red shoes and a red belt?
31. Modest Mouse, "Broke," *Building Nothing Out of Something* (Up Records, 1999).

Maintaining Your Shoes

Given the upfront investment you will make to purchase these vessels for your feet, there is a Law here worth heeding:

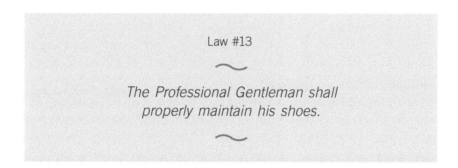

Law #13

~

The Professional Gentleman shall
properly maintain his shoes.

~

When you first purchase a pair of shoes, you typically will want to go to a cobbler and have the tips and heels covered. This is not essential, but it will allow your shoes to last longer and show anyone who is looking that you are a man to whom the details matter. Also, you should have new shoes polished as this will properly seal the leather, which might not come out of the box this way. Unsealed shoes will get damaged to the point of ruin in rain or snow if unsealed, so it is wise to do this.

Shoe trees allow your recently worn shoes to contract and dry out to their correct architecture. You should purchase unvarnished cedar shoe trees as they properly draw moisture (rain or sweat or the tears of your defeated opponents) out of the leather. You do not need to own a pair of trees for each pair of shoes. The proper time for using trees is pretty much right after you have removed the shoes from your feet. After a couple of hours, the shoes will have returned to their natural shape and the trees can be taken out.

A word on soaking-wet shoes: dry them away from direct heat. Direct heat can dry the leather way too fast, resulting in the leather cracking. This wrecks your shoes. Like, bankruptcy Chapter 7 ruins them (there's no Chapter 11 restructuring process for cracked leather). Stuff drenched shoes with newspaper and let them dry away from direct heat. Then insert shoe trees for a couple of hours.

Do not hesitate to take your shoes in for repairs when they show signs of wear. Heels, like M&A associates, are typically the first to be ground down, but they can be replaced. Any loosening of stitching should be addressed upon first notice. Scuffs and abrasions are usually solved with a longer than usual polish, or if on the inside of the shoes, by replacing the insoles or other affected areas. Also please remember to give your shoes a regular shine. The regular professional application of shoe polish not only makes the shoes look more attractive and cleaner, it also helps to keep the leather supple, moist, and flexible. This is essential to the longevity of the shoe.

Laces should be replaced every three years or more often if you are one of those dandies who likes to change up colored laces on occasion. I'm not in favor of this practice, as it evinces a touch of deliberation and fussiness. But if you fall within the Laws, and colored laces is your thing, God bless. It is just a lot of work on a regular basis to properly swap out laces. And matching your laces with, say, your tie looks very calculated, in potential violation of the Law of Insouciance.

A well-made pair of shoes should last your lifetime. *Ita vero.*[32] If you repair them regularly, they will serve. This reality will also help you to make the proper investment in your shoes. Given that they can last forever, why not keep truly beautiful examples healthy and on your feet rather than invariably spending more over time to replace one pair of mediocre shoes with another pair of mediocre shoes? Run the numbers on this. It's not like calculating the value of a municipal bond portfolio or a complex DCF analysis. It's simple math. Good shoes are worth the upfront investment.

Ignorantia juris non excusat.

---

32. It is true.

—6—

Sock It to Me

*"One that desires to excel should endeavor in those things
that are in themselves most excellent."*
—Epictetus

It's hard to get worked up too much over socks. Basic socks will provide a subtle texture and perhaps (but not often) color contrast from pant cuff to shoe. So the Professional Gentleman's basic socks shall be in black, gray (many variations), navy, and brown (light to dark). There is nothing remarkable about these socks—(there shouldn't be). Get your basic socks right and throw in your statement socks (discussed *infra*) from time to time.

The rules here are pretty simple. Black shoes look best with black or gray socks. Brown shoes look best with gray, navy, or brown socks. Dark green and burgundy are also considered basic sock colors and are acceptable with both brown and black shoes. White socks with dress shoes? Never.

Law #14

~

The Professional Gentleman shall not wear
black socks with brown shoes, nor brown socks
with black shoes, nor white socks with
dress shoes, ever.

~

Should the socks match another piece of your clothing? Not necessarily, but it's usually nice if they do. Many men prefer to have their socks generally match their trouser. This is a sound policy as it draws the least amount of attention to the sock. I'd just suggest you make sure there is a texture change or it can be a little visually confusing with solids. With tweeds this is no problem as you can select any one of the colors presented in the tweed weave and match it with a solid sock. This is another way of saying you can wear any basic sock other than black with most tweeds. What about the other elements of your ensemble? A sweater or tie perhaps? As basic socks stray more into color, my preference is to match them with a more disparate element of my wardrobe than my trousers (e.g. green socks and green cardigan or burgundy socks and burgundy and yellow rep tie).

"You choose your friends by their character and your socks by their color."

—Gary Oldman[1]

Wear socks that are comfortable, not frayed or damaged, and cover the entire area of your calf that might conceivably show if your pant cuff lifts up. Seriously, showing hairy mid-calf in any business situation is a breach of your duty of care. No one wants to see that. You don't want to show that. And listen, it is easy to address. Prefer mid-calf or higher socks, and replace

---

1. A fine actor often playing the elegant antagonist, Oldman is a Hollywood outsider who is nevertheless known for his high-style quotient.

socks once they show signs of wear or they have lost elasticity necessary to keep themselves up.

Like your underwear (which, sorry vato, is your own business and I'm not going to discuss in the Laws), socks are part of the basic layer of clothes that come in direct contact with your skin and should therefore be made from the best materials they can be given your budget. Bad socks will lead to discomfort and thus a lack of overall confidence (that essential factor to good style). All this said, it's difficult to get too ardent about sock quality and fit. Choosing good socks can be a hassle (which is why a number of vertically integrated socks manufacturers have sprung up to allow you to receive refreshers of socks on a subscription basis).[2] So we will quickly break down the different fabrics from which socks are made and look into what makes certain fabrics preferable to others.

Fabrication

Cotton

Cotton socks are probably what most of you wear, and that's fine. Me too. Cotton is a natural fabric, it is strong and versatile in terms of style, and it can warm you up in the winter and cool you down in the summer. It does not require special care, so cotton socks are fine to go in the washing machine (make sure you keep pairs together in the dryer). Moreover, cotton is relatively inexpensive, and let's face it, most Professional Gentlemen prefer not to spend too much on socks. Cotton is often blended with other fabrics to make socks, but while cotton socks come in all manner of colors and prints, they typically lack much in the way of texture. This lack of texture is the main drawback to cotton socks.

Wool

Wool socks are better for warmth as well as adding a little texture cotton socks lack. While likely more associated with warming the feet of Ivy

---

2. Like Sock Panda, Sockracy, Mack Weldon, and Nice Laundry.

League professors, woolen socks today come in very light versions. So wool socks don't need to be relegated to winter garb. Wool can both absorb and give off moisture. This is a very useful feature for socks. Wool socks can absorb 30% of their weight in moisture before they feel wet. Yes, revolting but true.

Brands to Know

Soxfords: This Upper East Side brand was formed in 2013 by men who sought to make men's dress creative and fun, but not absurd. That is why Soxfords designs socks that allow men to look professional, while still expressing their personality. Patterns range from subdued stripes to polka dots with a rubber duck, allowing any man to find the socks that best fit his style and needs. The brand has also expanded to sell creative ties, cufflinks, and tie bars.

Pantharella Corgi: Producing some of the finest quality socks, Pantharella has been manufacturing socks in England since 1938 and has continued to uphold its commitment to high-quality materials and superior craftsmanship. The brand is known for its innovation, as they were one of the first producers of lightweight, seamless men's socks. Their dedication to ingenuity and creativity is evident through their beautifully made socks, which are professional and refined while incorporating original elements such as vintage patterns, bright stripes, and houndstooth prints.

New & Lingwood: An English brand founded in 1865, New & Lingwood sells a full line of men's clothing, shoes, and accessories, including their collection of colorful socks. The brand is known for its quality and English style, and boasts retail stores as well as bespoke tailor shops. New & Lingwood socks range from solid bright colors, to contrasting polka dots, to skull-and-crossbone prints. In addition to their aesthetic appeal, the socks are made of fine fabrics and with expert craftsmanship.

Cashmere

Cashmere is known as an elegant fabric, mostly used for high-quality knit garments the Professional Gentleman favors. Cashmere, even though usage defines it as a type of wool, is in fact a hair, which is why it feels so different from standard sheep's wool. If you are wearing cashmere socks, you can be sure that your feet will be dry and comfortable. Cashmere socks are also very lightweight, which is another reason why they feel so delicious. As with your better wool socks, cashmere socks must be washed by hand in water with very little soap and air dried, or sent to your cleaners. This is a hassle and, along with their higher price, represents the downside of cashmere socks.

Silk

Silk is a fabric that is even finer than cashmere. Silk socks can be worn at formal occasions or to a formal function for a very dressy look. Generally, silk socks are not found in a lot of colors and are a pain to take care of. The Professional Gentleman can certainly get by without having silk socks.

Exotics

And then there are socks made from more exotic fabrics like camel hair to yak hair, alpaca, or vicuña wool. Other than as conversation starters, there is not much to recommend these special fabrics. As you likely know, yaks are found in the Himalayas, camels generally live in Africa, while the alpaca, which is a member of the camel family, and the vicuña live in the Andes. So if you are into the National Geographic channel and like to think of these beasts being domesticated for the benefit of your feet (and the local economies), go for it. The reason why the production of socks from these fabrics is so limited is because they produce a rather small amount of wool to begin with.

Many of the larger retailers like Harrods, Saks Fifth Avenue, and Barneys offer decent versions of basic men's dress socks, as do Brooks Brothers, Paul Stuart, Ralph Lauren, Paul Smith, and other brands.

Cashing in Your Sock Options

The circumscribed acceptability of loud socks will now be considered. Personally, I've been known to have what many would describe as a little "pop" in my socks. In fact I've been written up on the subject in the *Wall Street Journal*[3] and was somewhat embarrassingly quoted in a *New York Times*[4] profile as saying that I was okay with "my ankles looking like a piece of yummy candy." Not okay. At least not okay as a regular component of your sartorial presentation, and certainly not for those of you looking to present a subtle, gentlemanly air. But for those of you who really cannot resist a little whimsical play with bright color or garish pattern or—gasp—both, the sock may be the best place to show it. I say this for several reasons.

One reason is, quite obviously, that the ankle, with a traditionally cut trouser, rarely shows, and so your sizzling socks can remain mostly hidden. In most cases, your ankle will only flash when:

Crossing your legs boldly, which you are in complete control of (some of you may think you do this involuntarily; trust me, you do not). As professional men, we are somewhat prone to the wide cross-legged seated position by habit, example, or general inclination, but you are in control of your legs and can mitigate your socks' exposure.

Doing some uncharacteristic athletic or potentially heroic feat in your suit, like jumping a puddle on a rainy day, or helping that fetching executive assistant open some part of the copier you thought never existed.

In any event, the flash shouldn't come out too often—and I believe that is a good thing.

Another reason is that socks are probably the cheapest element of your wardrobe and the one that wears out the soonest. The result of this is that you can purchase colorful socks for a reasonable price and not need to work them into your rotation on a regular basis. Wearing the same memorable socks too often would be, well, it would be lame. What is interesting, and perhaps ironic, once, simply does not have the same impact until it is almost forgotten.

---

3. Steve Garbarino, "Exercise Your Sock Options," *Wall Street Journal*, March 2013.
4. Jacob Bernstein, "A Lawyer for Fashion Insiders Dresses the Part," *New York Times*, December 2014.

Law #15

~

The Professional Gentleman shall not wear socks with "pop" too often.

~

Doled out over time, mixed with many days of traditional black, navy, or brown pairs along with other potentially loud versions but not in the same genre, your statement socks will have lasting impact. When they show the slightest signs of wear, replace them with a different version to keep things fresh.

Brands to Know

Paul Smith: Selling socks in bright colors, bold patterns, and with accents that are sure to keep any man from getting bored, Paul Smith socks make a statement. Paul Smith began his brand over forty years ago in Nottingham, but his commitment to incorporating excitement and humor into fashion while not losing sight of traditional style elements has remained. His socks reflect "eclectic aesthetic," depicting details from skulls to strawberries, while remaining stylish and sophisticated. Paul Smith offers a full line of traditional yet wonderfully eccentric menswear.

Happy Socks: This Swedish brand began in 2008 with the aim of bringing excitement to something that was traditionally ordinary—socks. Happy Socks veers away from the mundane by incorporating creative elements into their socks, ranging from argyle and polka dot to patterns of animals and palm trees. Despite the company's commitment to colors and inventiveness, they have not sacrificed the quality and wearability required by socks.

MoxyMaus: With socks that are refined but exciting, MoxyMaus footwear is sure to add something extra to any outfit. Their socks incorporate color and geometric patterns, making interesting what would otherwise be boring. MoxyMaus socks are also versatile and could be worn with anything from a suit to denim. MoxyMaus is a Canadian company and can be found at their seasonal shop or their permanent retail location in Toronto.

Below are just a few examples starting with slightly unconventional and ranging to what I consider rather of-center (but still acceptable in a business environment). I would not wear statement socks more than two days out of the five traditional days of the work week, nor more than three out of the actual seven days of the actual work week for you strivers who realize every day is a day to advance your career.

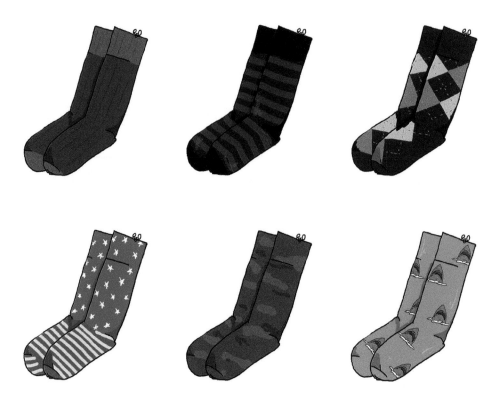

I'd view this small sample as follows and apply it more broadly:

- In relation to frequency of wearing—it should decrease as one moves to the more wild pairs.
- In relation to the quality one should purchase—it should be high for the pairs that will be worn more frequently and lower (subject to budget) for more whimsical pairs.
- In relation to the other clothes one is wearing—the level of formality should generally increase as the socks' formality decreases.

Below is another sampling of socks I consider entirely forbidden unless there are circumstances I simply cannot imagine going on at work.

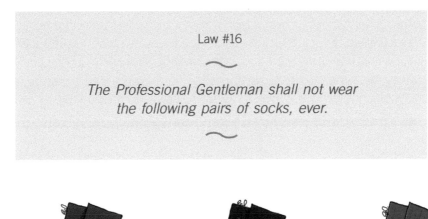

Law #16

~

The Professional Gentleman shall not wear the following pairs of socks, ever.

~

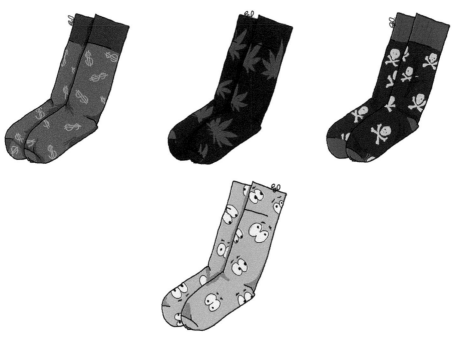

Sockless = Fearless

Not wearing socks is inherently casual—which is not usually advisable under the Laws.

- At best, sockless feet evoke insouciance, resort, vacation, the beach, summer, Bryan Ferry singing "Avalon."[5] (Please note that while these are all stylish and romantic associations, these are not things typically associated with great professional work product—very few clients want to think their Professional Gentleman is "at the beach" whilst doing work on their account.)
- At worst, sockless feet evoke germs, a sense of uncleanliness, sweat, smell, a disrespect for others, and a lack of civility. It doesn't take an Einstein to understand this tension.[6]

Nevertheless, there are some very limited occasions where going sockless is permissible. Based on the Laws, these will be dependent on the environment the professional finds himself in, the client he may be interacting with, and casual summer Friday permissiveness. These moments tend to be rare in professional situations, and if such a moment presents itself to the professional, he must always ensure that his ankles are worth showing.

So, if your skin is light and you've not yet established an appropriately even tan, wear socks. If your legs (lower legs) are hairy and that hair could reasonably be considered off-putting by anyone you might see, wear socks. If you have any sort of open wound, rash, bruising, insect bite, etc., wear socks. If you are wearing black lace up shoes, wear socks. If you are unsure if any of these apply and are not confident, wear socks. Dude, in general, wear socks.

Going sockless should be a rare and amazing occasion. Like when a public company CEO gives back his guaranteed bonus compensation after the company has a poor year financially. The Professional Gentleman does not go sockless often. As an aside that I hope is obvious to you, donning a sock liner to make it appear that

---

5. Roxy Music, "Avalon," *Avalon* (Warner Bros. Records, 1982).
6. As Albert Einstein himself put it, "Even on the most solemn occasions I got away without wearing socks and hid that lack of civilization in high boots."

you are going sockless when, in fact, you are not, is simply not done. Please, gentleman, if you are to go sockless, truly go sockless. While wearing these sock liners may provide comfort on that rare occasion, they smack of false-hood and disingenuousness.[7] These are not traits the Professional Gentle-man embraces. If you are inclined to wear a sock liner when the stars align for a moment to go appropriately sockless, it was not meant to be. Simply wear socks.

So the situations are scarce and the requirements are high. For these very reasons likely, pulling off the risky sockless look is a thing of beauty. Like a solar eclipse during a stroll on a summer night with a Brazilian *hermosa mujer* on your arm as your path leads wonderfully close to your apart-ment. When the situation permits it and the ankles are in form, a sockless look communicates casual elegance coupled with a degree of animal vitality. There is also a confidence in the look that says, "You must trust me. I'm so good I don't need socks. Not even my feet sweat." It's hard to replicate.

Ignorantia juris non excusat.

---

7. They are also very trendy—making the fashionable look put forth by menswear blogs showing sockless men more comfortable and accessible.

—7—

The Suit: Our Uniform

"Putting on a beautifully designed suit elevates my spirit,
extols my sense of self, and helps define me
as a man to whom details matter."
—Gay Talese[1]

We are all Professional Gentlemen. Ergo, we are men for whom details matter. Therefore, we should all wear the suit. It suits me to tell you, suits are the most suitable form of dress for the Professional Gentleman. At least four days a week they should be your wardrobe of choice, irrespective of office dress code. Wear the suit, but don't let it wear you. Suit up! But don't be a "suit."

Accept and Appreciate the Uniform

Okay, that's a lot of axioms and puns. Let me just break it down simply. As far as is reasonably possible in this day and age, the suit still represents the closest thing to a uniform for the Professional Gentleman. For some of you, this may be the very reason you eschew it. "Rebel, rebel, your face is

---

1. Talese is an American writer who helped define literary journalism with *Esquire* and the *New York Times*. He's also a totally natty dresser.

a mess."[2] Gentlemen, this is absolutely fundamental. The suit is our most dignified and balanced form of personal presentation.

> "To adapt a phrase from Le Corbusier, the suit is a machine for living in, close-fitting but comfortable armor, constantly revised and reinvented to be, literally, well suited for modern daily life."
>
> —Cally Blackman[3]

I recognize that many of you have opportunities to use business casual (whether just for Friday or all week long) as a cover not to accept this, but honestly, if you have issues embracing the suit in this regard, you are either:

- a lazy luddite who basically favors comfort over elegance and would prefer to relax in a tee shirt with your favorite sports team logo on it and sweats (perhaps with even the same sports team logo on it—if you went to the University of Michigan or USC) while on the job if you could get away with it; or
- a stylistic masochist who would rather toil with the difficulties related to choosing particular "outfits" every day rather than enjoy the ease and certainty of stylistic conformity with respect to your jacket, trouser, and choice of shirt as sanctioned by a longstanding and elegant code of conduct.

If either of these extremes is you, consider the following. First, as has been said before and will be said again, the suit represents the traditional uniform of the Professional Gentleman. The Professional Gentleman in a suit is what the client envisions when they think of a Professional Gentleman. The suit is the easiest way to look the part. There may come a time, a hundred years from now, when no one wears a suit, and the fashion industry has successfully moved the needle of men's preferences to other offerings. But you, Mr. Professional Gentleman, will not be the first wave of that movement. You are not the avant-garde, and you will not be "that fashionable guy." The first one over the wall always gets bloody. Let trends fall to

---

2. David Bowie, "Rebel Rebel," *Diamond Dogs* (RCA Victor, 1974).
3. Blackman is the author of *100 Years of Fashion Illustration, 100 Years of Menswear,* and *100 Years of Fashion.*

those who do not care about their careers or, better yet, who are not Professional Gentlemen.

Second, as we will discuss *infra*, the suit has a wonderful ability to hide bodily flaws and enhance the best qualities of the male physique. As it was developed during a time of neoclassical revival, the suit strives to present the wearer as a Greek athlete with a torso like the David's inverted triangle. I'm pretty sure that's still a solid look—particularly for someone who works in an office most of the day exercising their mind and not their body. If you are not sure, ask your significant other (or your trainer if you have one).

Third, as we will also discuss *infra*, short of Garanimals, the suit is perhaps the easiest way to get acceptably dressed in a coordinated way for any man, even one barely paying attention to what he is putting on. So to both the lazy luddite and the fashionable peacock, I say, get up and get into the suit! It's easy and, if well fitted and tailored to your specifications, can actually be quite comfortable. I'll even throw in a "go Blue!" or sing the "Tribute to Troy" if it will help.[4]

History

The designer Oliver Theyskens described a thing with classic style as "something beautiful and balanced that is culturally standardized." The suit is very much one of these things. The pre-history of the modern-day business suit is actually wrapped up in several interesting tales. The suit's origins are legal in nature. As a lawyer, I, of course, love this. Until the mid-seventeenth century, sumptuary laws[5] prevented commoners from wearing certain colors and fabrics in court. I don't mean in front of a judge—I mean in front of royalty (which in those days, perhaps, amounted to the same thing). In any event, colors like the royal purple, fabrics like velvet and satin, as well as fine furs were reserved for courtiers of various ranks, and sometimes for the royal family alone. However, after a fair amount of social unrest in the mid-seventeenth century, Charles II considered the elaborate court outfits to be a potential political liability. So he mandated that his courtiers begin dressing in more subdued tunics and breeches in colors you'll recognize as

---

4. "Go Blue" is a common chant for fans of the University of Michigan Wolverines. The Tribute to Troy is commonly sung at USC football games.

5. Sumptuary laws (from Latin *sumptuariae leges*) attempt to regulate permitted consumption. *Black's Law Dictionary* defines them as "Laws made for the purpose of restraining luxury or extravagance, particularly against inordinate expenditures in the matter of apparel, food, furniture, etc."

the fundamental business colors today (navy blue and shades of gray). Order in the court, indeed.

Still, it took a while for tunics, breeches, and stockings, certainly still ornate by today's standards of dress, to fall away. For that fashion revolution we have a single influential man to thank. George Bryan Brummel, a.k.a. "Beau." This iconic fashion figure was a friend of the Prince Regent, the future King George IV. He rejected the fashion modes of the day for a more modest look of understated, but well-fitted and tailored garments. Brummel wore mainly dark coats and full-length trousers. But these were impeccably tailored and assiduously clean. He is credited with introducing, and establishing as fashion, the modern men's suit, worn with a necktie.[6]

Somewhat ironically, the more recent origins of the modern suit (as a matching set of jacket, waistcoat, and trousers) became rooted in off-duty activities conducted in what was (around the turn of the nineteenth century) called a lounge suit. A lounge suit! Prior to its advent, the striped pants and frockcoat of bankers and lawyers (based on Brummel's example) were the only acceptable workwear. You don't see this look today outside of England or small anglophile gatherings. It now takes the place of an extremely formal mode of dress, but for social occasion, not business. So if you feel too dressed up in your business suit, just remember, only a couple of hundred years ago, men wore basically the same thing to kick around the house in. Go Trojans!

---

6. Ian Kelly, *Beau Brummell: The Ultimate Dandy* (London: Hodder & Stoughton, 2005).

The suit is one of those items, as designer Stefan Miljanic would say, are "a part of the cultural zeitgeist that has managed to rise to the top (and stay there) for a consistent and considerable amount of time, owing its longevity to its own versatility and universal message." While there is not yet any credible substitute for the business suit in many of the formal business settings the Professional Gentleman finds himself, with the advent of business casual and an upswing in men's appreciation of fashion, there has been a fairly constant drumbeat prognosticating the demise of the business suit.[7] Time, of course, will tell.

In my view there is a simple economic explanation for these dire predictions for men's suiting. Men's fashion is becoming a bigger and bigger business—expected to reach $40 billion in revenues by 2019.[8] Not surprisingly, it is starting to show some of the hallmarks of the development of women's fashion that have made womenswear as a business such a global phenomenon for the past century. Namely, that fashions must change so the consumer must constantly purchase new items lest he look *out* of fashion.[9] This is purely an economic argument, but one that explains why we hear so many fashion pundits announcing the death knell of the suit. I don't buy it—literally.

Construction

Like the shoe, the suit is a feat of engineering and construction, though most of these marvels are hidden from view. Let's start with the jacket. Most suit jackets consist of the outer fabric of the suit, a lining of the suit that your shirt rests against, and a middle lining that assists in maintaining the integrity of the shape of the jacket. Suit jacket construction is based on how this middle lining is affixed and what it is made of—fused or canvassed.

A fused jacket is typically mass produced and has a fusible middle lining between the outer suit fabric and the inner lining of your suit jacket. This middle lining is heated and then affixed (think glued—yech) to the wool shell of the suit both in the front panels and in the lapels. Fusing the jacket gives the jacket shape, but not necessarily one that conforms nicely to you.

---

7. Vanessa Freidman, "Banker Outfit Not Required," *New York Times*, April 21, 2016. Vanessa Freidman, "Catering to the Suit Haters," *New York Times*, April 14, 2016.
8. The growth of the global market for men's clothing was up 24% in 2015 and will reportedly reach $40 billion by 2019, according to a January 2016 report from Barclays.
9. Fellow NYU School of Law professor Chris Sprigman along with UCLA's Kal Raustiala use this premise as the basis for their analysis of the industry in "The Piracy Paradox: Innovation and Intellectual Property in Fashion Design," *Virginia Law Review* (Charlottesville: 2006), vol. 92, 1687.

Poorly fused jackets appear stiff and boxy, and you'll look like you are moving inside a costume rather than having the suit move with you. Avoid these. Also, fused jackets can delaminate, resulting in hideous bubbles (separation of the wool shell from the middle lining filled by air pockets). This happens over time with fused jackets and more often with frequent trips to the dry cleaners. Once it occurs, the jacket is dead—and the suit follows suit. Fused suit jackets are typically cheap, but not always. Hugo Boss and Armani Collezioni, to name just a couple of offenders, offer expensive fused suits from their tasteful and refined retail stores.

> "A vial of hope and a vial of pain.
> In the light they both looked the same."
>
> —Arcade Fire[10]

A canvassed suit jacket is far preferable. It has layers of wool or horsehair canvassing material, which is between the outer suit fabric and the inner lining of your suit jacket. While this canvas is hidden from view, it helps maintain the shape and balance of the suit. In the best examples, the canvas is hand stitched to the fabric somewhat loosely—the "floating" canvas. The effect is that the jacket can more easily move with you. What results is a suit that drapes more naturally to your form and hence looks much better. As you wear a canvassed jacket over time, the canvas itself, if it is made well, begins to conform to your body's shape, thereby becoming a better fit the more you wear it. That hopefully makes you feel a bit better while putting in the extra time on the job (in your canvassed jacket, of course). So the canvassed suit jackets drape better and last longer, and are accordingly more expensive. Many jackets are partially canvassed (and partially fused). If you are not sure at the time of purchase, ask. *Faber est suae quisque fortunae.*[11]

Shoulder construction is also important and is a key feature in determining a jacket's level of formality. Most business suit jackets will have some form of padding in the shoulder. A typical shoulder pad is made of a couple of pieces of spongy wool and a layer of canvas. It gives the jacket some structure and allows the fabric to hold its shape. It also allows it to fit men with different shoulder types. A shoulder pad helps build the silhouette of the wearer, especially on someone with a smaller physique or a body which bulges more in the gut than in the chest. Shoulder pads can increase width

---

10. "Neon Bible," *Neon Bible* (Slag, 2007).
11. Every man is the artisan of his own fortune.

up top to help hide this. Back in the 1930s, shoulders were cut big and broad as a symbol of machismo. Today, a large padded shoulder creates a retro look that is best reserved for long, full-cut jackets, if at all. A roped shoulder is usually lightly padded, but has a large sleeve head that extends upward at the shoulder line. This method of construction has become a style hallmark of many bespoke suit makers. The roped shoulder effects a rigid, almost Victorian look.[12]

Brands to Know

Sciamat: Sciamat was founded in 2002 in Italy by a junior attorney, Valentino Ricci, and his colleagues as an exclusive ode to masculine tailoring. The brand strives to be innovative for true connoisseurs of the suit. Now sold in Barney's RTW, this brand is famous for the Sciamat shoulder, which is a roped version—for many, *the* most perfect example. A fashion forward but decidedly manly take on traditional men's suiting.

Eidos Napoli: Founded in 2013 as a subset of storied Italian clothier Isaia, this brand is designed by Antonio Ciongoli. These suits are for the youthful and sartorially savvy Professional Gentleman who is unafraid of blurring definitive lines between sportswear and tailoring. It's a balance of forward-thinking fabrics and suits that can hold their own by themselves without traditional accessories. For high-fashion business casual.

Brunello Cucinelli: This Italian eponymous brand was founded in 1978 and sells ready-to-wear menswear, womenswear, and accessories. Headquartered in a fourteenth century castle in Italy, the company is well known for its commitment to "neohumanistic capitalism," Brunello Cucinelli donates 20% of its annual profits to its charitable foundation, The Brunello and Federica Cucinelli Foundation, and pays its employees wages 20% higher than the average employer in the industry. Brunello Cucinelli's is known for pared-back suits that are committed to traditional elements and natural fabrics while incorporating classic accents.

---

12. This style of shoulder can also be done using micro-pleats, which allow for greater freedom of movement and also showcase the level of handwork that went into the jacket (shoulder pleating is one of few manufacturing details that cannot be mass produced by machine).

Then there are unstructured jackets, which I personally prefer for many of my suits (even to the point of being profiled about it[13]). Without the interior lining, shoulder pads, or canvassing, the suit jacket wears more naturally. Due to the lack of shoulder padding, the line of the shoulder is more sloped and transitions smoothly into the line of the sleeve. It allows for more movement and comfort, and a silhouette more like your actual body's shape. Unstructured suits are typically of lighter, summer-weight fabrics because lighter weights of wool and materials like cotton and linen are more prone to wrinkle (and so using them with structured suits is problematic). Also, by removing the lining the jacket is quite obviously much cooler. However, certain less traditional menswear brands offer unstructured suits in a broader array of fabrics with heavier weights of wool.

Fabrication

Most suits are made of wool, due to this wondrous fabric's great versatility. Wool breathes extremely well and can be worn in both slightly hot as well as cool climates. It is also a relatively supple and soft fabric, which is comfortable and can conform well to a man's body. That said, wool also tends to be quite wrinkle free, allowing it to look sharp without too much fuss. The two main wool fabrications (or yarns) result in either (i) worsted (which is a fine smooth yarn spun from combed long-staple wool) in which the fibers are combined before spinning, and (ii) woolen (plain wool) where the fibers are not combined. These two yarns can be woven in a number of ways to produce tweed, flannel, cashmere, merino, and worsted—just to name a few.[14]

After wool, cotton is the second most common suit fabric. Cotton breathes extremely well and is also quite supple. However, it tends to crease very easily. Cotton suits are cheaper and are best worn during the transitional and warmer months of the year. Some prefer heavy cotton or wool/cotton blends as it allows the suit to retain its silhouette better. Personally, I opt for cotton only for warmer climates, as wool covers all of my other suiting needs.

Linen is a super lightweight fabric that is exceptionally breathable. Like cotton, linen tends to wrinkle easily. Annoyingly, it also tends to stain easily and needs to be frequently dry cleaned in order to maintain a fresh, crisp look of the fabric necessary if it is to be worn as a business suit.

---

13. Jean Palmieri, "At Work: Attorney Douglas Hand Pushes the Bounds of Tailored Clothing," *Women's Wear Daily*, July 27, 2017.
14. Cashmere and cashmere-blend suits can give off an unwanted sheen to a suit, which is not subtle and not generally advisable for the Professional Gentleman.

Other fabrics include polyester (made of synthetic materials), which is a decidedly lower quality fabric. Polyester (even polyester blended) suits are not an acceptable option for the Professional Gentleman. This fabric does not breathe, rendering it uncomfortable in all but the most perfect of climates. Plus polyester drapes horribly and shines, making suits made from this material look cheap, which they are. Velvet and silk are other fabrics suits are made with that, while not low quality, are more for formal or flashy events and not appropriate for the Professional Gentleman's place of business.

All suit fabrics come in a variety of weights to make many of them (certainly wool) a four-season fabric, depending on which weight you wear. To wit, below is a quick breakdown of weights from lightest to heaviest:

- **7 ounces to 9 ounces:** The lightest fabric weight you can find and is ideal for the Professional Gentleman during the warmer months of the year or for constantly balmy cities like Miami, Dubai, or Bangkok.
- **9.5 ounces to 11 ounces:** This weight is best for transitional seasons (early fall, late spring) when it's not too hot but certainly not cold. Perfect for most days in Los Angeles or Sydney and many days in Barcelona.
- **11 ounces to 12 ounces:** Middle weight. This is the most common and versatile fabric weight that is perfect to wear for the vast majority of the year. This is the perfect fabric weight to start with when building a formal suit wardrobe from scratch.
- **12 ounces to 13 ounces:** This is the second heaviest fabric weight. It's a decent option for fall/winter, but for summer it's really not wearable. This is a good weight for most days in Amsterdam, Montreal, or London.
- **14 ounces to 19 ounces:** These are the heaviest suit fabrics available. They are, well, weighty, but are easy to tailor and ideal to wear on a cold fall and/or winter day, or for constantly chilly places like, Copenhagen, Moscow, and Iceland.

Body Type and Silhouette: Delete the Negative; Accentuate the Positive!

Classic male physical proportions neatly fill the lines of a suit rather than spoil it. The suit is a garment that covers virtually all of your body. In terms of minimizing the negative elements of your physique that you do not like and maximizing the positive elements, the suit can be an amazing transformative vessel. A well-tailored suit can refine and perfect your inherent shape.

It can transform your silhouette into a more sporting posture, lengthen, broaden, and narrow. This is one of the great benefits to all types of men with the suit as a garment. It brings most body types towards an agnostic classical mean—rather than some hyper-proportioned one.

"Death is nothing, but to live defeated and inglorious is to die daily."

—Napoleon Bonaparte

For the shorter Professional Gentleman who wants to appear taller, who wants to be seen, who does not want to be looked down upon, who wants to speak from on high (or at least appear so), the vertical lines in a pinstripe suit help achieve this. The suit can also be a single button version which creates a deep "V" at the chest and gives the appearance of a longer torso.

"I wish to walk in such a line as will give most general satisfaction."

—George Washington

For the taller Professional Gentleman who wants to appear shorter, who feels ungainly and somewhat conspicuous and looming with his height (particularly in an elevator in Hanoi), the horizontal lines and pattern in a windowpane suit help break up his height. The suit can also be a three-button version, which matches the scale of his long torso and minimizes the "V" at the chest to reduce the appearance of height. Trousers with cuffs will also assist in breaking up the length of his inseam.

"It certainly strikes the beholder with astonishment, to perceive what vast difficulties can be overcome by the pigmy arms of little mortal men, aided by science and directed by superior skill."

—King Henry VII

For the heavier Professional Gentleman who wants to appear thinner, who feels corpulent and oafish, the single-breasted solid navy two-button suit will present a single block of uniform color with a broad enough shouldered suit jacket to minimize his girth. Pleated pants will add room and comfort, as will braces, in addition to not adding a belt, which would bifurcate his body in an unflattering way focusing on his midsection.

"Change will not come if we wait for some other person or some other time. We are the ones we've been waiting for. We are the change that we seek."

—Barack Obama

We don't have much sympathy for the slender man, as so much of today's tailored clothing seems to be cut to his dimensions. For the slim Professional Gentleman who wants to appear more substantial, who feels small and perhaps emasculated by his diminished size, the double-breasted glen plaid suit will offer a wide-buttoned stance, widening his torso while still looking sleek. The glen plaid's horizontal lines will also assist with broadening him. Roped shoulders would be a nice finishing touch.

This body awareness is not to be frowned upon. Being conscious of your flaws as well as your assets allows you to minimize the former and accentuate the latter. It allows you to suit yourself properly. As fashionable man's man Glenn O'Brien put it, "Some in the pack seem to wear suits that adhere more reasonably to their bodies, and we make a mental note that these are the young alphas, the future chiefs of that corporate tribe because men without vanity, with no ability to perceive themselves in the mirror, are fated to be drones."[15]

Styles and Suggestions

There are countless different styles of the suit, many (but by no means all) of which are acceptable as business attire. In terms of choosing styles, obviously adherence to the Laws is fundamental. If you are buying your first suit, or investing in your first made-to-measure or bespoke suit—start with the basics. One of my clients, menswear designer Jeff Halmos, told me that his personal style was "repetitive, simple, comfortable, easy, and tailored." This personal style credo should describe your basic suiting; your "go-to" suits; the basic four suits that serve as the foundation of your weekly wardrobe (the "Fundamental Four").

Law #17

~

The first four suits of the Professional Gentleman shall be the Fundamental Four.

~

---

15. Glenn O'Brien, *How to Be a Man: A Guide to Style and Behavior for the Modern Gentleman* (New York: Rizzoli, 2011).

Gray Flannel, Navy Blue Pinstripe, Charcoal Pinstripe, Navy Blue

The solid gray worsted wool suit in medium gray to dark gray. I struggle to think of an occasion to which this suit is not an acceptable ensemble. It goes with everything in terms of shirt, shoes, and accessories. Worsted can be worn most of the year in most climates. It is your absolute basic and should be invested in accordingly. You will wear it over and over and over again. Therefore, it would not at all be unwise to have the solid gray in more than one, even more than two weights of fabric. Put it on the tape![16]

The navy pinstripe worsted, which is more recognizably business in its orientation and, because darker than the medium gray, can also be worn out at night to social and business events while still striking a capable Professional Gentleman tone. It too goes with virtually everything in terms of shirting (though because of its stripes, you should default to solid shirts), shoes, and accessories. It is another core piece and should be invested in wisely (i.e., also invest in a heavier fall/winter weight fabric version and a double breasted).

The dark gray pinstripe is very conservative and financially/banking oriented. Let yours make you look like a billion dollars (or more appropriately, that a billion dollars is safe in your capable hands). This is also a solid evening partner and can be dressed up for business formal occasions. Best worn with black shoes and belt, as brown gets muddled in the darkness of this often charcoal or darker gray suit.

---

16. Back in the old days, trade orders to be executed by brokers came out on ticker tape—a long roll of paper constantly printing orders and emptying them out to the trading floor. Now all of this is done by computers, of course.

The navy blue solid worsted wool suit can be a bridge to adding more color into your basic wardrobe. Unhampered by pinstripes, you can add any number of striped, checked, or plain shirts to this suit, which makes it an extremely versatile companion for business and non-business. It is a very obliging business causal partner when worn without a tie. Please avoid the temptation to wear the jacket alone for a substitute to a blue blazer. A blazer is more than a blue jacket (as will be discussed *infra*), and so wearing the suit jacket as a substitute becomes obvious and embarrassing.

The Fundamental Four are absolute necessities and critical to your wardrobe. Each of them is subtle, professional, and is almost unrecognized as a foundation around which the rest of your wardrobe rests. Your first purchase of any of the Fundamental Four should be in an all-season fabric weight.[17] Every gentleman should have them all, and every Professional Gentleman positively needs them all. Invest in these items. I can't stress enough the importance of feeling and looking good in your Fundamental Four.

Law #18

~

The four suits of the highest quality in the Professional Gentleman's wardrobe shall be the Fundamental Four.

~

Before any fifth suit—a summer weight linen suit in, say, that off-white color many refer to as bone or a heavy brown and sage tweed suit that would look killer at a shooting party—are even considered, a great degree of your

---

17. Again, 9.5–12 oz. (285–360 g) should serve for most seasons. Just as data points: 14–19 oz. (420–570 g) is considered rare/heavyweight, 12–13 oz. (360–390 g) is considered midweight to heavyweight, and 7–9 oz. (210–270 g) is considered light.

sartorial budget should have already been dropped on the Fundamental Four. I would much rather you have a Fundamental Four of high quality in which you look elegant and capable and are supremely confident (i.e., a Fundamental Four that are expensive relative to your budget), than you have ten or more suits of variety and, due to your budget, you actually look elegant and capable in none of them. Trust that this is a sound policy. Given the understated nature of the Fundamental Four, it is not like people will be talking about the fact that you have only four suits. With your choice of shirting and tie/pocket square/accessories combinations, you can bridge the Fundamental Four into hundreds of looks—and all of them *good* looks.

Modifying Your Suits

"Trust not the heart of that man for whom
old clothes are not venerable."
—*Thomas Carlyle*[18]

Some of you may be asking yourselves, "Great. I get it. Spend as much as I can on the Fundamental Four, but what I could spend in my first year on the job is not what I can afford four years in, or now, am I to replace good suits with better suits and never have any other styles?" Great question. A+. Good students. My response is to modify those older versions.

One economical and fun tip I have for those of you who might find it hard to purchase a second traditionally cut blue pinstripe suit when you already have one that (but for the fact that you purchased it earlier in your career and you can now afford a better fitting better quality version) is perfectly serviceable, is to make a few modifications to distinguish the older version. The easiest and most noticeable way to do this, in most cases also the cheapest, is to swap out the buttons (which are likely to be in the same shade as the color of the suit itself) with buttons of another color entirely.

I've put white buttons on a light gray suit, brown wooden buttons on a navy blue pinstripe suit, and burgundy buttons (the same shade

---

18. Thomas Carlyle was a Scottish social commentator born in 1795 who is noted for his famous work on the primacy of heroes in history. See *On Heroes, Hero-Worship, and the Heroic in History* (London: James Fraser, 1841).

as the pinstripes) on a charcoal gray pinstripe suit. I don't wear any of these suits very often, but when I do, it's a pleasant bit of reminiscence coupled with a punch of sartorial whimsy. Kind of like I dropped a new engine in that old car I used to drive in high school, which is now a sort of hot rod version of a classic.

Other options include changing the lining of the jacket, or reversing the cuffs, or even adding elbow patches—which I know should not be on a suit if you are following the rules.

The Professional Gentleman who is worried that people think his wardrobe is too small and therefore focuses on obtaining low-priced suits of great variety is a doomed man. For while he may be able to turn his suits into hundreds (and hundreds) of looks—few of them will be good looks. This is because the framework upon which he is building his sartorial presentation will of necessity be less than it could be because his suits are cut-rate. So while he can roll out a jaunty French blue suit on the first bright day of spring (a perfect color for an April morning), that suit will very likely be ill-fitting, unflattering to his body, and perhaps even evidence of poor construction. While the spirit of his choice (to have seasonal suits for every occasion and temperature) is laudable for the man on a budget, he will look like the suit he is wearing—aspirational and cheap. Best to avoid that.

Beyond the Fundamental Four

Honestly, beyond the Fundamental Four, a Professional Gentleman (subject to climate) is best served obtaining similarly colored and cut suits in varying weights. So, heavier weight versions for winter or colder climates; lighter weight versions for summer and warmer climates.[19]

Perhaps more fun, and certainly no waste of resources, is to obtain similarly colored but differently cut suits. For instance, the charcoal gray pinstripe in a double-breasted jacket. Alternatively you could try single-button

---

19. Again, 14–19 oz. (420–570 g) is considered rare/heavyweight, 12–13 oz. (360–390 g) is considered midweight to heavyweight, and 7–9 oz. (210–270 g) is considered light.

(yes—some brands still make these) or three-button (not so much, unless you are tall—as has been said *supra*) versions of the Fundamental Four.[20] Or three-piece editions. Or cuff the trousers. Or pleat them. Or try a high-waisted version. If your versions are traditional English cuts, try one in Italian, say from Brioni, Ermenegildo Zegna, Caruso, or Attolini.

Brands to Know

Brioni: Brioni, a menswear couture house owned by French holding company Kering, was founded in Rome in 1945. Brioni is credited with the production of the first men's fashion show in 1952. (Other menswear brands can either thank them or curse them for this.) Known for its made-to-measure men's suits, sartorial ready-to-wear collections, and leather goods, Brioni has become a point of reference for the entertainment, institutional, and business worlds. Soon after the opening of its first shop, Brioni quickly attracted the attention of high-profile movie personalities, heads of state, and business leaders. In 1985, Brioni opened a tailoring school and has continually introduced new silhouettes, bold colors, and innovative fabrics to further its mission of being "one of a kind." I met the CEO at a dinner, and to hear him talk about fabric and construction is to hear a sermon on attention to detail and quality.

Caruso: Established in Soragna in 1958, this Italian design house is a favored brand of Italian men. Celebrities from around the world sport suits made by Caruso in the same industrial premises they occupied at the company's founding, assuring them the elegant accents and fine fabrics customary of garments "Made in Italy." Caruso prides itself on manufacturing suits of authentic Italian style, and its quality and craftsmanship is appreciated by fashion conscious men globally. The international appeal of the Caruso suit is evidenced by the brand opening their flagship store in New York City.

---

20. Preferable to the three-button, in most cases, is the three-roll two-button. The best of both worlds in some ways.

Attolini: Vincento Attolini, the Naples designer, was a pioneer in evolution of the men's suit. In 1930, he made an unprecedented suit, designed with a shape new to the industry and sporting accents that differentiated the garment from the standard English suit. Creating a suit that was extremely simple, yet elegant and comfortable due to the lightweight suit jacket, Attolini fashioned what has unanimously become known as "the jacket." Attolini transformed men's fashion, attracting even royalty to begin wearing his ingenious and beautiful designs. Today, Attolini sells suits that are simultaneously Italian and international. Attolini suits continue to be "handmade" in its workshop, and still display the elegance and sophistication that differentiated Attolini at the outset.

In addition to, or concurrent with, obtaining these Fundamental Four subsidiaries, you could also consider adaptations in color and width of the pinstripe versions. Red stripes. French blue. Tight and thin stripes. Chalk stripes wide apart. All of these renderings will look quite different and expand your wardrobe, adding many additional elements (shirts, ties, and accessories) that can handsomely be worn together in harmony.

If all of this sounds like an awful lot of blue and gray suiting, you're absolutely right. It is. That's because blue and gray suiting is what the Professional Gentleman looks best in. It is capable and elegant, and in it, you look like a Professional Gentleman. You are the avatar of capability and elegance. But once you have the basics well covered in a manner that flatters your body type, you can start to branch into suits that appeal to your more whimsical side or that are somewhat extreme in their seasonal appeal. You can be, as designer Lubov Azria[21] would describe, a "connoisseur with a visionary twist."[22] What are some of the elements you should strive for? Working within the Laws, only you know what is appropriate for you. Classic, subtle, colorful, masculine, refined, honest, vibrant, minimal, grandfatherly, bohemian, bookish, powerful, playful, sexy, preppy, Western, Eastern, exotic,

21. The wife of Max Azria, Lubov had designed for BCBG for years. DISCLOSURE: BCBG:Max Azria is a client of my firm HBA.
22. Council of Fashion Designers of America, *The Pursuit of Style: Advice and Musings from America's Top Fashion Designers* (New York: Harry N. Abrams, 2014).

clean, eclectic. Be YOU! (But within the Laws, my good man. Always within the Laws.)

Brands to Know

Anderson & Sheppard: English Savile Row tailors since 1906, they typify the fluid style that puts a premium on the way a man moves in his suit. This is the way most English Professional Gentlemen want to appear. Executors of the sloped shoulder, the limp silhouette, and the English drape, the Anderson & Sheppard suit is a refined thing of beauty. Very expensive.

P Johnson: This Australian brand was established in Sydney in 2008 and now has showrooms in Melbourne, New York, and London. P Johnson offers a unique approach to creating elegant and versatile wardrobes for the Professional Gentleman at a great value for the quality these suits represent. Drawing upon the lightness and deconstructed aspects of traditional Italian tailoring, P Johnson suits start at around $1,500.

Hickey Freeman: This US manufacturer of suits is based in Rochester, New York and was founded in 1899. The Hartmarx Corporation bought the company in 1964. Two young entrepreneurs named Jacob Freeman and Jeremiah Hickey built it in the early years of the twentieth century. Their plan was to bring high-quality hand-tailoring to men from coast to coast. As they envisioned it, a Hickey Freeman suit would be a testament to both the delicate artistry of hand-craftsmanship and the steady consistency of modern technology. A handsome conservative suit for the Professional Gentleman.

But let me assist with some practical advice. Some more exotic examples beyond the Fundamental Four that are potentially suitable for the Professional Gentleman include the following:

- the tan or olive green suit
- the seersucker
- the gray or navy windowpane suit
- the French blue pinstripe
- the tweed three-piece
- the black suit (the tuxedo)[23]
- the oyster white suit

23. I realize the tuxedo is formal wear but not business appropriate, and therefore I've not included a chapter on it. It will, however, be an important suit for the Professional Gentleman for charity benefits, client events, and other social occasions where clients (or potential clients) will be present. So I include it here.

There are many other varieties on these archetypes, but trust me, they do not stray into red suits nor orange ones nor light tones with pinstripes nor many, many other types of suits that exist. Just because a garment is a suit does not mean it is suitable for wearing in a business environment. As many of the courtside examples of wild colors and configurations worn by injured professional basketball players on the bench demonstrate, these types of suits are not the Professional Gentleman's mode. No, this is the mode of the sidelined, injured, young, physically gifted, oft misguided, professional athlete. This young man has no need of clients. If he's an established all-star, he may make more in a year than some of you will make in an entire career. His concerns and yours are very different. Take sartorial cues from him at your own peril. Let the Fundamental Four be your guideposts, and don't stray far unless the Laws compel you for some business reason or special occasion to do so.

Fit and Tailoring:
A Top-Down Approach

Few Professional Gentlemen have the physical build to be able to wear an off-the-rack suit without needing to visit the tailor. But let's start with your relationshipwith your tailor. In my experience, very few Professional Gentlemen actually have a tailor they know by name. This is wrong.

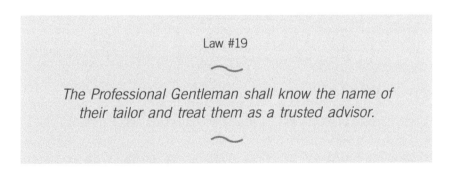

Law #19

~

The Professional Gentleman shall know the name of their tailor and treat them as a trusted advisor.

~

Your clients likely know you by name because you perform an important function for them. So too is the tailor's relationship to you. Thus, you should know your tailor's name and have an open and mutually agreeable relationship with them.

"I got a date with my tailor now, thanks for putting me so
straight."

—Joe Jackson[24]

Tip your tailor regularly and remember their birthday.[25] Also note that just as a paralegal is not a lawyer, just as an analyst is not an MD, a seamstress/seamster is not a tailor. In addition, the type of independent tailor you should engage does not operate out of a retail menswear location unless you plan on purchasing all of your tailored clothing from that same location.

The basic rules of fit are pretty straightforward. Everything starts with the shoulders and works down. The shoulders of the jacket should lie flat, and the seam should end where your natural shoulder ends. If this critical seam sits too high or too low, it throws the entire jacket off. So if you try on a jacket for purchase and the shoulder fit is sloppy, you, too, should throw that jacket off and move on. Shoulder alterations are the most difficult part of a jacket to adjust, and invariably that adjustment requires other modifications.[26]

The collar of the jacket should sit comfortably and flat against the collar of your shirt. One that is too loose will sit away from the neck and look unkempt—like a yoke for some beast of burden. If the collar is too tight, it will bunch up above the back and look uncomfortable. Either way, the line of your suit will be spoiled. A poorly fitting collar is usually due to a problem in construction elsewhere in the jacket—most usually the shoulders. It is not an easily administered alteration as a result.

Regarding the body of the jacket, please note that it is going to be worn both buttoned (when standing) and unbuttoned (when seated), so it's important the fit is checked both ways. The button should fasten without any fuss, and the material should not strain. Once fastened, you should be able to insert your hand (or that of a very close and attractive friend) into the suit under the lapels and cup your pectoral without the jacket pulling.

In terms of length of the jacket, if you are standing with your arms by your sides, the bottom of the jacket should fall in line with your knuckles—this should make it just long enough to cover your rear. But there are

---

24. Joe Jackson, "Look Sharp," on *Look Sharp* (A&M, 1979).
25. If you can remember to do so, send them a nice card on this date, or at least drop in with a small gift or tip.
26. Like when one of the parties to a long merger agreement becomes plural (i.e., the selling party becomes multiple selling parties) because all references to that party, as well as pronouns and other citations, will, by necessity given the way the English language functions, require changes.

cropped versions from certain brands, and a more English look is to prefer a slightly longer jacket fully covering your bottom. Button stance can vary, but the top button of the traditional two-button suit jacket should sit in line with, or just above, your navel. On a three-button design, this should be measured by the middle button.

Armholes in more sporting versions of the suit are cut high. In fitted versions, they can be quite small. This means you may have problems raising your hands over your head.[27] But as I like to tell myself (and my associates), the Professional Gentleman never surrenders. So don't worry about it. If you find yourself while suited with the urge to raise your hand in a meeting, put your hand down, buck up, and just speak, man! School is over, mate. A Professional Gentleman simply makes his statement or asks his question—forcefully but respectfully—he does not need to be called on.

Your jacket sleeves should hit about or just above where the base of your thumb meets your wrist. This will ensure that the cuffs of your dress shirt will be exposed by approximately a half an inch to ensure the "linen" shows. Arm length is fairly easy for a tailor to alter, providing the buttons on the cuffs are not functional and they are slightly too long rather than too short. If the cuffs feature working buttons, it's more labor-intensive and expensive.[28]

Now let's get down to the trousers. Your natural waist sits just below your navel. This should be the narrowest part of a man's midsection. When placed there, your trousers should not require a belt or braces to stay up. Fit in this area is critical to comfort. This is the one area of your clothing that you cannot modify with any decorum during the day. You can unbutton, even remove, your jacket without giving offense. You can roll up your shirt sleeves and even loosen your tie under the right circumstances. But unfastening your pants while doing Professional Gentleman business is just not acceptable.[29] The belt is the most common and yet the least comfortable way to keep your pants up. Having a strap of leather right where your body bends in an office chair is an odd form of self-inflicted torture, but the majority of men do it. Better trousers have side-adjuster or "daks-straps" which can modify the waist by a full size in a pinch. Braces are also a great option—which will be detailed *infra*.

The seat of your trousers is pretty self-explanatory, and the material here should drape with the natural shape of your backside. I'm not particularly keen to go into too much detail about your ass, but if you find that the mate-

---

27. When hailing a cab or waiving to a friend, please unbutton your jacket.
28. In that case, the sleeve has to be taken up from the shoulder rather than from the sleeve.
29. It's potentially even grounds for a sexual harassment claim if you meet with your colleagues in this sorry state of deportment.

rial in this critical area is strained or you are experiencing discomfort, it's too tight. Correspondingly, a noticeable sag in the material means the seat is too loose and should be taken in.

The traditional fit for trouser legs gives slightly more room in the thigh and then tapers below the knee. Slim-fitted versions have less room, and, if the fabric is straining when you put them on, you should avoid these versions.[30]

Trouser length dictates the "break" (the small fold of material that appears where your trouser cuff hits your shoe). Too long and your trousers puddle and you look sloppy but too short and *you* look like you are about to go through a puddle in waders. Thom Browne and the influence of his "shrunken schoolboy" aesthetic have had men wearing trousers shorter to the point that longer trousers look more conservative, even somewhat retro. Ultimately, trouser length is less about fashion and more about what compliments your body type and a sense of personal style. Less break will make a shorter Professional Gentleman appear taller, whereas a full break on a taller Professional Gentleman will make him look more proportioned.

For my money, I shoot for the slightest of breaks—a "shivering break" (as #menswear blogs would describe it), where the hem of my trouser meets my shoe's vamp without rumpling and making sure my ankles aren't permanently on show in my more traditional suits. For my unstructured summer and spring suits, I usually opt for no break.

Brands to Know

Sartoria Solito: This Italian family business was founded in the 1940s. The atelier is at Via Toledo number 256 in Naples and available through only a few select channels of distribution. The brand shares the Neapolitan preference for soft-fitted garments, but their jackets are recognizable for the high armholes, lack of shoulder padding, and with the most lightweight linings available. All their jackets tend to be a bit longer in the front.

Sartoria Formosa: Mario Formosa was a famous tailor in Naples. No two Formosa suits are made the same, but all share the easy comfort and

---

30. Refer to the cautionary tale of the "grab effect" on an unwitting QB at HBA's office *infra*. And I'm not talking about an illegal use of the hands.

rakish grace of the Neapolitan style. Formosa suits feature careful hand-work, soft construction, and elegant curves. Think soft natural shoulders, almost no padding, very round quarters, and generous lapels that roll to a low buttoning point. Bespoke at bespoke prices, but this brand is also available online through No Man Walks Alone.

Desmond Merrion: This is one of the most renowned tailors on Savile Row. These fine, tailored English suits are, however, wildly expensive (think mid-five figures for the "Supreme Bespoke"). All handmade with no machine touching the garment at any stage, this is the absolute pinnacle in tailoring. The finished product will appear as if it has been sculpted around the torso.

Pants may also be pleated or cuffed. If they are pleated, they should always be cuffed. But if they are not pleated, dealer's choice, you can still cuff them. Cuffs will look better on a taller frame, so for shorter Professional Gentlemen, consider leaving your flat front trousers un-cuffed. Cuffs will also add weight to the bottom of the trouser leg, which can enhance the drape of certain lighter fabrics.

In most cases, flat front pants are the preferred suiting option.[31] The unadorned waistline is sleeker, providing a silhouette that enhances the appearance of thinness. This is generally a good thing for the profile of the entire suit. Accordingly, pleats have been out of fashion for a while, particularly with the advent of slim fitting suiting options. However, pleats are a traditional trouser element—and for good reason.

I'm reminded of a meeting I hosted at our law offices for a client (a menswear brand) and a football player (who will go unnamed) with his advisory entourage regarding this athlete being the face of my client's brand for a couple of seasons (fashion seasons, not football seasons). Our footballer was a handsome stud; he was dating a major actress, and this was a push by his advisors to make him something of a style icon. It was all nice and aspirational and avuncular. He was dressed in a form-fitting gray Helmut Lang suit with flat front trousers. I'm not sure if that was a personal choice or some stylist's (the stylist was one of the few advisors who was not present at this particular meeting). Now, our jock was not a lineman or run-

---

31. As well as for all pants worn not as a suit (e.g., with an odd jacket, as casual trousers, etc.).

ning back; he was a quarterback, with relatively human proportions. But still, his slim-fit trousers were straining and because there were no pleats, it was visually pretty disturbing. When we finished the meeting and we got up from the conference table, the "grab effect" of the tight trousers on his manly, full thighs had them riding up and looking rippled. Roughing the passer! Indeed, this was unnecessary roughness. Certainly not the sleek profile Helmut Lang intended.

To be sure, most trim Professional Gentlemen can avoid pleated pants. And flat front pants are sleeker, providing a silhouette that enhances the appearance of thinness. But for larger men, whether portly or muscular, pleats will ensure that the silhouette of the trousers will not be sullied. There is also a potential retro cool to having pleats. They are on their way back as fashion's pendulum swings away from slim and cropped looks. Pleated trousers come in single-pleated and double-pleated versions. Just note that it takes a lot of waistline to fill out the double-pleated versions.

Maintaining Your Suits

Your suits are an investment. Care for them accordingly. Properly maintained, your suit can outlive you. You can put good suits in your last will and testament—I have.

Law #20

~

The Professional Gentleman shall maintain his suits in good working condition and treat them with care.

~

Don't wear the same suit two days in a row. This is not just a style tip. Your suit needs at least a day of rest to breathe, just like your shoes (see *supra*). Hang up your suit as soon as you're done wearing it.

Dry clean your suits as little as possible. The chemicals involved in dry cleaning can wear out the fabric. So if you have minor stains you can remove yourself with a good steaming or brushing, do so. If your suit is just a tad wrinkly, and not soiled, simply have it pressed rather than dry cleaned. Your suit will return just as crisp, but without having been subjected to the chemicals. If you must dry clean, point out specific stains so your cleaner can mark them. Once your suit comes back, get it out of the plastic bag (which does not let it breathe), off that wire hanger, and onto a proper wooden one, but you can leave in the tissue paper if you like and the cool plastic thing that brings the jacket together without buttoning it.

Storage is important. These are garments, not tax returns or corporate minutes. So don't store them the same way. Your suits require plenty of space. Keep them in a place where they can breathe, spaced out evenly and allowed to hang upright on a suit hanger, unhindered by objects below that might impact their drape.

Cedar wood hangers absorb moisture and work as repellants for moths. Moths can be a real danger to your suits. They lay around 100 eggs, and once they hatch, their larvae will destroy a suit. Mothballs can be used as a deterrent, but they reek, and they really only work in a sealed enclosure, like a suit bag. Since your suits need to breathe, this is not a good option. I am told that dried lavender leaves sealed in pouches and kept in pockets repel moths as well as smell lovely. Regularly cleaning of your closet and vacuuming the space regularly will do the trick better than anything. I certainly don't mean to sound like your mum here, but please try to make sure to have a proper closet cleaning done at least once a year.

Ignorantia juris non excusat.

—8—

Shirting

*"The boor covers himself,
the rich man or the fool adorns himself,
and the elegant man gets dressed."*
—Honoré de Balzac[1]

T he dress shirt is the underpinning of your business wardrobe. It is in physical contact with three of the main components of the business outfit—the tie, the jacket, and the trousers. Think of it as the overall holding company to a corporate organizational chart. Most Professional Gentlemen, in point of fact, typically spend more time in the office in just their shirt sleeves (i.e., without a jacket, let alone a vest, on). This makes the proper dress shirt a fundamentally important part of your wardrobe.

History

The modern dress shirt took shape at the end of the nineteenth century with the advent of buttons all the way down the front of the shirt (before then, the shirt was just pulled over the wearer's head, like underwear—which,

---

1. The famous French playwright and novelist, Balzac is regarded as one of the founders of realism in literature. Born in 1799, he's certainly keeping it real with this quote.

believe it or not, was what it was considered). As perhaps a snide aside, I hope this makes you all feel quite a bit more comfortable. Basically, today as a Professional Gentleman, you spend most of your day working in what was considered leisurewear a little more the 100 years ago.[2]

As we discussed briefly *supra*, until the end of the nineteenth century the white dress shirt was the true sign of an established (and moneyed) gentleman. This was because any form of manual labor would easily soil a white shirt and only someone wealthy could have shirts washed frequently enough to wear white shirts and keep them clean. While this is no longer true, as we know the *nom de guerre* for most Professional Gentlemen has been "white collar." This has even slipped into the lexicon of litigators when describing "white collar crime" such as accounting fraud, insider trading, and other culpable corporate shenanigans.

In any event, the proper dress shirt for Professional Gentlemen has seldom been altered in its general form since its twentieth-century incarnation. Sure, there have been shirt offerings designed to be untucked. These casual shirts are cut shorter and are finished at the bottom with a curved hemline. But without exception, brands that put forward these shirts, like the aptly named Untuckit, acknowledge that these are casual shirts—not dress shirts.[3] As a general rule, you will never wear such shirts because you will not wear your shirt in any mode other than tucked into your trousers. I'll now button down a Law here that should be rather obvious:

Law #21

~

The Professional Gentleman shall always wear his dress shirt tucked into his trousers.

~

---

2. And you are further even permitted to dress in what is considered leisurewear by today's standards. The slippery slope has had a mud slide, but more on that later. See Chapter 10 *infra*.

3. Certainly do not try to wear such shirts as if they were dress shirts. They will not stay tucked into your trousers for they are not made to do so. So rather than looking as neat as possible while trying to look casual (which is what these shirts are designed for), you will look as sloppy as possible while trying to look formal, which is a bad combination.

Another development over the last century worth noting is the advent of the breast pocket, which was introduced likely as a response to the decline of the three-piece suit and its pocketed vest. So if you are wearing a three-piece suit, please don't wear a dress shirt with a breast pocket. You might as well add cargo pockets to your trousers. Given that sticking pens or really any other items in the shirt pocket reeks of an IT service provider or archetype of a nerdy geek, best to simply do away with purchasing shirts with pockets all together. Your overall look will be sleeker, and I'm quite confident you can find a place to store pens, business cards, or the slim calculator you might have been tempted to slide into the breast-coat pocket of a dress shirt.[4]

There have also been technological advances in fabric and design, including flexible collars and wrinkle-free materials. We'll look at these below, but basically, the dress shirt has remained a basic and static article of clothing for quite some time now.

Collar: The Defining Feature of the Shirt

The shape and form of the collar is one of the defining features of every dress shirt. The spread of the collar with its inverted "V" shape always points toward your face and makes it stand out. Therefore, it is very important to have a collar that agrees with your neck and face, not to mention corresponding in width to the knot of your tie as well as the lapel of your jacket. Regarding pairing the collar to the length and width of your mug, the idea is to create balance. So, if you have a narrow or gaunt face, going with a spread collar, which is wide, would be your best bet. Similarly, if you have a round, wide face, going with a more narrow collar makes sense. By the same token, you want to make sure that the actual size of the collar corresponds to the size of your face. So if you have a massive head, face it, you are going to need a large collar.[5] And the longer your neck, the taller the collar should be.

The cut of the collar is one parameter determining the shape, while the distinction between the collar that stands up (the aptly named "stand-up" collar) and the collar that turns down (the just as aptly named "turndown" collar) is another.[6]

---

4. Please review Chapter 12 on accessories and how awesomely stylish the variety of accessories to store your gear can be.
5. If your face is large and narrow, it should be a large spread collar. If it's large and wide, it should be a large pinpoint collar. Get it?
6. Up to the end of the nineteenth century, various versions of the stand-up collar were the norm. The stand-up collar was gradually replaced by the turndown collar, and since the 1930s, the stand-up collar is usually only worn with tuxedos.

An old catalogue of styles of collar for dress shirting is set forth below.

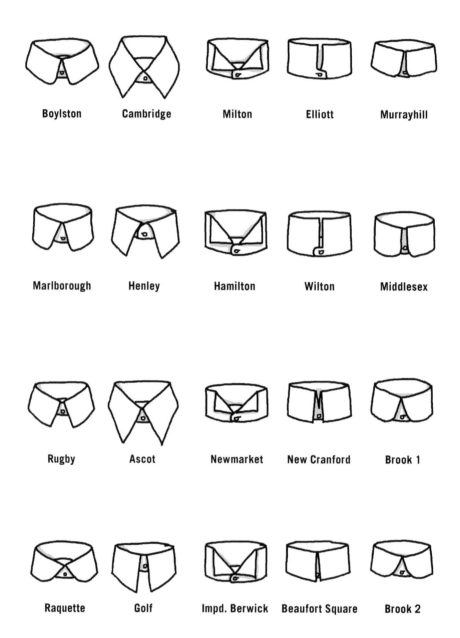

Many of these styles are obsolete. The stand-up collar is barely worth mentioning as it is hardly seen these days outside of formal dress. It is usually only worn now with a tuxedo, but even these sightings are becoming rarer. I mention it because, like a good contrarian trader, I'll boldly predict the stand-up collar is due to make a comeback in the next decade or so.[7] But please relegate any early adoption of this "blast from the past" to partner/MD dress.[8] The stand-up collar on a junior banker might make him look like a stand-up comedian in the context of business dealings—at least until it becomes more normal as it was two centuries ago.

Brands to Know

100Hands: This Dutch brand was founded in 2014 but is based on traditions centuries old. It shares a deep passion and appreciation for craftsmanship. Each 100Hands handmade shirt is crafted over a period of 1.5 to 3 days, where 100Hands' skilled artisans meticulously sew the body of each shirt. Each shirt literally goes through 100 skilled artisans' hands before it reaches the end customers. The artisans' stories are woven into the shirt during the unique production process. Only a limited amount of shirts get made per year; each shirt is truly a one-of-a-kind product.

Eton: This storied brand has been producing men's shirts since 1928. Eton's factory and headquarters remain in the same location—Gånghester, Sweden—where their first shirts were produced. Eton is a global leading shirt maker and can be found in the world's most exclusive stores. Classic, yet contemporary dress shirts for Professional Gentlemen.

Gitman: The roots of this brand go back to the 1930s. Gitman is one of the few remaining legacy American shirt makers with all their production still actually based in the United States. The shirts are well made and material selection is high quality. Gitman also makes ties.

Turndown collars are what virtually all Professional Gentlemen today prefer for the dress shirt. Some turndown collars (usually the more formal ones) have an interlining, giving the collar some bulk and heft. These are

---

7. Eat your heart out, Humphrey Neill. "When everybody thinks alike, everybody is likely to be wrong." See Humphrey B. Neill, *The Art of Contrary Thinking* (Caldwell: Caxton Press, 1954).
8. See Chapter 3, *supra*.

called fused collars. Unfused collars do not have this construction and are typically more relaxed.

Both kinds of collars usually feature collar stays in order to ensure (with the structural guidance of the stay itself) a smooth, unwrinkled collar. Some collar stays are sewn in and cannot be exchanged whilst others are removable.[9] Only soft turndown collars (like a button-down collar) do not have any collar stays.

Stays are typically plastic, but you can get stainless steel, brass, sterling silver, gold, wood, mother-of-pearl, horn, or bone versions as well. No one will know the difference, but plastic does tend to bend over time and certainly will bend and even melt if your dry cleaner does not remove the stays before washing your shirt.[10] So replace the stays when necessary. Metal collar stays are less flexible and heavier than other types. This gives the collar a sleeker look that many find appealing. Stainless steel and titanium versions are also relatively reasonable and will last forever, provided you do not lose them.

The size of collar stays is also important. If they are too long for the collar, the fold of the turndown collar will be adversely impacted. If they are too short, the collar may crease unnaturally. You should have a number of sizes to deal with this adequately. I once found myself in Tokyo for a couple of days on business, and I did not have the properly sized collar stays for one of my shirts. I tried using paper clips (the best thing at hand in the Japanese office I was working out of). The results were mixed.[11] Better to stay with the collar stay for the staying of the collar. So, stock up as these are inexpensive but important little things.

Unless you prefer to have exotic and rich collar stays. You can find them in 18 karat gold. You can have them engraved. You can spend a thousand dollars on them. Granted, they will do the same job of a $3 stainless steel pair, but you will know what lies beneath. If that's your thing, go with it. It may increase your confidence or just appeal to you to have a little luxury right under your nose. Just don't lose them!

---

9. There are many shirts with inferior glued interlining that have non-removable collar stays. After laundering and ironing, this collar is often deformed and the shirt becomes unwearable. But it should be noted that there do exist excellent bespoke shirts with glued interlinings and sewn-in collar stays that can last for years. So it is not, strictly speaking, necessary for a good shirt to have removable collar stays.

10. With most dry cleaners, removing the stays would be considered your responsibility; however, your relationship with your dry cleaner may rest on their proactive treatment of your garments. So when the first melted collar stay happens, let them know and encourage them to double-check your collars to ensure this does not happen again. Also encourage them to replace cracked buttons on shirts, suits, and the like. Tip your dry cleaner at year end if they have done a good job in all of this. You are a busy gent, and having your dry cleaner as a partner in ensuring your wardrobe is up to snuff can be invaluable.

11. Other office-ready substitutes for lacking proper collar stays in a pinch include cutting them out of sturdy business card stock as well as using clipped portions of wooden coffee stirrers.

Collars themselves are also removable on certain shirts. Like the stand-up collar, the detachable collar is a legacy of the nineteenth century when laundering shirts was more difficult and expensive. Since a gentleman rarely took his jacket off in those days, much less the vest he was surely wearing, the bulk of the dress shirt itself was rarely soiled. The collar, however, exposed to the elements, often was exposed to soot and grime (and let's hope, the occasional random passionate brush of lipstick). But by removing it, one could wash the collar and not the entire shirt. My English grandfather, Jack Ledwith, had collars like this.[12] According to my parents, I used to run around my grandparent's London flat when we visited with one of my grandfather's detachable collars on over my T-shirt as a boy and shouted things like, "Point of order. Point of order. The barrister must be heard at this time!" Yes, I was an odd but prescient lad.

Recently, Phillips Van Heusen, the world's largest (note: largest but not best) dress shirt manufacturer, introduced a flexible collar based on a proprietary technology that purports to give the wearer an added half inch of expanding collar without compromising the overall structure of the collar.

Please note that better fabrics and proper sizing have always been a solution to this issue as well. A dress shirt will eventually shrink due to washing (1–3% is common depending upon the fabric and tightness of its weave). It is inevitable. Typically the bulk of such shrinkage should be done by the third washing. Therefore, you should generally purchase shirts with a half inch of allowance for shrinkage, and you should not make any alterations to a shirt until after it has been laundered at least three times, because such premature adjustments may prove to be wrong.

Colors, Patterns

As we've discussed *supra*, the white shirt is the standard classic. It affords you the most options in terms of pairing with suits, ties, and the rest of your wardrobe. So the white dress shirt—in various weights and weaves of cotton as well as collar styles—should make up the bulk of your shirting inventory. Yes, my "white-collar" workers, the white dress shirt shall make up the bulk of the Professional Gentleman's shirts. In the same variety of styles, the blue dress shirt should be your secondary fundamental shirt. After that, a few

---

12. Beyond being a bit of a style icon to me, Grandad Jack was the last mayor of the London borough of Acton before it merged with the borough of Ealing in West London. Acton was the birthplace of The Who, of which all members (except Keith Moon—and really, he was kind of third fiddle) went to Acton County Grammar School. It's Queens Park Ranger territory.

shirts in basic stripes of white and blue or white and gray or white and red/burgundy are advisable.

Law #22

~

White dress shirts shall constitute the bulk of the Professional Gentleman's shirting inventory.

~

After that, and notwithstanding the opportunities for self-expression a shirt may provide you, I would still caution some restraint in terms of "statement" shirts or wild colors or stripes. Again, the shirt is a basic part of your wardrobe. It's hard to get excited about shirts. Let the shirt be the quiet and classic part of your overall ensemble it is generally meant to be.

That said, after you have covered the white and blue and basic stripe versions, there are a number of shirts you can add, which can serve your overall wardrobe well and not break any of the Laws.

Styling, Buttons, and Other Elements of Quality

Beyond the pattern and the collar, by far the two most noticeable elements of the dress shirt, there are other features in its construction that can have an impact on how the shirt looks and feels when worn.

The buttons traditionally are mother-of-pearl on dress shirts of high quality. Mother-of-pearl buttons are super hard and can absorb the damage of a sloppy dry cleaner who presses on top of the buttons rather than around them. Plastic often breaks at this rough treatment.[13]

Buttons should be firmly attached to the shirt without much looseness with the stitching in a crisscross "X" shape. This makes for a stronger button attachment. If the button is attached with two stitches in parallel that don't crisscross each other, it is a sign of a poor quality shirt. Another nice detail

---

13. Some higher-quality plastic/resin buttons can still last a long time, and other materials such as horn or Tagua nut also can be acceptable substitutes.

is if the buttons are "shanked." A shanked button will have another thread wrapped around the threads that hold the button to the shirt behind the button. This will result in the buttons standing out just a little. It looks sharp.

Where the button goes is also important. If there are loose threads around the button hole, or any sign of fraying, this is the sign of a low-quality shirt or one whose time as part of your business uniform has come to an end.[14] Well-made dress shirts will have more stitches on the button hole and clean openings with no sign of fraying.

If you took a typical factory-manufactured shirt from, say, Calvin Klein and compared it to a shirt from Hilditch & Key, Edward Sexton, or Turnbull & Asser, you'd see a noticeable difference in, among other things, how the buttons appear.

Brands to Know

Hilditch & Key: Beginning in 1899 with the partnership of two shirt makers taught at the famous Harman's of Duke Street, Hilditch & Key quickly became a favored shirt maker among fashionable Londoners. Opening stores on Jermyn Street in London and Rue De Rivoli in Paris, two well-known locations for stylish shirt makers, cemented the brands position in the men's shirt market. Today Hilditch & Key produces high-quality shirts with exquisite attention to detail that are classic in style with a modern touch. In addition to shirts, they also sell knitwear, ties, handkerchiefs, and loungewear. Their shirts emanate grace and elegance while maintaining prestige and tradition, as most of the brand's retail business is still done in the Jermyn Street and Rue De Rivoli shops. Until as late as 1981, the shirt maker did not sell its shirts outside of its own shops.

Edward Sexton: A bespoke tailor known for glamour, style, and taste, Edward Sexton is an icon in the menswear industry. Sexton has achieved a great degree of notoriety since he began working in 1969. In 1990 Edward Sexton developed his own workshop in Knightsbridge and has since trained others in his personal philosophy on tailoring. His tailoring

---

14. It should be mentioned that when a quality dress shirt has been well used and is no longer fit for service as part of your business wardrobe, it should always be put out to pasture as PJs for your spouse/significant other or as casual wear for vacations and weekends. These shirts are soft to the touch, broken in, might even carry a hint of your musk, and should communicate a lot of masculine, Professional Gentleman war stories. As the collars of much-loved dress shirts fray, I typically cut them off and wear the shirt in a slightly disheveled nehru collar style around the house, out walking the dog, or to the beach.

business has expanded with a line of accessories and an ecommerce website, yet Sexton's work still bears the same sex appeal and pioneering spirit that initially set him apart. Today, Edward Sexton continues to sell tailor-made goods, but also sells a ready-to-wear line that includes many elegant dress shirts.

Turnbull & Asser: Turnball & Asser is a men's bespoke tailor founded in 1885 in London. The gentleman's tailor has dressed many well-known persons from Winston Churchill to Picasso. Selling bespoke shirts and a ready-to-wear line, the menswear company sells shirts, ties, knitwear, jackets, and accessories. Known as a producer of the finest quality shirts, Turnball & Asser makes each shirt from 34 pieces of high-quality fabric and 13 mother-of-pearl buttons. Turnball & Asser was granted a royal warrant by HRH Prince of Wales in 1980, a testament to their superb product and unparalleled service.

The split yoke is another indicator of a well-made dress shirt. The shirt's yoke is the panel of fabric that runs across your shoulders, just behind the collar. A "split" yoke is where the yoke is made of two different pieces of fabric. A true split yoke will have the two pieces of fabric cut at an angle like on the shirts of one of my favorite brands, Paul Stuart. The dress shirt specialists at Ledbury also do this phenomenally well. The functional benefit of this is that when a fabric is cut at this angle (also referred to as "cut on the bias"), the fabric stretches more lengthwise. This means you have a greater range of motion when you're reaching forward. So when shaking hands with your boss or your clients in your split yoke Thomas Pink dress shirt, you (or at least your torso) will, literally, be a lot smoother.

There is stylistic benefit of cutting the fabric like this as well. If the shirt has a pattern or stripes, they will run parallel to the front seam of the yoke, producing a smarter look to the front of the shirt. In the back of the shirt, below the collar, the pattern or stripes will meet in a chevron pattern—which also looks pretty killer.

Brands to Know

Paul Stuart: Founded in New York in 1938 and named after the son of the founder, Ralph Ostrove, Paul Stuart has continued to be a well-known name in both men's and women's luxury apparel. Paul Stuart sells its ready-to-wear line from its stores in the United States and Japan, and also sells tailor-made suits. The wood-paneled store on New York's Madison Avenue demonstrates the classic and elegant nature of the brand, as the 600,000-square-foot store is filled with high-quality and beautifully made merchandise. The designer brand sells a menswear line, as well as the slimmer-cut Phineas Cole line.

Ledbury: While the company was founded by its owners on Jermyn Street in London, the roots of Ledbury began in Virginia and New Orleans. Emphasizing the traditional over the trendy, Ledbury is most known for its shirt, as the company founders aimed to make its shirt a flawless garment through the careful combination of shirt elements and fabrics. Coming in a classic and tailored fit, the Ledbury shirt is designed to appear tailor-made. With canvassed interlining under the collar and mother-of-pearl buttons, small attention to detail differentiates the Ledbury shirts from competitors.

Thomas Pink: Thomas Pink was founded in London in 1984 by three brothers. The brand was named after Thomas Pink, the London tailor who designed the first scarlet hunting coat, dubbed "Pink" after its creator. Beginning as a specialty shirt maker, Thomas Pink has expanded rapidly from its London roots, with about 90 stores across the globe. Despite their growth, Thomas Pink has held true to its commitment to an impeccable shirt. Their shirts are made of superior cotton and perfectly cut in order to provide a crisp and finished look.

Of course this is more expensive to manufacture. A split yoke requires more sewing and more expertise on the part of the shirt maker. But it gives you the functional and stylistic advantages over a single-yoked shirt and is a sign of high quality in a dress shirt—which will not go unnoticed amongst the initiated.

Dress shirt cuffs come in two primary styles: French cuffs and barrel cuffs. French cuffs, which are more formal, fold over and have no buttons, only holes, requiring a cufflink to close. I tend to reserve French cuff shirts to formal occasions as I find them just a little frilly as well as difficult to roll up the sleeves of during work, but Ike Behar, Finnamore Napolis, and Barba Napoli make fine versions. Barrel cuffs are more common, and are closed with the buttons sewn opposite the cuff's button holes. Cuffs are either fused or unfused in their construction—remember, fused means there is a bit of fabric "fused" between each side of the cuff to give the cuff itself more mass and weight, and unfused means the cuff is without this added bulk. The appeal of each depends on personal taste and level of desired formality. Fused will give you a clean, professional presentation, and unfused will result in a more casual look. Cuffs on quality shirts should be hand sewn, and this is where experience and skill of the manufacturer make a difference. It takes a lot of experience from the shirt maker, as well as focus and time, to get the details on the cuffs right, and it will show the most in the pointedness of the corners and the straightness of the stitching.

Brands to Know

Ike Behar: Founded by the Cuban American Ike Behar in New York in 1980s, this men's clothing company produces luxury ready-to-wear and custom men's shirts and apparel. Before Behar founded his own company, his talents were recognized by the famous designer Ralph Lauren, who employed the budding tailor to design shirts for his well-known clothing line. The Ike Behar brand has three different lines today. Ike Behar Gold Label is the luxury line made of the highest quality European fabrics and sold in luxury department stores and specialty stores; Ike Behar USA is the ready-to-wear line boasting refined and elegant apparel; and Ike By Ike Behar is a menswear line geared toward a younger man that sells quality garments at a more affordable price point.

Finnamore Napolis: Founded in Naples in 1925 by Caroline and expanded by her son and his wife in a large workshop in San Giorgio a Cremano in

1960, this family company has become one of the most forward thinking brands in the shirt industry. Their shirts, sold at high-end boutiques and department stores multinationally, stand apart because they are hand-made, allowing a great deal of attention to be given to precision and detail. The company has managed to keep their product current without sacrificing quality, still using the finest fabrics in constructing their garments. Finnamore has also expanded their luxury offerings, now selling ties and jackets in addition to shirts.

Barba Napoli: While the company began as a small producer of artisan apparel, today the company, located in Naples, employs over 110 people. At the company's outset, they only sold their shirts to the most selective clientele, but over time they have expanded to offer their beautifully made clothing to customers around the world. Barba has grown their shirt company, now crafting finely made men's jackets, suiting, and knitwear.

Above the cuff is the shirt sleeve placket. This is the part of the shirt sleeve that opens up when the cuff is unbuttoned. This extra length of opening is required so that you can get your hand through the opening of the sleeve or roll your sleeves up your arm. A well-made dress shirt will have an extra button in the center of this placket to prevent this part of the sleeve from gaping open. Without this little feature, you will have either a large gaping opening just above the cuff or a sleeve placket that is too short for the sleeves to properly be rolled up the forearm without being annoyingly tight.

Have a look at the sleeve placket and cuffs of a shirt made by Ascot Chang or Borelli, and you'll start to think Professional Gentlemen are not the only ones with superior patience and attention to detail.[15]

---

15. Or any of the "Brands to Know" set forth in this chapter.

Brands to Know

Ascot Chang: Mr. Ascot Chang began his work in shirt making at the age of 14 as an apprentice in Shanghai and began taking custom orders for shirts in 1949 in Hong Kong. Opening his first store in 1953 and expanding to open a New York store in 1986, Ascot Chang has grown to be a brand known for style and elegance. Making bespoke shirts, suits, and other apparel, Ascot Chang designs its clothing to suit each individual and has impeccable attention to detail and unparalleled precision.

Luigi Borelli: The Neapolitan tailoring house of Luigi Borrelli was founded in 1957 and features shirts manufactured with materials of the highest quality, hand finished by master embroiderers according to age-old Italian tailoring techniques. Since 1997, the company has expanded into tailored garments, outerwear, jeans, knitwear, and accessories. These shirts are designed for the most sophisticated Professional Gentlemen.

Single-needle side-seam stitching along the sides of the dress shirt and bottom of the sleeves is always desirable, as it results in a seam that is tight and well-made. Only one line of thread will be visible on the outside of the shirt, and the quality of the seam will ensure that no puckering can show when the shirt is washed and dried. Sewing the side seams in this way is more difficult and expensive for the shirt maker. Sort of like having a dense multiparty license agreement drafted rapidly by a well-credentialed Super Lawyer.[16] Such a complex task is obviously more difficult for a law firm to deliver and thus more expensive. In both cases, it is worth it. If double stitching is used for the side seam, it makes for a less expensive shirt but also a side seam that shows more puckering after washing.[17]

---

16. Super Lawyers is part of Thomson Reuters. It is a rating service of outstanding lawyers from more than 70 practice areas who have attained a high degree of peer recognition and professional achievement. This selection process includes independent research, peer nominations, and peer evaluations.

17. One exception to this is if the side seam is sewn such that only one line of stitching is visible from the outside, but two lines are visible from the inside. Technically not "single-needle" stitching, this is a bit of a compromise that is also a sign of good quality. It produces a clean look and a tight seam without the cost and difficulty of the classic single-needle side seam.

The side seam should end in a reinforcing bit of fabric called a gusset. This extra piece of fabric will prevent the shirt from ripping at the side seam that can be brought about by rough handling, such as tucking the shirt in quickly before going into judges chambers or having the shirt untucked by an overzealous amorous partner when you come home still looking dashing at the end of a long day at the office.[18] It also adds a minimal, practical design to the shirt. Indeed, Thomas Pink has featured the gussets on its dress shirts for years by coloring all of them in its trademark pink.

Materials

Your dress shirts will all be made primarily of woven cotton fibers. Thread count and type of cotton vary. The higher the thread count, the smoother the fabric, and the more expensive the material. Like stock quotes, thread count, and the value of material, is referred to with a number like 50s, 80s, 100s, 120s, 140s, up to 330s. These numbers refer to the yarn size, but a thread count above 100 usually means two yarns twisted together (known as two ply).[19] Types of cotton include Egyptian, Pima,[20] and Sea Island versions.[21]

Based on other materials that might be woven into it from warp (the lengthwise yarns) to weft (the widthwise yarns that go over and under the warp), as well as method of the fabrication process, dress shirting fabric may go by any number of names.

- Oxford—Putting aside the oddity that a single academic institution could have both a shoe and shirt named after it and yet not have a graduate-level school of law, Oxford cloth is like pinpoint (*infra*), but it uses a heavier thread with a looser weave. This results in a rougher texture but is decidedly more durable than other fabrics. It is a great casual option but not appropriate, in my opinion, to be worn with more formal suits.
- Pinpoint—With the same weave as oxford cloth, it uses a finer yarn and tighter weave. Pinpoint is more formal than oxford cloth, but less formal than broadcloth or twill. It's that middle option, like traveling

---

18. Yes, in my educated view, Professional Gentlemen who are well dressed have more passionate romantic encounters, as do hard-working ones, no sordid pun intended.
19. For example, 120s thread count means that two 60s yarns are twisted together.
20. Also known by the trademarked name, Supima. Thank you, IP lawyers.
21. These three are more desirable varieties of cotton because they are typically extra-long staple length (length greater than 1³/₈"), which allows them to be spun into finer, stronger yarns.

business class but not first class. Pinpoint fabrics are quite durable and slightly thicker and heavier than broadcloths.

- Broadcloth—Also known as poplin, this is a tightly woven fabric with very little sheen, which gives it little texture. Accordingly, it is a common Professional Gentleman choice. It is usually a thinner, lighter fabric which can wrinkle easily. I'm a big fan of broadcloth for warmer climates. In L.A. I seem to always wear broadcloth.

- End-on-end—A type of broadcloth woven with colored thread in the warp and white thread in the weft. From a distance it looks like a solid color, but it has more texture when seen from up close. It is a lighter weight fabric. It's important to recognize how this color effect will read with the rest of your ensemble, but the texture differentiation can be stunning.

- Twill—These fabrics have a very tight diagonal weave, giving the cloth nice texture. Twills will almost always have a bit of shine. Twill comes in extremely high thread counts and can be quite luxurious and soft. I don't like shine in my wardrobe by general principle, but then again I'm pretty subdued. Twills can be great and very expensive with the higher thread counts.

- Herringbone—Is basically a twill that is echoed when woven to create the sort of chevron, "V-shaped" look. Interestingly, the fabric's name comes from its resemblance to the bones of a herring fish. While I don't love herring, I truly love herringbone.

- Dobby—Can be similar to the thinness and lightness of broadcloth or thicker and heavier like twill. Dobby fabrics commonly have stripes woven into them. I don't wear it a lot, but I have an excellent Irish accountant colleague who loves this fabric and is a dandy.

- Chambray—The quintessential "blue collar" work shirt fabric, chambray has a similar construction to broadcloth, though it is generally made with heavier yarns for a more casual appeal. I would advise you to wear chambray only in business casual mode.

- Seersucker—Casual and for warm weather, seersucker is known by its characteristic, "puckered" appearance. This is due to the way the fabric is finished after the weaving process is completed. It's surprisingly effective at wicking away sweat and rendering hot climates more comfortable. Given that it is puckered already, it is also impossible to wrinkle severely and so travels very well.

Caring for Your Shirts

Because your shirt lies close to your body, whether or not you wear an undershirt (a practice for and against which there is certainly some fair debate), it should be laundered regularly and, as such, will be exposed to the most wear and tear of any of the items of your wardrobe other than your shoes.

The easiest way to care for your shirts is, like your other business apparel, to outsource their cleaning to reputable dry cleaners. As we've discussed, this relationship is an important one. If there are specific stains on your shirts that need to be addressed, point them out to your cleaner. If you are not sure if they will unbutton button-down collars before cleaning or remove collar stays, ask them. If they break buttons, ask them to replace them, and further, ask them to do this before they send your shirts back to you. You are a Professional Gentleman. Your cleaner should know that you are not a man who wants to walk into any professional situation with a broken button, a stain, or some other imperfection of his shirt that could easily be avoided by the partnership with a good cleaner. Tip your cleaner for good service. Give them respect. Develop this important relationship.

Law #23

~

The Professional Gentleman shall have and maintain a good relationship with his cleaners.

~

If you have the time and the inclination (or have a trusty housekeeper who does laundry well), cleaning and folding your own shirts is not only perfectly acceptable but may bring you into a more intimate relationship with your clothes—and not in a creepy way.

Ignorantia juris non excusat.

—9—

Ties and
Pocket Squares

"A well-tied tie is the first serious step in life."
—Oscar Wilde[1]

Ties are a wonderful contradiction. While their uselessness and ubiquity amongst Professional Gentlemen represents a degree of blind conformity, their variety and prominence in your frontal presentation offers a superb opportunity at distinguishing yourself from the herd of corporate drones as a man with style. They are also a very cost effective way to take the Fundamental Four suits and extend them into any number of viably killer looks. The right tie can change your whole look just like a different conjunction ("and" or "or") can change an entire written agreement.

---

1. The flamboyant and popular playwright, Wilde was known for his fine style sense and blistering wit. *The Picture of Dorian Gray*, his only novel, describes the hedonistic protagonist who sells his soul in order to maintain his youth and beauty while a picture of him records not only his age but his sins.

Origins and Transformations

The origin of the tie is oft debated and ultimately, like the tie itself, interesting but basically irrelevant. Like a lot of our more formal garments, the tie represents a thing we men are still wearing because a king hundreds of years ago found it fashionable. The commonly held view is that the roots of necktie originated during the Thirty Year's War (1618–1648) in France. King Louis XIII hired Croatian mercenaries who wore traditional small, knotted neckerchiefs as part of their uniform. Like most things military, these early cravats had functional relevance—namely tying the top of the soldiers' jackets together. But they also lent a jaunty, stylish look to the handsome Croats—a look that King Louis was quite taken by. He made these early versions of ties a mandatory accessory for French Royal gatherings and gave them the name "La Cravate" to honor the Croatian soldiers.

From this early cravat the world has seen the advent of everything from the small bowtie to the flowing Ascot tie. The tie as we know it today did not emerge until the 1920s and since then has endured through many subtle changes in design and construction, with wide ties holding sway until the 1950s with the introduction of the skinny tie. Tie width has oscillated between the "kipper tie"[2] widths approaching 6 inches to skinny ties as narrow as 1.5 inches. The traditionally observed standard widths for Professional Gentleman dress today is 3–3.5 inches based largely on the prevalence of traditional collar and lapel widths of tailored menswear to fit nicely within the range. More modern suits with narrower lapels and slimmer profiles—say those of Christian Dior, Helmut Lang or Jil Sander—demand ties from 2.5–2.75 inches.

---

2. The kipper tie was fashionable in the mid-1960s to late 1970s. Designed by British fashion designer Michael Fish, the primary characteristics of the kipper tie are its extreme breadth and often garish patterns and colors.

Brands to Know

Dior Homme: Starting in 1970, Dior Homme, Dior's menswear division, produced its first menswear line. Briefly called Dior Monsieur during the '80s and '90s, the menswear division was known for its characteristically slim silhouettes. Since 2008, under the direction of Kris Van Assche, Dior Homme has shifted toward a more formal yet minimalistic style paired with an almost religious attention to detail. Focusing on a darker color palette of blacks, grays, blues, and chocolate, the label has been popular amongst Professional Gentlemen. In addition to their seasonal collections, the label also has ready-to-wear, leather goods, shoe, accessory, and even skincare offerings.

Helmut Lang: Started by the Austrian designer Helmut Lang in 1986, the brand began in the era of minimalist fashion. His work featured severe lines and sharp cuts in garments made of high-quality and frequently high-tech materials. The brand is known for simple yet sophisticated style, but also for being a pioneer in the fashion industry. Lang was the first to show his collection to Internet viewers via live broadcast three days before the collection was to be shown to a New York audience. He also is partially responsible for the current timing of New York Fashion Week, as his decision to show his collection before NYFW and the Paris and Milan runway shows inspired other American designers to do the same.

Jil Sander: This minimalist German brand was founded by Heidemarie Jiline Sander in 1968 in Hamburg. Selling men's and women's ready-to-wear clothing and accessories, the luxury brand is known for no embellishment and austere designs. Raf Simons, now at Calvin Klein, served as the creative director for the company. Simons incorporated sculptural suits into the Jil Sander menswear line, which were readily accepted. The lines are sold in upscale department stores.

Wearing the Tie

I am not going to show you how to tie a traditional tie or even a bowtie. Candidly, you should know how to do both at this point, and if you don't, there are plenty of YouTube videos with very excited fellows happy to show you how. I'm also not going to go into the various knots you can use. All of them are fine, and it is a matter of personal preference which one you use. I *will*, however, give you a few simple ground rules on wearing the tie.

First of all, own it! *Wear* your tie, man. Put it on with pride and don't be ashamed by it. Jut out your chin and know you are flying the flag of the Professional Gentleman underneath your well-set jaw. Tie it firmly. The tie should ideally look neat and snug when on with a single dimple or no dimple at all. The tie will naturally loosen over the course of a day (and evening), so it is totally acceptable to discreetly check this from time to time and tighten it up. It should be worn on a dress shirt with a proper collar (not on a non-dress shirt with a collar that cannot handle it). Unless you are wearing a stand-up collar, the tie should not show at any point other than at the knot and below (so make sure your collar covers the tie on the sides and back of your neck).

Fit the knot of the tie to the amount of space created by the spread of your collar. If you are wearing a spread collar dress shirt, the tie knot should be similarly wide to take up the wide space. If you are wearing a short pin-point collar, the tie knot should be small. Moreover, fit the width of your tie to the size of your collar. A minimal collared dress shirt from, say, Band of Outsiders,[3] needs to be paired with a similarly proportioned tie in terms of width, as well as minimally sized lapel on the jacket. If the width of the tie, the collar, or the lapel are materially out of whack you will look wack.[4] The bottom of the tie should just hit your belt buckle or be a touch above it. If it goes below your belt buckle, you are pointing at your junk, and you are, literally and figuratively, going too far.

If you are wearing a tie in business casual mode, it is acceptable, though not always recommended, to wear it loosened with the top button of the dress shirt undone. I say not always recommended because while business casual is intended to cover less formal looks, the loosened tie can be consid-

---

3. Now run by a consortium not affiliated with the founder Scott Sternberg, creditors have revived the brand, under the moniker "Band of Outsiders Los Angeles." DISCLOSURE: my firm, HBA, has represented equity investors in Band of Outsiders.
4. According to Reginald C. Dennis, the former music editor of *The Source* magazine, back in the '70s, in NYC, the term *wack* was used to describe the drug PCP or angel dust. It was descriptive without being overly pejorative back then, but by the time "Rapper's Delight" dropped in '79, the word had taken on its current meaning, describing something as the opposite of *def*—which itself was derived from "the death"—meaning good.

ered by some more traditional clients or bosses as tantamount to a state of undress or sloppiness. So whereas you have a jacket and tie on, you end up looking sloppier than your colleague who is in much less formal clothes—like, say, a cashmere V-neck sweater over a polo shirt. As we have discussed *supra*, looking disordered relative to a peer is not good. Without more information, some may make the same negative assumption about your work product.[5] So this is a look to be worn with a careful consideration of the Laws—whom you are dressing for, what their expectations are, and where you stand in the food chain of the firm.

Another way the tie can be worn more casually is the somewhat obvious *sprezzatura* move of having the narrow end of your tie longer than the wide end. The same caution and reference to the Laws applies here, although you can at least refer to a figure like Gianni Agnelli as justifying your nonchalant splendor.[6] Note that the rest of your outfit should feel relaxed as well—even if it is a suit rather than an odd jacket. I personally recommend you only do this with ties that are thin to begin with. The more modern profile of the skinny tie coupled with the fact that even the wider end is not jarringly larger than the thin end helps with balance. Even safer, in my view, is to do this only with squared-off bottomed ties, particularly knit versions. Again, they are more casual by nature, and the uniform ends helps with balance. If you go for this move, really go for it. Make the narrow end at least two inches longer than the wide end. Preferably four or five inches longer.

Pattern and Textures

The mixing and matching of the tie with the patterns and textures of your other garments is an idiom all its own and will be covered at length in Chapter 11. Here I'd like to go over some of the properties of the ties every Professional Gentlemen should own to complement and broaden his wardrobe.

---

5. See Law #7.
6. Giovanni "Gianni" Agnelli was an Italian industrialist and principal shareholder of Fiat. Known as *L'Avvocato* ("The Lawyer"), he was the richest man in modern Italian history and was known for his impeccable yet eccentric fashion sense. Agnelli passed away in 2003.

Brands to Know

Vanda Fine: Vanda Fine Clothing was founded in August 2011, creating traditionally artisanal menswear of exceptional quality. Each product is handmade in Singapore with a unique touch that mass-production settings can never imitate. Their culturally distinct pocket square designs focus on the global perspective of Singapore. Meticulous construction, Asian design, and tasteful fabrics for the Professional Gentleman.

E. Marinella: This Italian company was founded by Eugenio Marinella in 1914 with a focus on neckties. It has standalone stores in Naples, Milan, Lugano, London, Hong Kong, and Tokyo, and is also sold at department stores globally. The company is one of the most prestigious luxury brands in the tie industry. In addition to ties, E. Marinella also sells bags, watches, cologne, accessories, and cufflinks for men. Their line of women's products include bags, scarves, perfumes, and accessories.

Tie Your Tie: This is the rare success story of a small local shop founded in 1984 that became a globally recognized brand. With a distinctive taste in apparel but particularly ties, the founders decided to open up their own tie workshop, which specialized in the airy, many-folded ties for which the Tie Your Tie brand became famous. The tie brand has outlived the store itself; the retail location in Florence has since changed hands and names. The only Tie Your Tie stores are now in Japan, but the ties are still made in Italy, with the same construction and unique aesthetic.

Ties are constructed of many different materials, with the most common being cotton, wool, and silk. Silks can be worn year round and are generally considered the most formal and business appropriate. Wool ties are heavier and connote a certain countrified air. They are best worn in the winter with suiting of similar weight. Cotton ties are best during spring and summer, again, with similarly weighted tailored clothing. It is good and right to have selections of each of these to match the season. Then, of course, there are many, many advisable ties that fall in between. Point is, you should have loads and loads of ties.

Law #24

~

The Professional Gentleman shall have many ties to choose from and shall mix them into his wardrobe.

~

This Law is also practical financial and logistical advice. Ties don't cost as much as suits. Moreover, they don't take up an inordinate amount of space. And, as has been said *supra*, ties can transform an entire ensemble. So a good selection can make a single suit into many potentially stylish configurations. I've been junked up on ties for years. Honestly, I am trading in size on ties and even bowties. Forgive the inundation of financial advisory terms here, but I'm triple long on ties. This is because it makes economic sense.

Types: Can You Give Me Some Color on That?

Color selection is personal, but it should be varied. Even if you have a ruddy complexion, red and burgundy ties should be options. Given that your suiting will be largely grays and blues, and your shirts white and blue, the pop of red can be necessary. Blue suit, white shirt, red tie is a prototypical look that will never go out of style given its inherent color balance. Moreover, many claim a psychological benefit to the red "power" tie.[7] Blues in hues that don't precisely match your suit or shirting blues are still very effective and versatile. They look smashing against all gray suits as well as brown tweeds. Gray ties, brown ties, and other neutral tones are useful if not particularly imaginative. But any color can be useful when the dominant statement of the tie still works within the color narrative of your outfit as a whole. Greens can be mean, yellows can be mello, you get it.

---

7. Common wisdom held that the red tie was more aggressive and assertive, giving the wearer a psychological edge over his competitors. Jury is still out on this—Robert Burriss Ph.D., "'Power Ties' Are Actually Powerless," *Psychology Today*, September 23, 2016, https://www.psychologytoday.com/blog/attraction-evolved/201609/power-ties-are-actually-powerless.

Solids

Solid colors are easy to pair with all manner of patterns and textures. They are far from exciting, but if the rest of your look has a degree of pattern in it, the solid tie is an appropriate grounding choice. Burgundy and dark blue are the safest, but any deep, rich color works. Other than the red "power tie," avoid bright colors and glossy silk surfaces, which make you look like an arriviste or a waiter, in favor of matte texture and sophisticated palette. Also, a note on the solid black tie favored by many who think they are a secret agent or a Reservoir Dog—you are not. The black tie is acceptable for black tie events, namely benefits, weddings, and funerals (though the first two of this list, the tie should be a black bowtie). It can be worn in the office and it often is—but mainly by pikers who don't realize they look more like a guy that's been dinged with FINRA sanctions than a Professional Gentleman.

Brands to Know

E.G. Capelli: Producing limited batches from a small workshop in Naples, E.G. Cappelli has been putting out some of the finest and most exclusive neckwear in the world since 2001. Famous for their flawless use of English printed silks, fastidious construction, and attention to detail, they have a devoted following of tie connoisseurs in-the-know. For the Professional Gentleman of taste and refinement who can afford it.

Viola Milano: This Italian brand understands that style and inspiration are highly personal and unique for each man. Accordingly, Viola Milano provides an opportunity through their ties and other accessories to express subtle uniqueness and personality. Very expensive and of the highest quality.

Shibumi-Berlin: *"Shi-bu-mi"* is Japanese for a concept of aesthetics, translated simply as "understated beauty." Not surprisingly, this brand is known for its tasteful, artisanal ties and accessories. Made in Italian and English factories, these are ties from a newer company but with a rich historical background and contemporary design sensibility.

Foulard

Foulard ties are ties with a symmetrical pattern in a gridded block array that doesn't change in size or spacing. This covers a lot of ground. The Professional Gentleman mainstay are the Hermès foulards, which feature patterns and even critters, and often play on the Professional Gentleman's keen awareness of economics and scarcity by offering limited editions of certain patterns. These sometimes whimsical ties can be found on MDs/partners on down the ranks whom can afford them. You won't go wrong within the firm with these French pillars of style, or their Italian cousins—the Ferragamo foulards—but candidly, the puckish foulards these brands tend to make can be difficult to integrate into a subtly elegant ensemble. There can be a lot going on with a bright foulard tie, making it an unintended focal point of the outfit. I think for this reason, many uninspired but well-intentioned Professional Gentlemen have gravitated to the high-priced and often lively foulard as an easy substitute of a way to dress audaciously under the cover of an acceptable and reputable European luxury house. If French artisans came up with this, and everyone at my club and in my firm is wearing this brand, how can I possibly be doing anything wrong? It's a wonderful pact between the luxury house and its core customers. I just don't respond to it visually.

The less the amount of color contrast within the pattern of the foulard, the more muted the tie will appear. In the best versions for business attire, most of the pattern should come from the same color family, with perhaps one minor contrasting color component as a highlight. The less noticeable this highlight, the better. Very inspired is the Professional Gentleman who can take that highlight and integrate it somewhere else in his look like his pocket square or his socks.[8] But the foulard can be as simple and useful as a navy blue tie with small white dots, which can be worn with any shirt and virtually any suit (other than your navy blue suits).

Rep

Rep ties (otherwise known as club ties) are simple and handsome with a wide variety of color combinations that are appropriate for suiting, as well as the odd jacket (in particular, the blue blazer). Basically these are colored ties with diagonal stripes, typically (although not always) in the same colors

---

8. See Chapter 11 *infra* regarding pattern and texture.

as a school's banners or sports uniforms, or a regimental color combination. They come in two stripes, if you will, university and regimental. University ties slant downward from left to right while regimental ties slant downward from right to left. Don't ask me why.

These come in traditional color combinations corresponding to the institutions they represent, but also in all other manner of color combinations. They are youthful and charming if somewhat insipid. However, please be aware that these ties actually mean something—particularly in England. To put this in a context perhaps many of my American readers can relate to, wearing a tie with university or regimental signifiers on it is kind of like wearing a T-shirt with something written on it. If you are wearing an orange T-shirt with "Princeton Crew" written on it in black, most people will assume you rowed for Princeton University or were a coxswain even if you are under 6'3". If you are wearing a vintage Hussongs Cantina T-shirt, many people from Southern California (as well as Mexico) will assume you've been to the original rowdy Hussongs in Ensenda, likely on a surf safari to K-38. If on the other hand you did not even go to Princeton or if you've never heard of K-38, wearing such a shirt makes you a poser. Please be sensitive to this and try not to wear a rep tie you do not know the origins of when meeting with Englishmen or women unless, of course, you actually belong to the school or regiment your tie represents.

Law #25

~

The Professional Gentleman shall not wear a rep tie if it represents a university or club he did not attend or does not belong to.

~

Brands to Know

Nicky Milano: This Milanese brand has epitomized the understated and elegant tie for discerning Professional Gentlemen since 1920, when founder John Nicky Chini returned from a trip to Africa and founded Nicky Milano. With exotic colors and patterns stylishly reduced to a more muted presentation, these ties represent a distinguished option between eccentricity and conservatism. Quoting Gabriele D'Annunzio, the brand encourages its loyalists to "remember to dare always."

Stefano Ricci: This Italian ultra-luxury brand is a distinctly Florentine operation known for individual statements in the men's accessory department—ties, belts, handkerchiefs. Stefano Ricci also offers a full tailored menswear, though some of the looks can be a bit over the top. Prices are not for the faint of heart, but the quality is undeniable.

Gallo: This Italian accessories brand has a long history of producing high-end accessories—as far back as the early 1900s. Gallo socks and silk knit ties are simply superb. In an array of colors and weights, the products include ties, bowties, and pocket squares.

Paisley

Paisley ties feature repeating, curved shapes that are typically ornately bordered and filled with abstract and often very trippy designs.[9] Paisley figures are often set against a solid background, sometimes with smaller floral figures in between. This is a busy frontal presentation, overwhelming the rest of an outfit at times like some of the brighter foulards can. But it can be useful for the same reason: namely it does not mimic a pattern that exists anywhere else. Just don't overdo it or you'll risk looking like Dr. Strange.[10]

---

9. Resembling a twisted teardrop, the fig-shaped design is of Iranian origin. Its western name "Paisley" originates from a town of the same name in Western Scotland, which was a center for textile production.
10. Dr. Stephen Vincent Strange (known as Doctor Strange) is a superhero appearing in Marvel comics. Created by artist Steve Ditko and writer Stan Lee, the good Doctor first appeared in *Strange Tales* #110 (1963). A former neurosurgeon, Strange serves as the Sorcerer Supreme, the primary protector of Earth against magical and mystical threats.

So how do you go about pairing these ties with the rest of your ensemble? Well, paduan, this is where things truly get interesting. We have an entire chapter to go through mixing and matching of patterns and textures, but your ties (and your pocket squares) are the best foot soldiers to add variety into your wardrobe both because of their frontal location and because you can (and should) have a multitude of them. One key is that the tie/hankie should offer up some degree of contrast to the rest of the outfit. So if the suit is navy blue and the shirt is white, the tie/hankie should be in any color but navy blue or white.

Tie Clips and Tie Pins

The tie clip can look deliberate and purposeful. Proper application is on the tie equal, vertically, just below the breast coat pocket, which is usually between the third and fourth button of the dress shirt. Note, the tie clip affixes the shirt to the tie (not the two ends of the tie together). I've noticed Professional Gentleman getting this wrong. The clip itself should not be longer than the tie is wide. If it is, do not wear it (or change your tie after, perhaps changing your suit and shirt to deal with a narrower profile).

Tie pins were very popular fifty years ago, and so this is a bit of a retro look. Because they present on the tie as a simple pin, they can be found in all manner of precious metals, shapes, and even with diamonds, rubies, or other jewels affixed. The tie pin typically has a little chain with a T-bar attached to it, which is put through a shirt buttonhole to keep the tie in place. This is similar to a lapel pin in that it pierces your tie and shirt to hold the tie in place. So while it works well for woven silk ties or coarser fabrics such as wool or cashmere neckties (because the little tack won't leave a mark), it does not work with fine silk ties since the little holes the pin makes may not disappear completely.

Going Tieless

Going without the tie while wearing a business suit, like participating in online gaming and Brexit, is one of those things that is widely supported by misinformed simpletons. I don't know if this is from a perspective of rebelliousness or men who simply cannot abide to wear a tie, but whatever the source, it is misguided.

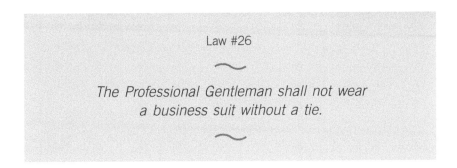

Law #26

~

The Professional Gentleman shall not wear a business suit without a tie.

~

Most suits absolutely need a tie. A suit's uniformity positively begs for more pattern and texture to be introduced to balance it. Moreover, the notion of mixing the informality of tielessness with the formality of the business suit is oxymoronic. Don't do it. If you vehemently do not want to wear the tie, forgo the suit for an odd jacket and trousers, or have a selection of more casual suits that you can wear with somewhat louder shirts so that the lack of a tie is less noticeable. You'll look better.

Pocket Squares

Designer R. Scott French once said, "Greatness is in the details."[11] Sure, the pocket square is the smaller stepchild of the tie, but she can be a beautiful one. She can peek out from the breast coat pocket with hope and expectation, picking up on a subtle color or texture element of the tie, the shirt, even the socks if you feel you can get away with it. Or she can boldly pop out of the pocket, corners blazing like a sunflower in unadulterated openness, and pronounce her color and/or texture on the rest of your ensemble—making it bow to her. The point here is, the pocket square's home is in a critical area of your frontal, chest presentation (just about the ground zero of personal appearance). This is a rare piece of sartorial real estate that gives you another opportunity to add color, texture, and YOU-ness within the boundaries of the Laws and personal taste.

---

11. Council of Fashion Designers of America, *The Pursuit of Style: Advice and Musings from America's Top Fashion Designers* (New York: Harry N. Abrams, 2014).

Brands to Know

Christian Kimber: Christian Kimber, a British-born designer living in Melbourne, Australia, designs with a distinct sensibility. Inspired by cityscapes and the world's great capitals, Kimber produces classically constructed pocket squares with a metropolitan twist. These unique pieces are largely wool-silk blends with hand-rolled edges.

Fort Belvedere: Established by Sven Raphael Schneider, the brand references the Duke of Windsor's royal residence. The Fort Belvedere product range covers pocket squares, knit ties, gloves, and other accessories. Pocket squares are sized based on material and are offered in wonderfully eclectic color varieties to help compose the desired dash of personalization to the Professional Gentleman's wardrobe.

Penrose London: Founded by Mitchell Jacobs in 2008 with a focus on handmade neckties, bowties, and pocket squares. With a wonderfully eccentric style evidenced in the brand's distinctive patterns and bold color combinations, each limited-edition textile is designed in-house and produced by expert weavers in England and Italy. Crafted of silk, cotton, and cashmere.

A few rules on usage are also worth noting. A very simple one is, if you have a pocket square, be prepared to actually use it. Nothing is more debonair than offering a handkerchief to a person in need (attractive woman or small child scoring extra points). Just don't put it back in its place if it becomes soiled. Replace it or go without. The only thing more ridiculous than a full-grown man wiping his nose with his hand or struggling to find a tissue when he is wearing the very tool for the job is the man who puts a soiled pocket square back into his frontal presentation. I don't spend too much on pocket squares, and I wear them all the time. As a useful article, I replace them frequently.

How do you square your square with the rest of your outfit? Often the last touch before you head out into the world dressed for battle. This can be daunting. Don't overthink it. Nothing need match perfectly—in fact, if it does it will look lame. Matchy matchy, like most of the commentators for NFL games. Those too-large panels of ex-players with one commentator, all of whom are dressed like car salesmen. So don't exactly match your tie! Try to *complement* a color in your tie, the more subtle the better.

Law #27

~

The Professional Gentleman shall not exactly match his tie and pocket square.

~

If that seems too obvious because the tie is of a single color (or only two), go with a pocket square with many colors where a minor component of the square is the same color as the tie. Or go with another item of your wardrobe. Your shirt is not off limits and is typically very easy to match. A refined and slight color running through your tweed jacket? Totally acceptable to pair with the square.

Brands to Know

Rubinacci: This Italian brand has a long-standing tradition dating back three generations, sitting between trend and tradition. Rubinacci has been able to incorporate theories and models of Napoli elegance into a unique style that is flawless and distinctive. Rubinacci is renowned for their highly detailed and exclusive pocket squares.

Alexander Olch: Wonderfully edited, filmmaker Alexander Olch began his eponymous line of accessories in New York in the early 2000s as a response to numerous requests from his friends to buy one of the handmade ties he had originally created as gifts for his film crew. Solid craftsmanship, local construction, and fine fabrics make Alexander Olch an attractive and distinctive option for the Professional Gentleman.

Tie Bar: This American brand headquartered in Chicago offers pocket squares, ties, and other accessories at a reasonable price. The styles are many and the quality is solid. This is a great resource for the Professional Gentleman on a budget.

There are many different folds to choose from, and they range from the conservative to the decorative, bordering on the outlandish. The fold many refer to as the "classic" is essentially the hankie folded nicely but imperfectly in the breast coat pocket so that a few of its edges show. In contracts, the "presidential" fold perfectly provides a single uniform edge of the hankie about ¼ to ⅛ inch uniformly and perfectly parallel above the breast coat pocket. The "puff" and "reverse puff" are less structured and add a bit of panache. The peaked folds like the "three peaks," "winged peak," and "angled peaks" require some precision but, can be polished. More intricate folds like the "rose" and the "stairs" are more deliberate and formal, but subject to your tastes, can be used effectively by the Professional Gentleman.

Ignorantia juris non excusat.

—10—

Business Casual

"You cannot climb the ladder of success
dressed in the costume of failure."
—Zig Ziglar[1]

In sartorial terms, the phrase *business casual* is an oxymoron. Like most oxymoronic statements, it came about as an attempt to put a label on a bad idea. That bad idea was rooted in the notion that clients want their Professional Gentlemen to look like anything but Professional Gentlemen. And that bad idea was compounded by us, Professional Gentlemen, as we allowed the lack of any set dress code to justify a sartorial anarchy the likes of which our professions have never before seen.

Casual Friday came online in the late 1990s with the advent of the dot-com boom where firms were looking to distinguish themselves as current (they thought "forward thinking") amidst what most of them perceived as a cultural shift toward clients who not only wore casual clothes, but moreover, the thinking went (or goes), who wanted their trusted Professional Gentlemen to share this casualness. Dudes in garages in Silicon Valley were wearing cargo pants from Old Navy and snarky T-shirts and becoming mil-

---

1. Hilary Hinton "Zig" Ziglar was an American author, salesman, and motivational speaker.

lionaires overnight.[2] The Professional Gentlemen had to somehow relate to this new business elite.

But let's all pause a beat and remember, we got a lot wrong and had some pretty depraved ideas back in the '90s: Y2K, pets.com, gansta rap, grunge music, the Hummer. And like those errors and debauched notions, the '90s business casual uniform was pretty dreadful. Looking like Bill Gates became a sad sartorial goal for many. A pair of khaki chinos and a polo shirt worn with boat shoes were the homogeneous and monotonous trappings of a generation. Honestly, from a style perspective this getup has to be considered the outfit of defeat. It is what sales people in chain electronics stores *have to* wear but not what any self-respecting Professional Gentleman should *choose to* wear. And yet many, many of us did just that. Sadly, some of us still do.

However, as times got tight again after the internet bubble crashed, and then more so after the financial crisis of 2007–2008 and the sub-prime mortgage crisis, wearing business casual on a Friday became a dicier play, and many Professional Gentlemen went back to the suit (even if usually without a tie—etch!) and took pains not to appear too casual.[3] As we've hobbled out of the Great Recession, and times seem better in most hallowed halls of firms in the financial sector and beyond, there has been an increasing erosion of the single-day-a-week casual workplace.

Firms have articulated many justifications in the movement away from requiring suits and toward full-time business casual: recruiting and maintaining millennials whom, we are told, are more casual; the demands of keeping junior associate ranks happy and comfortable so they do not leave for "funner" places they might prefer; following the reality that many businesses have gone casual and expect their Professional Gentlemen to follow suit; and even legal requirements related to gender equality.[4] Whatever the reason, casual Friday has now extended, for many firms, into a full-time business casual environment where the Professional Gentleman is not required to wear a suit and tie unless there are scheduled client meetings. This is the case at places like J.P. Morgan Chase & Co., Millbank, Tweed Hadley & McCloy LLP and PricewaterhouseCoopers, LLP.[5]

---

2. Jennifer Booton, "Facebook's Overnight Millionaires Begin Lavish Spending Spree," *Fox Business*, May 18, 2012, http://www.foxbusiness.com/features/2012/05/18/facebook-overnight-millionaires-start-luxurious-spending-spree.html.
3. Why it required people's jobs to be on the line for this sartorial shift to occur is a mystery to me, but there it was.
4. The New York City Commission on Human Rights announced new guidelines in 2015 that expressly prohibit businesses enforcing official dress codes, uniforms, and grooming standards that impose different requirements based on sex or gender. So no employer can require that men wear ties unless women are also required to wear them.
5. Ray A. Smith, "Wardrobe Advice for Men as Office Fashion Returns to Casual," *New York Times*, August 10, 2016.

This full-time casualization in dress may represent a power shift from employers to employees, from institutions to individuals.[6] *Optime!*[7] But it has also made it quite possible for certain Professional Gentlemen to revert to adolescence. To what got them by stylistically in college or grad school. In short, it's gotten ugly out there.

> "Our grandchildren will taunt us as the generation that allowed our jeans and our sweatpants to become one: 'Was everyone that lazy, Grandpa?'"
>
> —Jon Caramancia[8]

Why this ambivalence amongst us? Discouragement at the prospect of having to find a style? Generalized apathy or listlessness over one more thing to get wrong? Acedia?

Town & Country menswear editor G. Bruce Boyer put it, "It is both delusional and stupid to think that clothes don't really matter and we should all wear whatever we want. Most people don't take clothing seriously enough, but whether we should or not, clothes do talk to us and we make decisions based on people's appearances." Isn't there an inherent and annoying cavalierness in the adoption of business casual that says to the client, "My job is so easy, any slob can do it"? I think there is.

Does business casual mean the Laws are just "not held"[9] and that you are free to riot in your own interpretation of what is appropriate? No, compadres, it does not. In fact, the Laws in this Chaosrealm[10] actually become much, much more important. There is both a challenge and freedom in being invited outside the relatively safe uniform of the suit. Doing it right and communicating competence and aptitude in one's "casual" presentation is the goal.[11] However, the bar is high. As we have discussed *supra*, the suit is the proper uniform of the Professional Gentleman. When executed well, it both hides physical flaws and enhances our finer points. Most "sportswear" or casual clothing often do neither of these things. So there is less of

---

6. See, Vanessa Friedman, "The End of the Office Dress Code," *New York Times*, May 2016,
7. "That's great" in Latin.
8. Jon Caramanica, "Critical Shopper: A Brief Visit with My Inner Diesel," *New York Times*, March 10, 2016.
9. In trading terms, this means you're free to go to the market.
10. The Chaosrealm, also known as the Realm of Chaos, is a realm in the *Mortal Kombat* video game series.
11. "If you do it right. You can go all night. Shadows on you break out into the light." Daft Punk, "Doin' It Right," *Random Access Memories* (Daft Life and Columbia Records, 2013).

an acceptable formula with business casual and more options that, candidly, will look much better on certain physiques than others. There is also the basic issue of frequently having to mix (rather than just match as a suit does) bottom and top. High degree of difficulty.

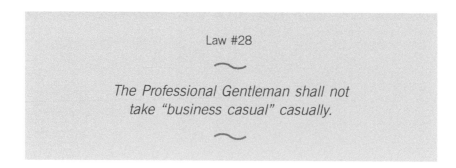

Law #28

~

The Professional Gentleman shall not take "business casual" casually.

~

Not to fear, there are brands out there, and retailers as well, attuned to these new challenges.[12] While the very wealth of options is intimidating and increases the level of difficulty, they also make dressing well outside of the suit a thing of beauty. Let the Laws be your guide through some capable and elegant yet casual outfits.

The Odd Jacket

The term *odd jacket* does not mean weird or peculiar. It simply means a jacket that, unlike a suit jacket, is designed and made to be worn with contrasting trousers. The odd jacket and trousers with dress shirt, polo, or knit underneath, and with or without tie, is the prototypical conservative business casual look. It is, for all intents and purposes, a suit that does not match, and therefore, while more difficult to pair together with style, is very safe as a business casual form of presentation for the Professional Gentleman.

---

12. Menswear geniuses like Eric Jennings formerly of Saks Fifth Avenue and others have recognized the great retail opportunity this shift to casual represents. To wit, Saks Fifth Avenue published a six-page "how-to" manual, *The New Office Casual*, which updates business casual styles for the beginner under Eric's watch.

The Blue Blazer

This is the most traditional and safest non-suit option for the Professional Gentleman and yet is still very stylish. My friend Tommy Hilfiger has told me he feels most himself in "a perfectly worn-in pair of jeans with a crisp, white button-down, a navy blue blazer, and loafers." Putting Tommy's (and the most of the world's) denim fetish aside, the basic formality of the blue blazer, its ubiquitous acceptance as elegant, durable, and sharp, argue in favor of it becoming your standard basic go-to piece of casual wear when not in a suit.

To be sure, blazers also come in other colors.[13] Some pretty wild colors in fact. Don't wear these other colors unless you've won the Masters or the Congressional Cup.[14] Strictly speaking, a blazer is any odd jacket of a solid color (or with bold colored stripes and/or with contrasting piping— you won't be wearing one of these unless you are headed to a regatta in England). The blazer can be single breasted or double breasted, with the most distinctive feature of them all contrasting buttons made in brass, pewter, silver, or mother-of-pearl. The blazer can also sport a crest on the breast pocket of some storied association to a college, sports club, or brand. Avoid these at all costs.

Brands to Know

J. Press: Founded in 1902 on Yale University's campus by Latvian Jacobi Press, the company now operates stores in New York, Washington, D.C., and Cambridge, Massachusetts. Big in Japan, in 1986, J. Press was acquired by the Japanese apparel company Onward Kashiyama, who had previously been his licensee for 14 years. Since its founding, J. Press' clothing has remained much the same. The company produces

---

13. Indeed, one theory has it that the term *blazer* itself comes from the hot red jackets worn by the *Lady Margaret Boat Club* (founded in 1825 by twelve members of St. John's College, Cambridge). Since their jaunty jackets *"blazed,"* they were named *"Blazers."*

14. The winner of the Masters Golf Tournament in Augusta, Georgia, is awarded a green blazer, while the Congressional Cup Regatta at the Long Beach Yacht Club bestows a crimson blazer upon its winner.

the vast majority of its off-the-rack jackets in the traditional "three-button sack" style.

Brooks Brothers: Opening its first store in 1818, Brooks Brothers is the oldest American clothing retailer. Introducing ready-made clothing in 1848, Brooks Brothers continues to be a major seller of ready-to-wear suits, apparel, and accessories for men, women, and children globally. Through their "Made to Measure" line, Brooks Brothers has continued the tradition of custom-tailored suiting that the store first boasted in 1818. The brand has come to symbolize fashion innovation and high quality while maintaining its modest prices, allowing the brand to preserve its prominent place in the global market.

Ring Jacket: This Japanese brand has a rich history that dates back more than 60 years of producing tailored clothing with a full-canvas construction that utilizes the hand-sewing skills of the artisans in their Osaka workshop. Known in part for their distinctive fabrics, Ring Jacket collaborates with some of the finest mills in the world to develop unique cloths that are exclusively their own. A beautifully made Japanese garment with a distinct Italian flavor—classic clothing reinterpreted in a modern and comfortable way for the Professional Gentleman.

The blue blazer goes with almost anything—just don't try to wear trousers in a matching shade. So, to best contrast the deep blue of the blazer, light button-down shirts from white to any shade of color are all fine. Even a polo shirt underneath the blazer is passable as long as it is similarly in a light shade. All manner of trousers work—even denim jeans if you must—as long as the shade of blue is lighter:

- Chinos—A nice nod to the blue blazer's military associations, if a bit pedestrian. The blue blazer can be worn with all shades of chinos. You can even pull off white (but in summer only) or Nantucket red if you are looking to be that uber-preppy lad. With or without a tie is fine.
- Flannel—The classic presentation of the blue blazer for business. This combination is failsafe and the closest thing to a suit the Professional Gentleman can wear. The flannel trousers should be light gray, charcoal, or camel, worn with a white or blue dress shirt with a tie.

- Corduroys—An advanced sartorial move. Make sure the blazer has enough heft and texture to pair with cords (i.e., think flannel not linen or even the classic Navy serge, which is quite flat and untextured). Avoid wide wale cords. Deep rich colors look great, like burgundy or rust. Pair with a dress shirt and knits if it is very cold.
- Moleskin—Same considerations that apply for the corduroy trousers apply for moleskin trousers. A heavier weight blazer is needed with some texture, and a dress shirt is a must, although you can look to more casual fabrics like denim or chambray (which look attractive next to navy blue). Shades of brown moleskin will work best.

A few other minor details to note when wearing any blue blazer ensemble: Try to match your hardware. So if your blue blazer has, as most do, gold, brass, or silver buttons, then try to match your belt buckle and any other metal you might be wearing on your person (e.g., belt buckle, watch, monk strap buckle, cufflinks).[15]

The Tweed Sport Coat

The tweed jacket is another essential that has great style and versatility. The rough wool of tweed is exceptionally moisture-resistant and durable, and able to withstand harsh climates. As such, hundreds of years ago it basically became a very early form of "athliesure" on the English islands. The tweed blazer came about as the garb of choice for the sporting activities of English noblemen expanding their life of well-dressed diversion. After Prince Albert's purchase of Balmoral and the design of a corresponding tweed, estate tweeds became a *thing* amongst the landed gentry, and other estate owners followed suit, commissioning their own particular tweeds.[16] Must have been fun.

Harris tweed is the world's only commercially produced handwoven tweed and the only one with its own specific law, defined in the Harris Tweed Act of 1993 as cloth which is "Handwoven by the islanders at their homes in the Outer Hebrides, finished in the Outer Hebrides, and made from pure virgin wool dyed and spun in the Outer Hebrides." Tweed is a rough wool usually woven with a plain weave, twill, or herringbone struc-

---

15. See Chapter 11 *infra* regarding mixing and matching.
16. In 1848, Prince Albert led a rush on Scottish estates when he purchased Balmoral. Although the foundation of the castle wasn't laid until 1853, he designed *the Balmoral Tweed* earlier. Blue with white sprinkles and crimson in color, it was no coincidence that it looks gray from afar, resembling the granite mountains around Balmoral, as it was designed for deer stalking in the area.

ture, and the various color effects in the yarn are obtained by mixing dyed wool before it is spun.

Popular patterns for the tweed jacket include houndstooth, windowpane, Harris tweed, gray Donegal, Prince of Wales check,[17] and herringbone. There are many, many more. For a first jacket, purchasing a Harris tweed is a good choice.

Most tweed jackets pair nicely with shirts whose colors pick up any one of the many colors present in the tweed. You will want to go with a heavier weight of cotton to match the weightiness of tweed fabric. As far as trousers, anything heavy works well. Certainly corduroy (preferably wide wale) is a good match as well as flannel. Calvary twill, moleskin, and denim (gasp) can also work for the Professional Gentleman. Chinos can work with lighter weight tweeds, but note that lighter weight versions of tweed can ring false with British aficionados as tweed is not a fabric designed to be worn in warm weather. Sort of like putting a rear spoiler on a truck.

The Unstructured Blazer

More casual blazer options take on the typical shape of the odd jacket but without the structure. These jackets are supple and more relaxed. The biggest difference between the structured blazers I've described *supra* and unstructured blazers is their drape. Unstructured jackets hold less shape, they aren't cut quite so close to the body, and the padding, inner workings, and linings we discussed in Chapter 7 on suiting are removed to give them a far softer, casual fit.

These blazers follow your shoulder more closely, ensuring the jacket drapes nearer to your body. This gives a more natural fit to the jacket compared to the constructed drape of the structured blazer. While usually lighter in fabrication, they can also come in heavier versions. Of course the Italians, with their more casual flair, do this best, and Brunello Cucinelli is the most notable purveyor of these beauties, but other brands that execute this well include Boglioli, Berluti, and Massimo Dutti. Reasonably priced versions

---

17. Prince of Wales check was originally commissioned by Edward VII.

can also be obtained from Steven Alan, Reiss, and LBM 1911. Consistent with its more laid-back nature, deconstructed blazers typically are unlined (or just the arms are lined) and feature exposed seams, external patch pockets, and working cuffs that can jauntily be rolled up without looking at all odd. They also can come in more than two buttons, with versions featuring three and even four buttons, which, if used, reduce the lapel and render the jacket even more casual.

For a first purchase of a desconstructed blazer, opt for a versatile color like dark blue, brown straying into oatmeal, or gray hues. Pair it with similarly casual pants. Chinos in a contrasting color work well. Not that I'd advise it for the Professional Gentleman other than when he's on vacation, but I've seen enterprising and well-dressed Italian gentlemen wear blazers like this with drawstring high-cuffed pants and espadrilles.

Brands to Know

Berluti: The Italian shoemaker Alessandro Berluti founded Berluti in 1895 as a shoe company focused on fine craftsmanship, incorporating traditional elements with flair. Today, Berluti is based in Paris and is a subsidiary of LVMH. While Berluti maintains its strong traditions in the footwear industry, it has also expanded into the ready-to-wear and bespoke tailoring menswear markets with its acquisition Arny's, a Paris tailor house. The brand now sells suits known not only for their flawless style and attention to detail, but also for their focus on comfort.

LBM 1911: Luigi Bianchi, from the Italian province of Mantova, founded his label in 1911 for luxury menswear. Bianchi's company, like many of the great Italian houses, is now a family affair, but it has evolved from a single line into a tailoring house with two distinct imprints: the more relaxed LBM 1911, and a more classically minded offering aptly titled Luigi Bianchi Mantova. Both lines blend exquisite fabrics and expert fabrication to create Professional Gentleman splendor.

Orazio Luciano: Echoing their fine suits, the odd jacket from classic Neapolitan tailors Orazio Luciano features a flair for color and pattern with soft construction, shirt shoulders, and curved pockets. With hand finishing everywhere—from the buttonholes to the double rows of edge stitching—plus parallel attention to detail inside. These are expensive garments.

Once the basic odd jackets are obtained, in good quality and with proper fit, you can move on to the more esoteric pieces: seasonal versions in ultra-appropriate fabrics (think winter heavy tweeds and summer lightest linen or seersucker), unusual colors, patterns, and the like. Some examples of these rare birds follow.

Law #29

~

Only after obtaining a blue blazer, tweed sport coat, and modest unstructured blazer shall the Professional Gentleman purchase more esoteric odd jackets.

~

More Tweeds—Houndstooth, Striped/Checked

Fall/winter appropriate and in multiple colorful varieties, tweeds make great odd jackets. Houndstooth is characterized by an almost checked appearance made up of a specific repeating geometric block. Created in Scotland and dating back to the 1800s, the term *houndstooth* comes from the protruding jagged teeth that define that particular block. Striped and checked tweeds add one or more stripes to form a windowpane pattern over the basic plain twill tweed to add color and distinction. A tweed blazer can feature leather elbow patches and leather buttons. In its traditional brown versions with forest green and burgundy windowpane (or narrower) accents, it is eminently sporting. Black and white versions are more modish and city appropriate. But there are almost unlimited color combinations. As an odd jacket, the tweed jacket makes a capable companion and pairs wonderfully with heavier trousers like corduroy, moleskin, and denim, as well as more formally with gray flannel trousers.

Corduroy

Corduroy is a ridged velvet fabric made of cotton. Its surface is covered in "wales" (the vertical pipelines of soft fabric running down the jacket), and corduroy is described by the number of wales per inch. The more wales per inch, obviously, the smaller those wales have to be, so the 16-wale corduroy has a much finer and less visible texture than the 8-wale corduroy (standard is around 11). Fine corduroys higher than 16-wale are sometimes called "pincord" or "needlecord."

Inherently casual and autumnal, the degree of the wale divides corduroy jackets into differing levels of formality. Pincord is somewhat formal and can even be used as a material for navy blazers, while wider wales are used to make more countrified colored sport coats in browns and greens. To suit their casual nature and use in fall, these odd jackets feature flap pockets and a leather button flap to hold the lapels closed in bad weather. The corduroy should always be in a single, solid color. Elbow patches are encouraged in leather or suede. Corduroy goes best with smooth, solid garments that help bring out its unique texture. So light cotton slacks with a tight weave will certainly pair well.

I love the corduroy odd jacket, but they can be hard to find in quality versions. I have a couple from Steven Alan that have held up well. Other American brands put them out regularly like Ralph Lauren, J. Crew, and even Orvis, but higher end versions are usually not offered by better brands seasonally. So if you've complied with Law #29 and see one from a brand you like, jump on it.

Brands to Know

Massimo Dutti: A Spanish brand founded in 1985, Massimo Dutti began with a focus on men's fashion. Now, with over 869 stores, the brand has expanded into the womenswear and children's markets. The brand describes a Massimo man as one who focuses on individuality but has a multicultural sensitivity. The brand's clothing is intended to be worn by a refined, urban man who appreciates attention to detail. Massimo Dutti combines different textures and fashions to create a unique look. The brand offers a ready-to-wear line as well as personal tailoring for men, a service that is accessible at 60 of its stores.

Steven Alan: This American fashion brand has become well known and loved by the fashion-forward. Steven Alan Grossman founded the Steven Alan boutique and showroom in 1994, where he sold the apparel of other designers. Alan launched his own ready-to-wear collection in 1999. The line is known for adding edgier and avant-garde elements to more traditional pieces, such as the signature "Reverse Seam" button-downs and dresses that were sold in a variety of patterns and bright colors. DISCLOSURE: HBA represents Steven Alan.

Reiss: In 1971, David Reiss founded Reiss as a menswear brand, selling men's suits and specializing in tailoring. Since its inception, the brand has focused on providing inventive, high-quality fashion items. Today, the brand continues to emphasize the importance of creativity in its menswear and womenswear lines. Many consumers are attracted to the company because of their commitment to value and attention to detail, including celebrity clientele like the Royal Family. Today, this UK company has over 160 stores, but its most famous store is the flagship location in London, which has won multiple awards for its design.

Linen Unstructured Blazer

A summer essential for having a jacket to wear on hot days. A linen blazer has to be unstructured and feature all of the benefits detailed in the description of the unstructured blazer *supra*. The crumpledness of the fabric must be accepted to be worn with any degree of confidence. In fact, I purposely have my linen blazers absorb a few bends and buckles before wearing so there is no dismay at the first, inevitable crease.

The light linen blazer worn with a crisp, white cotton shirt creates a still professional contrast in textures on a hot day. Loro Piana and Boglioli make lovely versions of the cream and oatmeal linen blazer. Wearing the linen blazer is a somewhat senior move in accordance with the Laws. It goes without saying that the linen suit is also reserved for MD/partner ranks.

Plaid Madras

Madras fabric is a plain, cotton muslin that is overprinted or embroidered in elaborate patterns using colorful dyes. The weave is simple, producing a breathable light fabric befitting a humid climate.[18] The Madras patterns are most associated with the summer wardrobe of Northeastern preppies and became very popular in the 1960s in the form of jackets (as well as shorts) for Ivy League elites.[19] The Madras blazer can come in virtually any color combination but is generally not subdued. Because of its bold nature, it will pair best with a solid tie, a solid dress shirt, and contrasting solid-colored pants.

There is also the uber-prep patchwork Madras jacket which stiches together multiple swatches of Madras fabric in a sort of "go to hell" ("GTH") version of a blazer—which essentially tells everyone you are going to wear what you want, and if they don't like it they can go to hell. A GTH version of the Madras blazer is not appropriate for the Professional Gentleman in the office. Trad clothiers like J. Press, Brooks Brothers, and Ralph Lauren offer multiple versions of the Madras blazer. As a spring/summer business casual wardrobe item, one or two are advisable—no more.

Brands to Know

Loro Piana: The Loro Piana family started as merchants of wool fabrics at the beginning of the nineteenth century. An Italian company specializing in luxury cashmere and wool products, Loro Pianna is vertically integrated, "from sheep to suit." It is one of the biggest producers and only sells its own cloth. Consequently its suits, knitwear, and other clothing are exquisite.

---

18. The Madras fabric is named after the Indian city of the same name (now known as Chennai) from where it first made its way to the West. It is hot there.
19. Perhaps to underscore this link to the Ivy, it should be noted that Madras first made its appearance in America in 1718 as a part of a donation made to the Collegiate School of Connecticut by the then Governor of Madras Elihu Yale and the college was later renamed Yale University in his honor. Ironically, Madras is not popular in India as it is associated with a certain types of sarong worn predominantly by the labor class.

Boglioli: A leading Italian tailor and suit maker based in Brescia, this family-run company is committed to excellence in the men's and women's apparel industry. The brand is well known for their suits, which feature lightweight designs and a clean cut. They sell suits in a range of fabrics from silk-wool blends to textual corduroy.

Knits

Knits cover all manner of clothing, but what we are primarily talking about here are sweaters (or "jumpers" for you anglo inclined). Knit materials range from cottons, which are good in the summer, to wool, which is for the winter, and cashmere, which is the softest and most desirable material and can be worn all year round.

The sweater takes many forms from the functional and rugged to the sleek and refined. For the workplace, there are a few acceptable styles that are comfortable and appealing. There are also many styles that should be avoided.

Wearing large bulky sweaters makes you look large and bulky and can ruin the sharp, clean lines you want to create for the office.[20] Moreover, these very functional outdoor knits can overheat you. The office is a place that is always approximately 70 degrees, so any sweater you are going to leave on for the day should be light. So leave the Irish fisherman cable knit and the large Nordic toggle versions for outdoor activities. This will also allow you to wear most of your knitwear under a jacket or coat, creating a nice textural difference as well as another color option.

Also, solid colors are best. Your knits are going to be worn in the office as part of an overall ensemble. They should not compete for attention. So leave the Fair Isle patterns and prints for leisure activities.

---

20. The sole exception to this general rule is the cardigan worn as a jacket—as detailed *infra*.

Given the modern fitted silhouette that most knits come in today, one caution is to know your own body and what you can wear and what you cannot wear. Warning sign.[21] Unlike a fitted sport coat, the fitted sweater will leave very little to the imagination regarding the state of your shoulders, pectoral muscles (or lack thereof), arms, and belly. I'm reminded of an intellectually (but not physically) gifted securities lawyer I knew early in my career. At some point in his 30s, working long hours, living on Shun Lee Palace takeout in the office, and going over '34 Act disclosure documents, he had let himself (his body) go. Nevertheless, he maintained a sentimental and misguided hold on his lovely cashmere sweater collection from his earlier more svelte days as an undergrad at Dartmouth. How he managed to get himself into these old sweaters strained credulity, and his jutting midsection and rounded mounds of chest and back fat strained the very fibers of his poor sweaters. He looked like an anti-hero. Like Newt Gingrich in tights about to perform some unsavory performance art routine. When he wore his J. Press "shaggy dog" sweater, he really looked like a shaggy dog. It was sad. He was so much better than he looked. The lesson here is that if you want to wear fitted sweaters, get in shape.

Brands to Know

Berg&Berg: Founded in 2009, this Norwegian brand creates a line of menswear products of the highest quality. Their goal is that every product will become a trusted friend in your wardrobe: loved, cared for, and enjoyed for many years to come. Berg&Berg knitwear is made in the two countries most famous for premium knitwear. In Scotland, they work with Johnstons, one of the most famous knitwear and scarf manufacturers in the world. In Italy, they work with a family company that specializes in fine merino and cotton knitwear.

Uniqlo: This Japanese knitwear powerhouse originated in 1949, as Yamaguchi-based company Ogori Shoji which opened a unisex casual wear store in Hiroshima under the name "Unique Clothing Warehouse." Price points are low and style points are high as Uniqlo puts forth simple, fitted, quality knits.

---

21. The Talking Heads, "Warning Sign," *More Songs About Buildings and Food* (Compass Point Studios in Nassau, 1978).

Sid Mashburn: The Southern-oriented retailer also puts forth solid private label sweater offerings. Sid Mashburn has a touch of the collegiate running through the line, which balances athletic looks in a refined color palette for the Professional Gentleman.

Crew Neck

The crew neck sweater is a classic, simple, functional item. A knitted long sleeve T-shirt—for all intents and purposes. It is important to note that when you are wearing a shirt and tie underneath, a crew neck will show very little of the shirt (just the collar and the cuffs) and of the tie (just the knot).[22] So consider how your tie looks against your sweater and its balance against the shirt collar. Opting for a heavyweight, knitted or textured tie can be overkill; instead, stick to classic silk versions and concentrate on your color/pattern mixing. You can go a little more crazy with the tie or the shirt, since so little of either will be seen. Just don't go crazy with both—as the tie knot and collar will clash. Also, there is a prominence placed on the quality of your tie knot. Strive to create a good dimple and nice balance to the knot.

The basic nature of a crew neck sweater allows you to consider a textured version when assembling your smarter looks. A waffle knit or subtly ribbed jumper in a rich complementary hue is best. This will add a solid point of interest to a suit or odd jacket with tie ensemble while maintaining a degree of correctness. If you want to punch it up a bit, go for more daring colors like burnt orange, teal, or blends, but only do so under a jacket or you risk overwhelming your outfit.

V-Neck

The V-neck sweater is a similarly classic item. Again, it is important to note that when you are wearing a shirt and neckwear underneath, a V-neck will not show much of the shirt (just the collar, the cuffs, and a little of the chest) and of the tie (just the knot and the first few inches of the tie). But since the V-neck gives your neck and chest a tad more room to breathe, you

---

22. Obviously, much less of the tie will show than if you are wearing an open cardigan, and a bit less than if you are wearing a V-neck sweater.

are allowed to better show off a considered shirt and tie combination. Use color judiciously, but note you can be more daring if you keep it under a jacket. For those with a shorter neck and/or round face, the V-neck helps create the illusion of length and a leaner appearance. Never, under any office circumstances, wear a V-neck (or any deep-necked knit) without a shirt underneath. You will look like a club owner, not a Professional Gentleman.

Law #30

~

The Professional Gentleman shall not wear deep-necked knits without a shirt underneath.

~

Polo

The Professional Gentleman can wear the polo collar in a variety of ways suitable for the office. Because it has its own distinct collar, the polo can be worn quite effectively without a jacket. Layered over the top of your shirt and tie with a couple of its buttons left undone or unzipped to better display the majesty of your neckwear, the double collar creates a distinctive look that can be quite smart.[23]

The polo collar can also be worn underneath a blazer alone (with just an undershirt), for a dressed-down feel. When doing this, I'd encourage you to wear an undershirt that does not show (e.g., a V-neck or wide scoop neck) and button the polo up all the way or just go with one button undone for a cleaner look. The polo can also be worn under a jacket and with a shirt and tie like the crew neck and V-neck versions above. However, the triple collar effect ("Triple Collar Effect") of this presentation, where jacket lapel, polo sweater collar, and shirt collar meet usually appears chaotic.[24]

Polo sweaters work well with soft shouldered or unstructured suits. The formality of crisp tailoring does not jibe with the informality of the polo.

---

23. The polo jumper comes in buttoned and zipper versions. Under most jackets, the buttoned version looks more appropriate. The zippered version reads more modern and fashion forward.
24. It's really a lapel (the jacket's) and two collars (the polo and the shirt), but it is nevertheless too much in most cases.

Brands to Know

Scott & Charters: Established in 1955 in Hawick, Scotland, an area well known for its local knitwear tradition. The third generation of Charters maintains the brand as an independent family business still manufacturing all its products in Hawick. Scott & Charters draws strength from its independence, allowing it to source the best fibers, buttons, and zips, wherever they may be found. Cashmere and Geelong yarns come mainly from Scottish spinners Todd & Duncan, whose stringent and high-quality levels ensure a beautiful and consistent yarn to knit with. There is quite a bit of handwork to these sweaters: rib cuffs and skirts are linked by hand to the front, back, and sleeves panels; sweaters are cut by hand; all components (neck trims, buttons, pockets, zips, ribbon) are stitched or linked by hand.

The Armoury: This shop was established in Hong Kong in 2010 born from a passion for classic menswear and interest in the stories behind well-crafted products. They have a New York location as well. Selective with the wholesale accounts they stock, they also offer private label knitwear, which shows the same high level of integrity and discrimination as the brands they carry. Quality craftsmanship, outstanding design, and timeless style.

Shawl Collar

The shawl collar features a draping neckline often of ribbed knit, which can stand up and wrap elegantly around the neck and upper chest. Layering a shawl collar sweater under a jacket can be a challenge though. While this collar produces an arresting silhouette (offering more to the eye than a standard V- or crew neck), it also adds bulk. It has a tendency to spill over lapels in a somewhat sloppy manner and is also heir to the same Triple Collar Effect as the polo is. For the Professional Gentleman attempting to wear one under a jacket, make sure to get a quality version that can, literally, stand up to the task. Worn correctly, this neckline gives your layers a true sense of depth and brings an extra dimension to a simple shirt-and-tie combination.

Worn on its own, the shawl collar can be acceptable in a business casual environment. The depth around your neck and upper chest frames your tie impeccably, showing the knot and a few inches of the tie to great effect.

Cardigans

Cardigans can look scholarly and unassuming. As such, many Professional Gentlemen prefer them as a business casual standard. But no need to go for the granddad look here. Over the past decade, cardigans have gotten a nice overhaul, and many brands offer versions that are more fitting and slim cut. The traditional cardigan is still a perfect match to the plaid shirt, but a well-cut heavier cardigan with leather elbow padding and large leather or even toggle buttons can substitute for a sack jacket, and with a tie be the basis for a business casual look that is distinctive and smashing.

Thin cardigans can be worn in the same manner as the shawl collar and polo collar jumper. Beware the Triple Collar Effect, by opting to wear thin almost colarless versions with a jacket. Keep the buttons done up (except for perhaps the top one, and always leave the bottom one undone). Unbuttoned, a cardigan will almost always look sloppy. Not capable. Not elegant.

Sweater Vests

The sweater vest is a great option. It fits nicely under jackets since there is no added bulk under the arms of your jacket. Worn without a jacket, the sweater vest allows more of the shirt to be seen (more than just the collar and cuffs), allowing for more pronounced contrast in your outfit. Solid sweater vest with plaid or striped shirt in complementary colors is a failsafe business casual look. The lack of arms allows for more comfort in office temperatures.

The sweater vest comes in cardigan, crew neck, and V-neck versions. The cardigan version is best without a jacket (avoids a front assault of buttons) while the crew and V-neck in thin cashmere or merino wool versions work best under a jacket.

Turtleneck

The turtleneck (or roll neck) sweater is a far more daring item, often invoking images of the creepy Dianetics auditor or the French mime. But the turtleneck has improved greatly over the last decade with some brands offering super thin, softer, and more relaxed versions that look cooler and also just literally are cooler. Still, heat regulation is one general caution here: wearing the roll neck in the office, a Professional Gentlemen can be apt to overheat. So plan accordingly. Don't wear a dress shirt underneath; just wear the lightest of T-shirts. And do not get bulky versions of the turtleneck. Not only will you get steamed, but these versions will not fit under a jacket and are far too casual for the office.

Wearing the turtleneck with a suit is a nice casualization of a classic standard and can look quite edgy. For the full effect, you can go for the turtleneck under a double breasted jacket but be in adherence with the Laws (i.e., best to have some seniority here). To pull this off, make sure the roll neck is flat and even rather than slouched down.

As far as color choices, because so much of the sweater is on display, go with neutral colors like gray, camel, and the somewhat sinister but ultimately versatile black. Navy and burgundy will go far for you as well. Create a subtle contrast or try similar hues to your jacket—both will work quite well—and you are good to go.

Trousers

The separate pant is often viewed as a necessary evil. I mean, you have to wear pants. But because of their less-pronounced area on the human body, they can be used as an opportunity for some sartorial caprice, bringing some gusto into an otherwise staid outfit. While the Laws do not permit the prep-school lad favorite GTH pants in the office, there are some risks that can be taken if the rest of the ensemble is in need of some oomph.

There are many different types of styles and fabrics appropriate for the Professional Gentleman in business casual mode.

Chinos

Made from cotton twill or gabardine, the chino is ubiquitous in business causal settings. The chino is formal enough for the Professional Gentleman to wear into the office while clearly not being the trousers of a suit. The chino can be worn in all seasons but winter (in temperate zones—wearing chinos during the winter in LA is fine) and are comfortable enough to be considered casual wear.

Brands to Know

J. Crew: Headquartered in New York and boasting hundreds of retail stores in the United States, J. Crew is an American specialty retailer serving customers through a variety of channels, including its retail stores, website, and factory stores. Selling men's, women's, and children's apparel and accessories, the brand sells everything from suiting to leisurewear to swimwear. The brand emphasizes the concept that clothing should be lived in and encourages color-blocking, daring patterns, and upbeat colors. Their fashion-forward pieces are accompanied by reasonable prices.

PT01: This Italian brand advances a more casual but no less sophisticated style of trousers. Understated elements and polished adornments add a subtly sumptuous touch. Expect luxurious natural fabrics worked into frame-flattering fitted shapes. Sporadic striking patterns and tapered versions lend a touch of irreverence.

Bonobos: A brand built on the Internet, Bonobos was created in 2007 with the mission of finding the perfect fit for every man outside of the expensive realm of custom tailoring. The website provided "tailors" for the modern age, termed *Bonobos ninjas*, customer service representatives tasked with the charge of finding the perfect fit for each shopper. Expanding into brick and mortar stores in 2012, Bonobos created the concept of a "Guideshop," which provides men with the opportunity to make an hour-long appointment at a Bonobos store in order to receive personalized assistance finding the best fit for the individual.

Khaki is the most popular color of chino; however, just to confuse men, many people refer to khakis as a separate, less formal type of pant. Chinos come in all colors, and given their wearability, should be obtained in at least three colors: khaki, stone/cream, and olive. Navy and gray won't serve you wrong, but given that you'll likely have navy and gray odd jackets, they may be less useful. I'm also partial to certain colors bordering on GTH pant territory, like lime green, Nantucket red, and yellow. But no critters! While the color selection one can have is amazing, it should be noted that chinos do not offer a great amount of texture and can read a bit dull and smooth (again, in texture, not color). Given that, I feel it is best to mix some texture into the jacket or knits the chino is worn with as well as the belt. Also note that chinos should not be worn without a belt (e.g., not with suspenders and not beltless). Hence all chinos will have belt loops. As has been discussed *supra*, flat front works best for thin men while pleats should be worn for men with larger legs and midsections.

Flannel Trousers

The flannel trouser is another standard that can be worn all year round, but is best in fall and winter, and should be obtained in light gray, charcoal, navy, and camel versions. Flannel is tightly woven wool, brushed to create an extremely pleasant suppleness.[25] The brushing process creates a smooth, napped surface. It's somewhat fuzzy, and the color is not totally consistent throughout the trouser, which adds great texture.

Flannel is generally considered to be softer than worsted wool. So flannel doesn't hold a crease as firmly as a formal pair of worsted wool trousers—which is the fabric used for most suits. This feature makes flannel the ideal complement to the more formal end of the scale of business casual outfits (e.g., odd jacket ensembles).[26]

Flannel is undoubtedly one of the best fabrics to make trousers for cold climates. It's warmer, and it has been a favorite for decades in winter because it wears and drapes so damn well. But it should be noted that flannel comes in light enough weave weights to be worn as pants in summer.

Law #31

~

The Professional Gentleman shall own a pair of gray flannel trousers.

~

25. The word flannel is believed to have a Welsh derivation. The French term *flanelle* was used in the late seventeenth century, and the German *flanell* came about in the early eighteenth century. In the nineteenth century, flannel was made in the Welsh towns of Llanidloes, Montgomeryshire, and Newtown.

26. Certainly flannel is used for suits, and the gray flannel suit is an absolute standard.

The well-appointed Professional Gentleman should have both a fall/winter and a spring/summer gray flannel trouser. Gray works with everything in terms of shirts, shoes, even jacket (other than of course gray). The added texture of the flannel also works with everything. Trust me fellas, these things are workhorses of business casual and should be invested in accordingly.

Brands to Know

Zanella: Since the 1950s, Italian brand Zanella has been producing sartorial trousers handcrafted by skilled tailors. With a keen eye for detail, the brand's sleek clothing is tailored in wool, cotton, sharkskin to suit different body types. From pants in regular sizes to pleated and flat fronts, the Zanella trouser collection offers great comfort in classic designs. The prices are reflective of the tailor's touch.

Ambrosi-Napoli: Bespoke elegance. Salvatore Ambrosi started making trousers at the age of eight, keeping alive the legacy of his father and grandfather. He has produced trousers for some of the most well-known tailoring houses, including Attolini, Sartoria Formosa, Rubinacci, and Sartoria Solito. By all accounts, this Neapolitan has elevated trouser-making to an art form. Visiting Naples isn't an obligation, as Salvatore has partnered with some of the greatest establishments in menswear across the globe (e.g., The Armoury in Hong Kong and New York, Leatherfoot in Toronto). A signature pair of Ambrosi trousers are light and feature an extended tab fastening belt, a thick waistband, one or two pleats, and ample cuffs. *Multo costoso.*[27]

Luciano Barbera: Launching his namesake label in 1971, Luciano Barbera has become world-renowned as the arbiter of "classic original Italian style"—a provider of fine fabrics for Ralph Lauren and Armani, and a fastidious designer of handmade men's cashmere and wool suits. Barbera's durable and lightweight superfine wools are woven on state-of-the-art looms, then stored in an Alpine cave to protect them from humidity—he calls it his "spa for yarn." A team of master tailors oversees the final production of Barbera's clothing. His trousers are things of beauty.

---

27. "Very expensive" in Italian.

Moleskin Pants

Moleskin is a sturdy cotton fabric which was traditionally used in outwear and trousers for British farmers.[28] Moleskin is woven with a twilled weave to form a dense cloth (the denser the better), giving it weight and shape. Like flannel, moleskin is also brushed to form the nap, giving the trouser its trademark texture. Typically a fall/winter fabrication, moleskin trousers are best paired with a tweed or separate colored jacket, a denim shirt, and/or with knits. Colors are all shades of brown, fall greens, and burnt versions of orange, yellow, or red. Navy blue also works, though it is not a color that is traditional to the fabric. It is a trouser that reads to the eye as heavy, and thus what you wear on top should have similar visual weight. A thin dress shirt or linen V-neck sweater paired with the moleskin trouser would look wrong.

Corduroys

Corduroy pants are a nice textural change the Professional Gentleman can most easily work into his wardrobe through trousers. As I've mentioned *supra*, corduroy is a ridged velvet fabric made of cotton.[29] Wales are the vertical pipelines of soft fabric running down the trouser. Corduroy is described by the number of wales per inch. The wider the wale, the more casual, so the Professional Gentleman should opt for 11-wale and higher for trousers. I prefer these to wide wale cords which I think make normal fellows look plump and thin fellows look too skinny. Corduroy is a sturdy and yet soft fabric most stylishly worn in fall/winter in seasonally appropriate colors like browns, sage greens, burnt orange, or yellow, but navy blue and burgundy also work well and are versatile. The existence of the high-texture wales places cords on the casual end of the spectrum, but it is certainly appropriate for business casual for the Professional Gentleman. The vast majority of cords are a flat front, and given its weight, it is a non-cuff trouser. Corduroy trousers pair best with a tweed jacket or smooth, solid knits that help bring out its natural ribbed texture and pair with the fall/winter character of the fabric.

---

28. Moleskin is often associated with British heritage menswear and workwear/performance brands such as Barbour and Hackett.
29. Sometimes wool is added to the cotton, so called "wooly" cords. Avoid these.

Brands to Know

Beams Plus: This Japanese brand started as a small shop in the Hara-juku district of Tokyo in 1976 and has since grown into a significant retail force. The men's line, Beams Plus, which was launched in 1999, is the rugged, heritage- and workwear-inspired range from the company. The cords are perfect for the Professional Gentleman.

Incotex: The Italian Slowear Group comprises of four different specialist labels: Incotex for well-cut trousers, Zanone for knitwear, Glanshirt for shirts, and Montedoro for jackets. Between them, the Slowear family of brands covers most casual wardrobe requirements in a classic-yet-modern way for a reasonable price. Their fabrics are made of fine cotton, wool, and linen, treated, washed, and dyed with modern techniques brought about by continuous experimentation.

Denim Jeans

Why do so many Professional Gentlemen insist on wearing denim blue jeans into the office? With all of the other trouser fabrics mentioned above that offer greater variety, comfort and (lest we not forget) formality, why would the Professional Gentleman still opt for dungarees? Is he wrangling cattle after work? Laying down railroad ties? Mining for gold?

Personally, I do not wear jeans in professional environments. And listen, I'm not the most buttoned-up formal Professional Gentleman you'll come across. I just find I have so many better and business-appropriate options to pair with an odd jacket or knits. Sure, I wear jeans on weekends with the kids, out at night for non-business functions, when I'm fishing or I'm breaking broncos, etc. Despite the fact that I know many of you do wear jeans into the office, I am going to ask that you strongly consider not doing so to both distinguish yourself and, in fact, be more comfortable. I'm not making a Law of it, but consider it a strong suggestion.

If you are going to ignore my suggestion, here's how the Professional Gentleman should pull off wearing jeans into the office. Choose dark jeans with minimal wash and absolutely no distressing. That means little to no fading. Basically a deep navy blue. It also means no rips, no white patches around the knees or pockets. If possible, also avoid high-contrast external stitching and rivets, which basically are neon sign-like advertisements to the fact that you are wearing jeans. In most cases, playing it safe for the Professional Gentleman means to treat jeans as a direct substitute for chinos. A straight fit is vital: neither too skinny (too trendy and uncomfortable), nor too baggy (which will just look awful). Your jeans will finish on the shoe without the need for a conspicuous cuff (where the lighter denim underneath shows). Brown to tan shoes will work best with a matching belt. Black shoes never go with blue denim—not for anyone.

Law #32

~

The Professional Gentleman shall not wear black shoes with blue denim.

~

Pair with a button-down and an odd jacket for the most benign presentation. For me, a knit tie never hurts and stays within the tone of the informal ensemble while reading very much capable and elegant (i.e., very Professional Gentleman). Rag & Bone, Richard James, 3x1, A.P.C., and Paige, among others, make jeans that fit more like a trouser and can properly be worn with a dress shirt and blazer.

Polos and Sportswear

"Men's fashions all start as sports clothes and progress to the great occasions of state. The tailcoat, which started out as a hunting coat, is just finishing such a journey. The tracksuit is just beginning one."

—Angus McGill[30]

---

30. The witty and genial McGill won the British Press Award as Descriptive Writer of the Year 1968; he became a founder member of the SDP in 1981; was awarded the MBE in 1990.

Polos are more typically worn in short-sleeved pique cotton knit versions, often with a logo of a polo player, alligator, or some other critter affixed or woven into the upper left chest.

Brands to Know

Lacoste: Rene Lacoste won the 1926 tennis US Open in a version of the modern polo shirt he designed by removing the sleeves from his long-sleeved white tennis shirt as well as the buttons, and adding the "tennis tail," which allowed the back of the shirt to be slightly longer than the front and therefore more comfortable to tuck in and keep in place, particularly when serving a tennis ball. The brand offers colorful versions in a variety of weights and fabrics.

Fred Perry: This historic brand was born in England in the 1940s by Fred Perry, a multiple winner of Wimbledon, who decided to create a line of sportswear. In 1952 he launched his cotton pique polo shirt with slim fit by a laurel wreath embroidered on the chest. Sporty and refined defines the Fred Perry brand. One of the best traditional brands of clothing for tennis if you are able to play without moisture wicking fabric (unfortunately, I cannot). This lack of performance fabrics makes it all the better for the office.

Sunspel: This British standard in men's sportswear was founded in 1860. It was owned by the Hill family until 2005, when it was sold to Nicholas Brooke and Dominic Hazlehurst. Ever since the brand began making the polo shirt in the 1950s, they have focused on combining an exact fit with the finest cotton fabrics for a contemporary look and luxurious feel.

The polo shirt is sportswear. Its very name carries with it the sport of polo—even though its roots are in tennis.[31] Polo shirts are worn regularly for not only tennis and polo, but also golf, sailing, and a variety of other athletic and semi-athletic activities. They are also worn regularly by many

---

31. The iconic Lacoste logo stems from Rene Lacoste's nickname "The Crocodile," which he got from his somewhat shockingly long nose.

workers forced to wear them as part of a uniform (from Best Buy to Barnes and Noble to Starbucks) and given this, perhaps surprisingly, by many Professional Gentlemen voluntarily into the office. I'd like this to be an infrequent occurrence for you, but when you do wear a polo shirt, let it be in the following format.

Law #33

~

The polo shirt shall be worn to the office infrequently and under specific guidelines of business appropriateness.

~

- Avoid logos. I realize that for some consumers the iconic Ralph Lauren polo player in mid-swing, the Lacoste alligator, or the Fred Perry[32] laurel wreath are status symbols. The Professional Gentleman eschews logos as drivel (unless he's an IP lawyer).[33] Keep logo polos on the court or on the course. Loro Piana, Sunspel, Paul Smith, newcomer Feldspar Brook,[34] and even J. Crew make very nice logo-less versions.
- Never wear a polo shirt together with an undershirt under any circumstances.
- Never wear a tie with a polo shirt (or any shirt other than a dress shirt).
- Do not "pop" your collar indoors (and really think long and hard about it if doing it outside).
- Tuck in your polo shirt (as you would tuck in any shirt) when wearing it in the office.
- Avoid wearing the polo shirt with a blazer. The cuffs won't show (obviously). The collar will not sit properly unless its "popped,"

---

32. Another tennis great, the English Perry was the first player to win a "Career Grand Slam," winning all four singles titles at the age of 26 and going on to win six more majors in his career.
33. By way of a reference point for how inappropriate logo dressing is for the Professional Gentleman, I "designed" a logo for polo shirts for my bachelor party (an embroidered hand with a halo above it), which I handed out during my crew's first round of golf.
34. DISCLOSURE: HBA represented Feldspar Brook in its formation and initial establishment.

which it shouldn't be in the office. The dress shirt looks infinitely better and is designed for wearing with the blazer.

- Never wear a performance fabric polo for anything other than athletic (or quasi-athletic) activities (i.e., not into the office).
- Wear polos in the late spring and summer only. The polo is short-sleeved and made of piqued cotton; it is not meant for any other season even if it comes in fall/winter seasonal colors.[35]
- Don't be afraid of a slight pop of color. Certainly every man should (and most do) own a white and navy version of the polo shirt. But since I'm not recommending that you wear the polo shirt into the office often, and further that you only do so in the late spring and summer, you should dabble with the multiple colors available. Greens, yellows, pastels. As Rene himself might have said, *"devenir fou!"*[36]

Performance Sportswear/Suiting

Are there acceptable pieces of performance sportswear the Professional Gentleman can wear into the office? The simple answer is no, not really. Elements of performance fabrics offering stretch, moisture wicking, and water resistant qualities are creeping their way into more tailored clothing. I'm certainly not against that. But true sportswear is for sport. And the technologies and pockets and racing stripes and other doodads that accompany sportswear do not belong in the office, at least not your office, at least not according to the Laws.

Law #34

~

The Professional Gentleman shall not wear sportswear/gym clothing into the office.

~

Many of the early versions of what some consider office-appropriate performance sportswear had these features to call out their performance-based roots. I get it from a branding perspective, but from a style perspective,

---

35. Because of this rule, fall- and winter-colored versions of the polo should never be purchased as they are a total waste of money and closet space.
36. "Go crazy!" in French.

they don't work for the Professional Gentleman. Nevertheless, brands like QOR, Isaora, RYU, Lulu Lemon, Patagonia, and others are having a go at this potential market.

Better options are found with the more traditional brands that are subtly integrating these fabric advances into more conservative tailored clothing. According to a recent consensus of menswear retailers, 20–65% of their apparel mix involves some type of performance fabric.[37] Brands like Ermenegildo Zegna (with its Trofeo fabrics), Loro Piana (with its innovative Storm System fabric), Paul Smith (with its Travel Tailor-Fit line), Thom Browne (whom together with American Woolen Company developed "Cool Wool"),[38] Theory (with its Wellar HC Suit),[39] and Perry Ellis (with its Comfort Stretch Portfolio Suit), among others, are integrating stretch and water-resistant properties into their suiting without shouting from the top of the gym rock climbing wall about it. Others, like newcomers Ministry of Supply (which uses performance fabrics throughout its entire line) and Mizen & Main, are certainly making bold performance bids but are at least paying heed to traditional menswear style and don't feel the need to affix too many other sporty embellishments.

Brands to Know

Thom Browne: American brand established in 2001 and debuting a ready-to-wear collection in 2003, Thom Browne is celebrated for his iconic shrunken suit silhouette. This distinct take on tailored clothing arguably was a watershed moment in recent menswear fashion, leading to a slim-fit suiting trend that is on its second decade (though in my view Fonzie is currently riding his chopper up the ramp to jump the shark tank on this trend). Known for theatrical runway presentations, Browne expertly distills his creative vision into looks that are based on traditional modes, but with a wink.

Theory: This American brand makes affordable modern suiting for men and women. Clean lines and a minimalistic esthetic are pervasive throughout the line. While generally fused, these suits are affordable for the young Professional Gentleman and represent a quality cut and tapered design.

---

37. Karen Alberg Grossman, "High Performance: Tailored Clothing Gets Technical," *MR*, April 20, 2016, http://www.mr-mag.com/high-performance-tailored-clothing-gets-technical/.
38. Cool Wool involves high twist yarns that stretch two ways, and mechanical stretch with added elastic yarns for a more complete stretch in all directions.
39. Which has 3% Lycra in its fabric and a vented back to the jacket.

Perry Ellis: Warning Sign. Another mid-tier American brand, Perry Ellis has been around since the 1970s. The suits are fused, and often the materials are not of high quality. To be avoided by the Professional Gentleman.

Ministry of Supply: This Boston-based high-performance tailored menswear brand was launched in 2012 via Kickstaster by former Massachusetts Institute of Technology students using some of the same temperature-regulating material as NASA astronauts in their clothing. These suits are made from stretch polyester and cannot be recommended as formal business attire, but as a viable business casual alternative for the active Professional Gentleman they perform well and are cheap.

Mizen & Main: Another American company, Dallas-based Mizen & Main specializes in performance menswear—dress shirts and blazers using synthetic performance fabrics. They do not offer suits. For the active Professional Gentleman, Mizen & Main makes an affordable and comfortable business casual alternative.

My buddy Josh Peskowitz, founder of the Los Angeles menswear store Magasin, was quoted in a *Vogue* article as saying, "The idea that there is a difference between what a man needs to wear for off-duty and on-duty is over." Peskowitz clarified, "We're always on duty; we're always on call."[40] The addition of fabric technology should allow some men who just are more active in their tailored clothing to remain in it longer. A good thing for those rare but important occasions when you bump into you client or your boss on the street, and you are still dressed every bit the Professional Gentleman.

Ignorantia juris non excusat.

"Here comes your man."

—The Pixies[41]

---

40. Alexis Brunswick, "A Menswear Street Style Star Opens L.A.'s Coolest New Store," *Vogue*, March 17, 2016, http://www.vogue.com/13417417/magasin-josh-peskowitz-la-store/.
41. "Here Comes Your Man," *Doolittle* (Elektra Records, 1989).

—11—

Patterns and Textures: Mixing and Matching

"To achieve the nonchalance,
which is absolutely necessary for a man,
one article at least must not match."
—Sir Hardy Amies[1]

Patterns and textures involve a high degree of risk. As any student of finance knows, with higher risk there is often (or should be in an efficient market) higher return. But patterns and textures can be a sartorial minefield. So many choices; so many varieties; so many ways to cock it all up. The art of mixing and matching is an essential skill in dressing that will help to break up the monotony of your wardrobe. Brands like Paul Smith, Etro, and Ring Jacket have distinguished themselves by playing boldly with patterns and textures in their designs. Indeed, subtle and not-so-subtle blending of both patterns and textures can be one of the highest forms of artistry and subtly acceptable individuality. Like that mistreated rug in *The Big Lebowski*,[2] the right mix of patterns and textures can really tie your look together.

---

1. English fashion designer famous for his work as official dressmaker to Queen Elizabeth II from 1952 to 1989. Amies also created his own fashion label, Hardy Amies.
2. The one that was "micturated upon."

Law #35

~

The Professional Gentleman need not mix and match patterns and textures, but in doing so properly, he shall attain degrees of style.

~

For the Professional Gentleman, the art of mixing and matching textures and patters is best approached soberly and conservatively. It should be done as an acknowledgment to the small details in dress in an otherwise impeccable outfit. Legendary, and well-dressed, UCLA basketball coach John Wooden said it best: "It's the little details that are vital. Little things make big things happen." Understanding the smaller details, like patterns and textures, applies to a much larger picture in a Professional Gentleman's overall presentation. "Everything in its right place."[3] It speaks volumes about who you are not only as conscientious dresser, but as a detail-oriented person who clients and employers can trust and also esteem.

What Do You Mean by Patterns and Textures?

These concepts are nuanced. They can be easily lost on someone becoming a more deliberate dresser, like game theory or obscure accounting comments from an SEC examiner.

Pattern is somewhat self-explanatory. Any of you who are quants know it—the consistent and repetitive presentation of stripes, polka dots, paisley, critters, etc., on an article of clothing. Pattern is found everywhere, and likely at least one piece of the prototypical professional uniform contains a pattern, usually the tie or pocket square, or perhaps the shirt. Patterns can also present themselves on suits, or the odd jacket and trousers: pinstripes, windowpane lines; the subtle chevrons of houndstooth; the muted plaid of

---

3. Radiohead, "Everything in Its Right Place," *Kid A* (Capitol, 2000).

tweed. As we've canvassed shirting, knitwear, ties, and pocket squares in previous chapters, we've discussed patterns in some detail.

It is the texture element that is often forgotten by careless or simply uninspired dressers. This is also the reason it offers the most exciting element for refined self-expression and distinction. Perhaps the best way to portray the concept of texture in apparel is to think of it concurrently with the four seasons and what we, at least in less-temperate climes, wear to address the climate. Fall and winter dressing are generally made up of wools and heavy cottons, tweeds, flannels, and other "fuzzy" fabrics. Summer and spring are usually synonymous with that of lighter weight crinkly cottons, linens, and silks. Each season has its own texture, so to speak, which leads us to break up the Professional Gentleman wardrobe in possibilities based on these options.

There is nothing wrong with a worsted wool blue suit with a classic silk rep tie. This is a classic look that will likely be around as long as the suit remains relevant. It is a mode of presentation, that although has some pattern (the tie), will likely contain little contrast in texture, which is fine. *Pas de problème.*[4] If you are mailing it in. If you are cool with a C+/B–. The same goes for a fuzzy gray flannel suit with a solid shirt and tie (no pattern)—for sure there is a sober efficiency to a minimalist look at times. However, a fuzzy flannel suit, blue striped shirt, dark blue grenadine tie, and perhaps a silk paisley pocket hankie is much more interesting, no? Come on, you guys. If you know you are strivers, strive!

---

4. No problem.

Balance is an important attribute when adding elements of pattern and texture successfully. That is, to combine them in a way that works cohesively and is complimentary. This takes a style calculation for which there are no real hard and fast formulas. The key thing to be mindful of is that no one element should control your sartorial presentation as it will draw undue attention to itself and away from you and the rest of your ensemble.

Law #36

~

The Professional Gentleman shall not wear just a single item with a pattern or texture that monopolizes his sartorial presentation.

~

Think of this edict as an anti-trust regulation—a menswear Sherman Act.[5] So, navy worsted wool suit, white shirt, white pocket square and red, orange, purple and green paisley tie, is going to have everyone you meet starting at your vivid tie. This outfit needs another pattern to neutralize the blazing tie. Douse this sartorial fire in the making by opting for a tweed, windowpane suit (rather than the solid navy). This has echoes of the tie's color palette and would work well.

Keeping things scaled is paramount and allows each garment to be optically delineated. A large-scaled pattern should be paired with a smaller-scaled pattern. Somewhat counterintuitively, this prevents a clash and an overstimulation of visuals. Avoid two or more patterns of the same size (large or small) together as the eye will read similarly sized patterns as the same. Each item should be able to be defined visually, and if this can be done artfully with other patterns rather than solids, it can serve to soften the edges a bit more.

Although this may seem like tricky business, relying on your eyes usually works—if it hurts to look at, it's not a good look. Putting this into some perspective: have you ever looked at an object that had a variety of similarly

---

5. The Sherman Antitrust Act was passed in 1890 and prohibits certain monopolistic business activities. The act has also been used to oppose combinations of entities through M&A that could potentially harm competition.

sized stripes and zigzags that made the room spin? Like a stock ticker when you are down, or the tax code, or the footnotes in an amicus brief? This can happen easily with your clothing if a look is unbalanced.

The more patterns and textures you throw into your dress, the easier it is to become unbalanced. A quick Law here:

Law #37

~

The Professional Gentleman shall not attempt to integrate more than three patterns or textures into the same outfit.

~

While an adventuring sartorialist at Pitti Uomo can try to pull off more—you are not adventuring here, and you are not a boulevardier at a menswear trade show. Really sticking with two patterns or textures as a maximum is the safest path—but I want to be mindful that often patterns need other patterns to accommodate the anti-monopoly Law #36 *supra*. Windowpane suit, polka-dot tie, and keep everything else low key with a solid shirt and solid pocket square if you so choose. Striped contrast collar shirt, foulard tie, perhaps best to keep suit solid, and, if you want more patterns, limit them to the pocket square or the socks. Getting a feel for this?

With respect to balancing textures, this is usually easier. Typically, the seasonality of your choices will dictate a balance of texture on its own. But to the extent you are not sure, heed a simple Law that will also keep you comfortable.

Law #38

~

The Professional Gentleman shall not wear fabrics that are suitable for fall/winter together with fabrics that are suitable for spring/summer in the same outfit.

~

One of my colleague works with several companies doing business in Dubai. As most of you know, from an apparel seasonal perspective, Dubai has two seasons: summer and summer-on-the-planet-Mercury. On one of his trips there, he left the office in January in a 13-ounce tweed suit he loved from Cad & The Dandy. A striking suit and fine for a New York winter, insanity for even the cool "summer" season in Dubai. Since he didn't pack with foresight, he brought only one other suit. The rest of his choices were sensibly made with a nod to how hot it would be. So he had brought two pairs of tan loafers (suede and pebbled leather) from JM Weston, lightweight dress shirts, and a few seersucker ties. The only other suit he brought with him, a lightweight navy worsted, performed fine. But the tweed suit simply did not properly pair with the rest of his summer pieces. He actually did what any smart Professional Gentleman would do under the circumstances. Made a quick trip to The Dubai Mall,[6] headed straight for Alfred Dunhill (even though he does not smoke, his tailored off-the-rack clothier of choice), and picked up a simple light gray worsted off the rack and had them cuff the trousers on the spot. Given exchange rates, however, he spent more than two times what he would have in New York.

Brands to Know

Cad & The Dandy: An independent tailoring company based in London offering bespoke suits, manufactured from English and Italian fabrics at a lower price point than the traditional Savile Row houses. The company was founded in 2008 by James Sleater and Ian Meiers, two Professional Gentlemen who were both made redundant from their banking jobs in the 2008 financial crisis. Cad & The Dandy tenders a remarkable value for money. Fully canvassed bespoke suits are under £1000.00.

JM Weston: This French shoe brand was founded by Édouard Blanchard in 1891, in Limoges. It offers a full line of dress shoes as well as leather goods ranging from belts and briefcases to luggage items. The company's most famous model is the 180 Moccasin (a classic penny loafer).

---

6. The Dubai Mall is a shopping mall in Dubai and the largest mall in the world by total area.

Alfred Dunhill: This English brand, specializing in ready-to-wear, custom, and bespoke menswear, leather goods, and accessories. The company is currently owned by Richemont. Alfred Dunhill the man was an English tobacconist and inventor. Known for conservative tailored clothing, though quality is somewhat mixed based on conversations I've had with my colleague. The suits are made in Italy, not England.

So keep hefty wools, corduroy, and other heavy fabrics together. Similarly, keep linen and light cottons together. This will also serve for certain color palettes as well—for instance, pairing a burnt orange and brown striped wool tie with a light blue seersucker suit would be wrong just as pairing a canary yellow linen tie with a heavy brown tweed would be.

Heavy Metals and Leather

The Professional Gentleman is not clad head to toe in leather, nor in metal. We are not motorcycle cops, nor are we knights, though at times we might feel like both. But in those areas of our outfits where leather or metal are located, those leather or metals should match.

Law #39

~

The Professional Gentleman shall have his leathers and his metals in his ensemble match or be bridged with matching colors/patinas.

~

Let me explain what I mean by way of example.

Imagine a Professional Gentleman in a pair of Crocket & Jones double monk strap dress shoes, with a Coach leather belt, a Salvatore Farragamo leather briefcase, and a Breitling Montbrillant watch on a leather band.

Brands to Know

Crockett & Jones: Established in 1879 by Charles Jones and Sir James Crockett in famed (for footwear, at least) Northampton, England, Crocket & Jones specializes in the manufacture of Goodyear-welted footwear and produces three collections (Hand Grade Collection, Main Collection, and Shell Cordovan Collection). These are shoes of the highest quality, reliability, and strength. Perfect for the Professional Gentleman.

Coach: Founded and still based in New York City, Coach is a multinational accessories behemoth. Originally known as a purveyor of all manner of leather goods, they have expanded, with mixed results, into outerwear, ready-to-wear, scarves, sunwear, and watches. The Professional Gentleman should stick to the leather essentials from Coach for solid, stylish quality belts, wallets, and bags.

Salvatore Ferragamo: An Italian luxury goods company that started in shoes, then expanded into leather goods, and now covers ready-to-wear for men and women, as well as eyewear and watches (under licensing agreements). Despite its size, this is still a family-run operation. I went to business school with James Ferragamo, the women's and men's shoes and leather goods division director.

Now, if the belt is oxblood and the shoes are light tan, and the briefcase is black, and the watchband is gray suede—the Professional Gentleman will look debauched. All of the aforementioned items of leather should match in color, or there should be a deliberate complementary contrast that is bridged by an item (or items) with both shades in it (a "Bridge"). So, if the belt and shoes are black, and the briefcase is your Bridge in oxblood with a black leather handle, then your watchband in oxblood is totally acceptable.

Indeed, it's pretty awesome. Obviously, all black leather is also acceptable, although less interesting or inspired. Like somewhat grubby distressed debt deals, it's high risk but high return when swapping leathers.

Ditto for your metal hardware. Try to match it or Bridge it. So, imagine the same Professional Gentleman described above. Ideally, his belt buckle, the buckles on his double monk straps, the casing of his watch, and the hardware on his briefcase, and the metal of his tie clip (if he's wearing one) would all be in the same metallic finish whether that is near black iron, silver, metallic gray, brass, or gold. Perhaps there are other metal surfaces or accessories like a ring or a metal bracelet or the metal details on a pair of glasses. Again, ideally, these too would match the same metallic patina of the other items in the Professional Gentleman's presentation. If there is a variety of, say, silver and gold, hopefully there is some Bridge between the two. As far as Bridge items in metal, typically a sports watch or bracelet offer the most metallic surface area, particularly given that the Professional Gentleman no longer wields a shield and sword and does not wear a cowboy-sized belt buckle. So it would be wise to have at least one watch or bracelet or other item which has components of two of your favorite metals—most useful is obviously silver and gold—to have an appropriate Bridge item with which you can pull other disparate metallic items together.

Ignorantia juris non excusat.

—12—

Functional Accessories

*"A lawyer with his briefcase can steal more
than a hundred men with guns."*
—Mario Puzo[1]

We are Professional Gentlemen. We work from the office, from hotel rooms, from airport lounges, from planes, trains, and buses, from home. We transport confidential documents and computers containing proprietary information wherever we go. We carry phones with critical contact information and access to our e-mail lifelines as well as our hopes and dreams of looking handsome. Our need for accessories has, arguably, never been greater, and yet this wonderful style opportunity is, unfortunately, lost on most. Designer Tom Ford talks about carrying a briefcase to school as a boy. While not a Professional Gentleman, he's undoubtedly one of the most stylish men alive today. Do you need more encouragement?

A Brief Case for the Briefcase

Lawyers commonly use briefcases to carry legal briefs to present to a court, hence the name. Your briefcase is not only a functional container for corpo-

---

1. The author of *The Godfather* (New York: G. P. Putnam's Sons, 1969), which became the epic three-part film saga directed by Frances Ford Coppola.

rate secrets; it also carries a message about you professionally.[2] Let yours be a well-expressed reflection of professional skill and standing. Think of your case as "trade dress" for your Professional Gentleman work product. Tiffany does not sell even the most modest of its silver baubles in anything other than their signature Tiffany blue box packaging. No matter what the item is, this trade dress enhances it and makes it special.

Law #40

~

The Professional Gentleman shall carry a briefcase.

~

I'm reminded of a merger closing involving two public companies. The impressive conference room was full of exceptional investment bankers, attorneys, and their clients. Accordion files spanned the long walnut conference room table with closing documents in each slot. Only a few items were missing. The room was jolly—awash with goodwill and anticipation for the moment of completion.[3] When the lawyer delivering the critical finishing pieces of the merger (original signature pages to several of the final ancillary closing agreements) placed his beaten Eddie Bauer canvas satchel on the closing table to draw the signature pages out, the very dowdiness of his "briefcase" sort of sullied the whole affair. Honestly, it was a palpable letdown to what should have been a pristine moment of congratulations, not only for the two companies but for the hapless lawyer with the crappy bag.

Your briefcase is a major purchase. You are not going to grow out of it. If well made, it will improve with age. Indeed, a good briefcase, like a good Professional Gentleman, should never look new or underemployed. The best ones are expensive, but worth it. Few accessories in your wardrobe show as

---

2. Lawyers commonly use briefcases to carry legal briefs to present to a court, hence the name.
3. Sadly, face-to-face closings are becoming rare. The speed and efficiency with which closing documents can be delivered and saved have made many of today's closing virtual affairs—taking place by an exchange of documents via e-mail or by Dropbox.

much commitment to your profession and dedication to your career's success and longevity like the briefcase.

Brands to Know

T. Anthony: Dating back to Theodore Anthony's launch of the brand in 1946, T. Anthony is known mainly for travel luggage but also makes serviceable work accessories with the same durable and basic stylistic qualities. Most feature locks, and the high-end versions in alligator are quite refined. Synonymous with the Professional Gentlemen of the Upper East Side of Manhattan, the longstanding flagship store still stands on Park Avenue and 56th Street.

J.W. Hulme: Founded by John Willis Hulme in 1905, J.W. Hulme Co. defines itself as a company of makers. The Hulme brothers started their business making military tents for both World War I and World War II. Made in America and crafted to last a lifetime, J.W. Hulme bags and leather goods are made with the finest of American leathers and meticulous hand craftsmanship. Describing true luxury as a beautiful piece that can be handed down, withstands fashion, and is immune to trends, J.W. Hulme is making heirloom bags with luxurious craftsmanship. The company is devoted to maintaining that craftsmanship and employs an apprenticeship system so that knowledge and skills of the trade are continually passed down to the next generation of artisans.

Jack Georges: A third-generation leather craftsman, Jack Georges started his eponymous brand in 1987, which features a number of reasonably priced men's business accessories. With their factory in New Jersey, many items are made in the USA. Jack Georges represents classic styling in conservative colors and finishes. The brand's Sienna collection represents its most stylish pieces.

Serapian: Serapian Milano (which has a larger women's accessories offering than it does men's) provides a more fashion forward briefcase at a luxury price point in both traditional and non-traditional colors (like blue, light gray). Known for a sleek profile and more relaxed construction, these items are a bit too sumptuous (not to mention expensive) for junior Professional Gentlemen, but can fit nicely once more senior (and confident).

I have had three briefcases virtually from the beginning of my career. All of them are capable and elegant. A brown leather case from T. Anthony with brass clasp, a black leather case with silver locking clasp that Barney's put out in the '90s (they likely still do), and a no-nonsense, very Bond-like, ZERO Halliburton metal case. All share some handy similarities:

1. All have locks (as a Professional Gentleman you are carrying confidential information, proprietary financial reports, and attorney-client privileged communications; the lock is essential—this should be abundantly obvious).

2. All are subtly monogrammed (this element also has a functional rationale if the case goes lost or, more commonly, is against several others unclaimed in a coat check), which just looks sharp and communicates how dearly you view not only the accessory but the items contained within it.

3. Not one of them has a strap that would allow me to throw the briefcase over my shoulder (because, quite frankly, then it would cease to be a briefcase and become luggage—and furthermore, who in their right mind would do this to their suit or odd jacket?).

4. All can fit a laptop, a few documents (100 pages or so), a couple of sections of the *WSJ*, and a few pens. You shouldn't need more room than this. More room strays from briefcase and into luggage, and you shouldn't need or want to take luggage into work unless you are traveling.

The leather cases have accordion bottoms, like legal redwelds, which expand if necessary. I now have a couple other briefcases too but honestly, a brown and a black case in leather is all you need

If you are involved in some of the highly confidential arts of transactional or litigation work, the metal case is a viable (as opposed to laughable) option. Just note that you'll feel a need to modernize your wardrobe a touch to harmonize things. But make no mistake, it is a bold entrance you'll make to covert business discussions in a slim fitting Gieves & Hawkes suit, black monk strap To Boot shoes with silver buckle (perhaps even Chelsea boots with side zipper?—I'm pressing), divers watch (think an aggressively metal Panerai), and high-end ZERO Halliburton briefcase. You can also get matching luggage, which is a pretty cool touch—but don't overdo it, or you risk straying into some form of ROBO-attorney ridiculousness.

Brands to Know

ZERO Halliburton: The ZERO Halliburton story began by creating the first aluminum travel cases. Globetrotting oil field engineer by trade, Halliburton was often disappointed with luggage that failed to protect his wardrobe and documents when exposed to the harsh conditions of extreme dirt, heat, and dust. Drawing upon the engineering knowledge of his staff, Halliburton guided the development of the world's first aluminum cases. Contemporary design, unsurpassed quality, and protection meeting military specifications define the essence of the company. Security, durability, and reliability were the top priority 78 years ago and remain the same today. As travel has changed, so has ZERO Halliburton. From adding a series of lightweight attaches and travel cases to the addition of advanced wheel systems, ZERO Halliburton has products fitting the needs of today's travelers. In addition, ZERO Halliburton provided slightly modified cases to NASA in 1969 to use on Apollo 11. The aluminum cases were used to safely carry moon rocks back to Earth.

To Boot: To Boot designer Adam Derrick has created many exciting casual styles that are modern, versatile, and wearable, as well as powerfully elegant new dress shoes for business and sartorial dressing. To Boot recognizes that a shoe is only as good as the materials it's made with and uses only the finest Italian and French calf leathers. The skins are hand selected and hand cut to ensure the highest quality products. From cutting to sewing to polishing, each pair of To Boot shoes is touched by over 200 skilled hands before it is finished. Adam styles his collection with his clients' varied lifestyles in mind. Menswear is so often based on enduring classics, Adam feels it is his job to rethink, refresh, and redesign the classics so that they work in any modern man's wardrobe.

Panerai: In 1860, Giovanni Panerai opened up his first watchmaker's shop, which served not only as a shop and workshop, but also as Florence's first watchmaking school. Panerai created both Radiomir and Luminor, paints designed to give luminosity to the dials of sighting instruments Panerai supplied to the Italian Royal Navy. Panerai watches played a huge role in assisting the frogmen of the Decima Flottiglia MAS in their operations during World War II. By 1970, the company ceased to produce watches for the military and focused its efforts on the civilian market. Panerai makes many of its watches as either limited or special editions, intentionally producing fewer watches than the market demands in order to maintain an image of exclusivity, which allows it to command a high price. Retailers may only receive a few limited-edition pieces each per year, and there are long waiting lists for popular models.

Wallets: Where's the Money?

The Professional Gentleman must recognize that he will pull out his wallet from time to time in front of clients (e.g., picking up the tab at Nobu, Il Cantinori, or Smith & Wollensky), as well as with colleagues (e.g., pulling out your ID to get into the office building, settling last night's lost bet, tipping the valet). As such, the Service Professional's wallet should, at a minimum, be presentable. Since, pursuant to Law #40, the Professional Gentleman shall carry a briefcase, his wallet should not be burdened by much. Don't overstuff it.

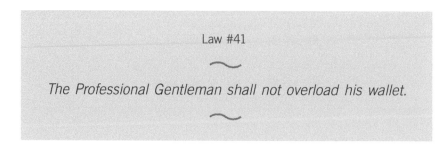

Law #41

~

The Professional Gentleman shall not overload his wallet.

~

Receipts, other people's business cards, notes, random phone numbers, or other scraps of information jotted down on paper all have a home—most likely in your smart phone or in your briefcase. Your wallet should carry no more than a little cash, credit and bank cards (really no reason for more than three of these),[4] health insurance card,[5] building ID, as well as legal ID (presumably your driver's license).

A thin wallet profile will not adversely impact the line of your suit. It will not hurt to sit on if it is in your back pocket—though if you are wearing a jacket, your wallet should always be in your breast coat pocket. Pulling your wallet out of your trousers' back pocket makes you look like a teenager. Pulling your wallet from your breast coat pocket makes you look like a man. Bi-fold or simple no-fold (so-called "minimalist wallets") leather versions work best. Both are sleek and simple. For the cross-border Professional Gentleman, the travel wallet is also essential. It is large enough to include your passport and keeps that important piece of identification with your other items.

Every Professional Gentleman should have a black leather wallet. It is the most versatile and formal and basic. If you are a stickler for matching your leathers, then also getting a brown leather wallet is also not a bad idea. Just note that transferring cash and credit cards and ID to a new wallet can be a bit of a pain. Personally, I leave cash in both. That way it is just a simple transfer of cards. A more daring alternative, and a caveat to the black leather wallet requirement, is a color your belt and shoes will never be, a color these items have no business being, like blue, purple, or red. These colorful versions can work and get you out of any concerns about being matchy-matchy.

As far as the patina of leather, the options are fairly broad. Alligator skin, ostrich, cordovan—you can get whatever you want. If you want to monogram your wallet, nice touch, go ahead. Just steer clear of leather wallets embossed with imagery, embroidery, or anything like the *Pulp Fiction*-inspired "Bad Mother Fucker" wallet.[6]

---

4. Unless you travel extensively and use multiple cards, but then you should be using a travel wallet which, as discussed later, is larger to accommodate your passport as well.

5. Evidence of health care insurance coverage is, of course, good for ensuring you are well taken care of if, God forbid, you ever wind up passed out in the emergency room, but you can also take comfort that if you are dressing according to the Laws, few doctors or hospital administrators will take you for someone unable to pay their hospital bills.

6. The BMF wallet is actually more common than one might think. Obviously, they are to be avoided.

While there are plenty of other materials wallets are made from, the Professional Gentleman's wallet should be leather. Canvas sports wallets or synthetic weaves, which usually have Velcro closures, are the domain of teenagers and backpackers and are forbidden.

Law #42

~

The Professional Gentleman shall not carry a sports wallet with a Velcro closure.

~

I will note here that the money clip is also a potentially acceptable accessory that substitutes for a wallet. My beef with the clip is that it makes getting out one's cash a bit of a conspicuous production. I've pressed a few Professional Gentlemen who employ money clips on this, and after a cross examination, they admit they always feel on show while using it. One accountant I know told me he always feels like he can only carry $20s or higher denominations lest he look not "flush."[7] But if you have no such hang-ups, try a money clip. Some do come with other Swiss-Army-like features making them useful (but beware trying to board a flight if one of those features is a serviceable blade).[8]

Business Card Holders: Case Closed

Like it or not, Professional Gentlemen are involved in the sales of services. As one of my early mentors put it, "Without clients, we are false esquires, overeducated men without anything to do." Given this reality, the business card is still a necessary tool of the trade. It is your calling card and your

---

7. I think that right there says it all. An accountant of all people should understand the utility of denominations below the $20 bill. Sad.

8. I did this once with an "EveryTool" I was given prior to a trip to Africa. I didn't realize there was a blade in it, and, while I flew from Tanzania to Amsterdam with the thing in my carry-on, I was stopped from boarding a flight from Amsterdam to New York. Good thing I was articulate and dressed, even while traveling so far, according to the Laws as I was allowed to proceed (without my EveryTool of course.)

name tag within the firm. For these reasons, these cards should be treated with respect.[9] Ramming your business cards into your stuffed wallet is a bad idea as they risk crumpling. And seriously, don't prospective clients deserve better than you scrounging around your wallet, waiting while you sift through your gym ID card, receipts, and random other papers (like other people's business cards) for your business card and then accepting this now potentially grungy paper representation of you and your firm? Juxtapose this with how gracious it looks when you smoothly remove a card case from your jacket pocket, it snaps open, and a immaculate card slides out into your hand. Capable and elegant.

The most common types of cases are metal card holders and leather card cases. Metal cases can be as expensive as budget allows for. Some are made of gold, rhodium, or a variety of other precious metals. But even the least expensive cases sold online usually have the ability of being engraved with a basic monogram, giving them a degree of personalization. Some metal cases will feature other quality accents like being two-toned[10] to ones with velvet or silk interiors.

Purchase what you like and what you can afford, but pay heed to the Laws regarding where you are in your career. A silverback litigation partner can, perhaps, have a whimsical card holder (say with an engraving of expressionist Edvard Munch's *The Scream* on it) while a junior associate should stay with something simple and tasteful—no more than initials. Make sure the hinges work and that the edges are not too sharp (lest your suit lining and breast coat pocket suffer rips as a result). Please also note that since some firms have moved away from traditionally sized cards to more bespoke shapes and sizes, you'll also want to make sure your firm's cards fit in a case before purchasing it.

Leather cases are another viable option. Some leather card cases are so thin, they slide effortlessly into even the tightest pockets, while others have metal interiors to support the exterior structure and better protect your cards.[11] There is a cornucopia of types and styles of leather cases available. From cheaper but serviceable leatherette (faux leather) cases, to exotics such as alligator, ostrich, or lizard, you can find leather cases to suit any budget in different colors, patterns, and qualities. Note your leather colors and

9. When presented, the business card should be held with each hand's finger and thumb on the upper corners and then presented over to the other person. This custom is still observed in Southeast Asia. It's sharp and reflects well on the presenting party.

10. Not particularly helpful as a metallic Bridge item, but it won't cause you consternation no matter what belt buckle–watch combo you might be wearing, so a good choice if you don't want to feel forced to have more than one case.

11. Leather-only holders may bend with minimal pressure just as your wallet can. Obviously this can allow damage to your cards.

consider whether you want more than one color to match the rest of your attire. If that seems too strenuous for you, consider getting a Bridge version that contains both black and brown (a combination that can be troubling to some) or a leather color that you will never wear as belt and shoes, such as blue or red.

The stylish amongst you will likely opt for more than one card case. And listen, *mon amis*, it is not too much bother. Stock all of them with current business cards and leave them near your wallet and keys. Take the one that suits your outfit for the day as you exit. Done.

Belting Homeruns

The Professional Gentleman will have belts to match the Foundational Five shoes. That is, he will have a simple black dress belt and a simple brown dress belt and a simple cordovan dress belt (the "Three Requisites"). With the Three Requisites, he has successfully paired his Foundational Five shoes. Any other shoes he intends to wear with a belt (as opposed to with suspenders or nothing securing his trousers) should also be paired appropriately. So assuming the Professional Gentleman's sixth shoe purchase is a light tan loafer, he should purchase a simple light tan belt.[12]

Law #43

~

The Professional Gentleman shall have the Three Requisites and a belt to match any other pairs of shoes he regularly wears.

~

---

12. It is often best to do this at the same time of purchase (assuming you are at a department store or large shoe retailer that also sells belts) as any sales person worth their salt will guide you to the proper match. I failed to do this with my first pair of oxblood balmorals and was forced to wait a full six months before actually being able to wear them as I did not have the proper belt.

This can become somewhat difficult with suede shoes or leather shoes in non-traditional shades. Yet for dress shoes it must be done. Coach, Andersons, and many menswear retailers have a full selection of proper belts.

Pairing your belt with more casual shoes, such as sneakers, is even more challenging. So much so that in some cases you might want to consider simply not wearing a belt if the pair of trousers you plan on pairing with sneakers fit you well. In general, the belt should share the same casual characteristics as the shoes. So don't wear a dress belt with non-dress shoes. Instead, casual shoes need to be paired with a casual belt. One problem here is that there really are not a ton of viable casual belt options. Most are canvas or braided leather or perhaps beaded belts. Another issue is you are further relaxing your overall outfit into casual territory—one more reason not to do it at all, but let's press on. The upside here is that unlike with dress shoes, you need not match the belt so much as you should coordinate it. So if I'm wearing white leather sneakers into the office (trust me, gentlemen, a rare occurrence—more like a hypothetical), I could pair them with a navy blue belt with white stripes from J. Crew. Similarly, if I have on Rag & Bone brown leather high-tops, I could pair them with a brown and tan braided leather belt from Il Micio.

Brands to Know

Andersons: Started in Parma, Italy in 1966, Anderson's is synonymous for high-end Italian leather belts and accessories. Still family-run, their products are manufactured entirely in their workshop by 50 trained artisans.

Il Micio: Tucked away on a small side street in Florence, Hidetaka Fukaya's workshop creates small leather goods and bespoke shoes that showcase his unique personality, blending old world craftsmanship with bright colors and interesting raw materials.

A few points on the functionality of the belt as a Bridge item. If you want more options with the other leathers in your ensemble (shoes, watch band, briefcase), the belt can serve this purpose well. For example, a dark brown and light tan interwoven braded belt builds a perfect Bridge between both colors, allowing you to wear either color shoe with it and be comfortable, similarly, with either color leather watchband or briefcase. So you can mix and match both shades. Less easy but also possible is to use the belt buckle as a metallic Bridge. The simple reason for this is that the buckle on most dress belts is small and rarely permits more than one metal to be featured. Please don't go for some of the more large outlandish buckles with, say, gold and silver in them. Buckles like that look like cowboy buckles. Unless you are in Texas doing nothing but oil and gas deals, the cowboy buckle should stay home on the range. Don't force the Bridge, mate. Building a Bridge on a shoddy foundation may have you falling into the drink—sartorially speaking.

The belt is rarely a statement accessory. Let's face it, for all but the fittest of Professional Gentlemen, our midsections are not where we want people's attention focused. Beaded belts have a business casual acceptability, particularly in the South, but must be worn, like most multicolored objects, with a high degree of caution and in otherwise muted surroundings. Also, matching belt to shoes can be challenging. Try to pair the main color of the belt's beads with the shoes of the underlying leather if it shows. So if you are going to wear that beaded golf belt on a summer Friday, make sure you do so with khaki chinos and ideally a solid white or blue dress shirt. Unless you have a simple tie that pairs nicely with one of the main colors in your belt, I'd probably avoid the tie altogether. So if the occasion calls for a tie, avoid the beaded belt, paduan.

Suspend Judgment

The advent of suspenders (or braces, as the English call them) as a Wall Street fashion statement in the go-go '80s has given suspenders a bad rep. We've all seen the image of the fiend with garish doodads on his suspenders or the bright red versions worn with MD contrast collar shirt and the dark pinstripe suit. As we know, that villain, while perhaps a style icon to many business school students, gets burned in effigy at Occupy Wall Street rallies. But suspenders are underrated. If more of us know how suspenders worked, how comfortable they can be, and further knew that you can purchase quite conservative pairs in muted, solid colors like tan and navy, more of us would wear them.

Brace yourself, while they may look overelaborate, suspenders are actually a basic and venerable element of pants suspension that works better than the belt and is certainly more comfortable. Albert Thurston introduced the first suspenders in 1822 as a basic undergarment in response to the high cut of pants at the time, which made a belt unrealistic. Basically, suspenders are a fabric worn over your shoulders to help hold your trousers up from the front and the back. This is important to consider when thinking about your silhouette; suspenders do not artificially interrupt the drape of your trousers. In most cases, this is a good thing. When the three-piece suit was the standard, suspenders were hidden from view and considered underwear. So when the vest went out of fashion, men preferred to hold up their trousers with a belt since showing their suspenders was tantamount to showing their knickers. And thus, through shyness was a fairly perfect sartorial device rendered obsolete. This makes no sense today.

Brands to Know

Albert Thurston: Founded in England in 1820, Albert Thurston has been making braces and armbands for kings, presidents, and royalty. They work just fine for Professional Gentlemen too, with muted colors and quality components.

Bretelle & Braces: Established by Rosanna and Mirco Merlo, the Italian brand Bretelle & Braces makes all of their products in their workshop by hand, showcasing their incredible attention to detail. They make both clipped and buttoned versions, the former of which I do not recommend for the Professional Gentleman.

By contrast, the belt is a rigid piece of leather that cinches around your waist by an uncomfortable square of metal. When seated (as we know most of us are most of the working day), the belt can dig into your midsection unpleasantly. Many Professional Gentlemen will, no doubt, admit that when settling into a long (read three to six full hours, seated) session of drafting a PowerPoint deck presentation or merger agreement, they have unbuckled for comfort.[13] By contrast, suspenders do not interfere with your midsection

---

13. It's potentially grounds for a sexual harassment claim if you meet with your colleagues in this sorry state of deportment.

at all when seated (or when standing). That's not all; whereas the belt draws attention to your stomach, suspender straps attractively frame your shoulders and torso. For all but the most absurdly fittest of Professional Gentlemen, this change in focus is welcome. Moreover, like a well-tailored jacket, suspenders help you auto-correct your posture to erect perfection. Their connection to your shoulders and midsection help you align these areas smartly. The Professional Gentleman needs to recognize the superior technology of suspenders and should wear them not as a fashion statement or a focal point, but as a subdued element that enhances the rest of his ensemble.

Law #44

~

The Professional Gentleman shall wear subdued suspenders to enhance the rest of his ensemble.

~

Suspenders can either be clipped on (which is not ideal) or buttoned to the *inside* of your trousers. If you take this more desired later route with your trousers, you will need to have buttons sewn into the insides of the waist. You may want to also seriously consider removing belt loops from the trousers. It looks way cleaner but it, quite obviously, prevents you from wearing the trousers with anything but suspenders. This is just a cost benefit analysis for you to go through. If you wear suspenders frequently, then removing belt loops makes sense.

Wear suspenders as follows. Match relative width of the suspender generally with the width of lapel and shirt collar. Regarding colors, think mellow but with contrast. So go with navy, tan, and black but wear in contrast to your shirt and jacket. Also match, generally, with your shoe color pallet as you would with your belt. Avoid novelty or statement braces. They don't match with much and can look downright absurd. Match the texture and formality of the material

with the rest of your look. So silk suspenders should be reserved for more formal circumstances. Grosgrain, jacquard, and Oxford cloth versions of braces are the most versatile and typically include some elasticity. They can be used with a variety of outfits. Leather braces are another option but look a bit heavy and lack the elasticity of more typical suspenders. They do, like belts, match more directly with a Professional Gentleman's dress shoes, but that is quite a lot of leather there, Maximus.

Glasses

Glasses are considered a necessary evil by many Professional Gentlemen. Silver lining: they do present a great sartorial opportunity to not only enhance the shape of your face, but also to look more studious and professional. Materials and colors for the frames should be traditional, like metal wire rims of gunmetal or copper, tortoise shell, or just black. Never wear red frames or white frames or really any color in the frame unless you want undue attention.

Suit your glasses to the shape of your face. A symmetrical oval face will take all styles well. But for other face types, there are some easy rules.

- If you have an oblong mug, give it a sense of balance with glasses that don't extend beyond the widest part of your face. Round or square frames will work well on you, but make sure you go for larger styles lest your features look too small.
- For the round face, you should favor angular frames that lend some much-needed definition. Your cheeks will appear slimmer with frames that are slightly wider than your face. Also, angular styles will help to elongate your temples and lengthen your face. Do not echo your spherical countenance with round frames, and best to opt for solid acetate styles to create a defined silhouette.
- If you have a square face, you have a lot of good options as long as you stick with the curves. Round out your blockheadedness with rectangular-shaped frames with softer corners. Avoid enhancing your sharp angles with angular frames.

- A diamond- or heart-shaped face will take many styles well. With a defined chin, wide cheekbones, and forehead, you can wear retro, rectangular styles.

Glasses for general vision problems that include distance issues must be worn at all times. Reading glasses, however, need only be worn when reading. The question then becomes, where does the Professional Gentleman place his reading glasses when not in use? This annoyance (and I can assure you as one who wears reading glasses, they are annoying when not in use or in sporadic use when I feel I'm sliding them on and off and on and off) is a sartorial opportunity. Since, as we've already established, glasses look aged, bookish, and serious, they can be a feature accessory. So, if you can stand it, wearing reading glasses on the bridge of your nose is best. You can use the glasses in this fashion as well as look up from them to view things out of the reading glasses, short range. This can lead to headaches in cases of prolonged use, as you will invariably end up looking through the reading glasses at things out of range, like a colleague when speaking to them. But the slant of the glasses on the bridge of your nose and the invariable arched brows and furrowed forehead when you look up to establish eye contact with others is a thing of Professional Gentleman beauty.

Brands to Know

Oliver Peoples: Founded in 1987, the company opened its first boutique in West Hollywood. In addition to being sold in Oliver Peoples boutiques and via oliverpeoples.com, the eyewear can be found in a variety of notable fashion boutiques and department stores throughout the world. Classic with some twists, these are great items for the Professional Gentleman. My reading glasses are all Oliver Peoples.

Moscot: This multigenerational, American eyewear brand was founded in the Lower East Side in 1915 by Hyman Moscot, making it one of the oldest local businesses in New York City. Recognized by its bold take on classic designs, and downtown aesthetic. The frames, eyeglasses, and sunglasses together are categorized under the MOSCOT Originals and MOSCOT Spirit Collections. Materials vary from acetate to metal and beta-titanium. Moscot has done brand collaborations with Johan Lindeberg, Todd Snyder, and Chris Benz, among others.

Robert Geller: This German-born American designer debuted his men's line in 2007, receiving the GQ/CFDA Best New Menswear Designer Award in 2009. His apparel line is progressive with distinctly Teutonic influences. I've worked some of his fine knits into my business casual arsenal. He recently launched eyewear with his typical attention to detail putting forth a high-quality high style but still very Professional Gentleman appropriate product.

Tom Ford: Founded by the former Gucci creative director and all-around Renaissance man, Tom Ford the brand launched in 2015 with eyewear as a component. Ford's penchant for provocative designs and his trademark aviators make this a brand for the bold Professional Gentleman with bold aspirations.

Selima Optique: This trendy eyewear brand was founded by Selima Saluan in New York. It has a distinctly whimsical French Mediterranean vibe, but several of the designs may appeal to the more youthful Professional Gentleman.

The other place to logically place your reading glasses when they are not in use is your jacket's breast coat pocket. If possible, placing the glasses inside the pocket with just one arm showing is preferable and most subtle and useful. Sometimes if there is also a hankie competing for real estate, there is not enough room to put the frames inside the pocket, in which case just a single arm can be placed in the pocket, or you can hold your glasses. In any event, our reading glasses should be ever at the ready. We are Professional Gentlemen; reading and perusing numerical data is a constant reality. When your glasses are in proper position, you look capable. When your glasses frame your face properly and are well designed, you look elegant.

Future's So Bright: How to Wear Shades

Sunglasses are sexy. They can make you look suave and mysterious. They can also make you look like a douchebag. There's something about not being able to see a man's eyes that is a bit sinister.[14] Accordingly, they are to be

---

14. Indeed, apparently judges in China's top courts would wear prescribed sunglasses in order to conceal their eyes while questioning witnesses.

approached warily by the Professional Gentleman. We want to look suave but also trustworthy. So one absolute rule for the Professional Gentleman is that his use of sunglasses must be purposeful:

Law #45

~

The Professional Gentleman shall only wear sunglasses outside in bright environments or while operating a vehicle.

~

Sunglasses are innately useful. They shield your pupils from intense light to aid vision when it's compromised by sun or glare. Using them in any other environment is disingenuous and smacks of trying too hard to showcase personal style and flair. So don't wear shades inside. And while Corey Hart may have worn his sunglasses at night[15]—he was not a Professional Gentleman.

Sunglasses are available in all shapes and sizes. In most cases, it is best to go with styles based on the old standards: Aviators, Clubmasters, Wayfarers, round Corbusier models, Persol 649s. Materials and colors for the frames should, again, be traditional, like gunmetal, tortoise shell, or just black.

Brands to Know

Ray-Ban: The original American branded sunglasses, Ray-Ban was founded in 1937 by Bausch & Lomb. The brand is best known for the Wayfarer and Aviator styles of sunglasses. In 1999, Bausch & Lomb sold the brand to the Italian Luxottica Group for a reported $640 million.

Persol: This Italian luxury eyewear is one of the oldest eyewear companies in the world, and, like Ray-Ban, is currently owned by the Luxottica group. (Hart Scott Rodino filing, anyone?) The name is derived from the Italian *per il sole*, meaning "for the sun." Formed in 1917 by Giuseppe

---

15. "Sunglasses at Night" from Corey Hart's debut album *First Offense* (EMI, 1982).

Ratti, Persol originally catered to pilots and sports drivers. Its trademark is the silver arrow (often referred to as the "Supreme Arrow"), and several of the company's glasses feature this symbol.

Garrett Leight: This LA-based eponymous brand founded in 2011 makes optical glasses and sunglasses with a California edge at a competitive price. The founder comes from a line of excellence in eyewear design, as his father was the founder of Oliver Peoples. DISCLOSURE: HBA represents the company.

Warby Parker: The venture capital darling that makes great wearing, reasonably priced glasses and sunglasses is a brand Professional Gentlemen should know beyond just the Harvard Business School case study *Vision of a "Good" Fashion Brand*.[16] Warby Parker makes virtually every frame a Professional Gentleman should wear.

In addition, try to suit your glasses to your face's shape. The same rules apply as with glasses, so I will restate those easy rules as they apply to shades.

- If you have an oblong face, balance it out with glasses that don't extend beyond the widest part of your face. Go for larger styles so your features do not look small. Aviator styles are a solid option as the tear drop silhouette helps to accentuate cheek and jaw bones.
- For the round mug, you should favor angular frames that lend definition.
- A square face should go with curves like aviator styles or rectangular-shaped frames with softer corners. Avoid enhancing your sharp angles with angular frames.
- A diamond- or heart-shaped face will take many styles well. If you feel your chin is weak, detailing like that on the classic Clubmaster or tortoise shell frames will draw attention toward the top of your face.

Ignorantia juris non excusat.

---

16. Christopher Marquis and Laura Velez Villa, *Warby Parker: Vision of a "Good" Fashion Brand* (Brighton, MA: Harvard Business Review, 2012).

—13—

Outerwear

"Dressing well is a form of good manners."
—Tom Ford[1]

Hats

There was a time when most men would not, indeed the Professional Gentleman wouldn't dream of, leaving the house without a hat on. The hat was a daily accessory. That ended 60 or so years ago. Cultural shifts in menswear style in the 1960s for the Professional Gentlemen were perhaps galvanized by style icon JFK, who started making public appearances *sans-chapeau*. This seems to have been the infraction point for hats, starting a trend toward general hatlessness.

The revival of the hat since then has had its fits and starts. I own a few, and on the streets of true walking metropolises like New York, London, or Paris, I don't feel conspicuous. I know men who wear hats all the time, but I have to admit they are known by many as "hat guys." I'd rather have you known as a "well-dressed guy" or just "that guy with style," so if you want to wear hats, do so with a touch of restraint and in compliance with the Laws.

---

1. Ford was the creative director at Gucci and Yves Saint Laurent before launching his eponymous line in 2006. A creative Renaissance man, Ford designs and maintains Tom Ford–branded menswear and womenswear, as well as having directed Oscar-nominated films.

Basic hat styles suitable for the Professional Gentleman include the following.

The Fedora

The classic men's hat. A fedora is typically creased lengthwise down the middle of the crown, then "pinched" near the front on both sides. Despite its mob associations, Indiana Jones (a professor of anthropology no less) as well as countless Professional Gentlemen of note have donned this hat. A proper felt fedora has a durable but malleable brim that can be "snapped up" or "snapped down" in the front or back, allowing you to mold the brim and achieve the desired snapped up back and sides and snapped down front. The more you wear it, the better the shape and fit will become. Brands like Larose, Stoffa, Pascal, and Borsalino offer wonderful lightweight felt versions that are crushable and therefore packable. Brown versions are most useful for the Professional Gentleman, but you can branch out to black or navy as well. Once comfortable in your fedora, you might even try a jaunty side tilt.

Brands to Know

Larose: Larose was established in 2012, working with professional milliners in the south of France. They started with making five-panel caps and eventually expanded the collection but remained committed to being classic and understated. The brand is focused on creating a product that is both timeless and chic.

Stoffa: Stoffa was created in New York City, making high-quality classic accessories. Stoffa believes in responsibly producing well thought-out items from raw materials. Stoffa has now expanded to include made-to-order outerwear and trousers. Products are priced reasonably considering the materials and craftsmanship that go into each product. DISCLOSURE: HBA represents Stoffa.

Borsalino: Borsalino was established in 1857 in Italy. The brand is most well known for its fedoras, which are both classic and iconic. The brand uses high-quality raw materials and expert craftsmanship to create products that will endure the test of time of both style and wear.

Homburg

The homburg is a more formal if less cool version of the fedora. It is also made primarily of fur or felt, and is a solid choice for a formal business look. The homburg has the same center-creased crown as the fedora, sometimes with the side pinches, sometimes without. The brim, however, is stiffer and has an upturned lip all the way around, which cannot be angled down. It is this last feature that can make the wearer look a little dorky if not worn with supreme confidence. Rap moguls have been able to pull this off, which translates to a high level of difficulty for the Professional Gentleman.

The Trilby

The trilby has a narrower brim, which is angled down at the front and turned up at the back, versus the fedora's wider brim, which is more level and flat. The trilby also has a slightly shorter crown than a typical fedora design. The trilby is objectively a cool-looking hat. A cool that has been appropriated and run into the ground by many, including boy bands of the '90s. Perhaps too trendy for the Professional Gentleman, but since it is a great design and it has been so appropriated as to likely once again be cool in truly cool quarters, I'm actually not going to turn you off of it. Being the contrarian, I'm fairly certain the subtle trilby is due for a revival of sorts. If you do opt for this hat, make sure to purchase a quality version in a muted brown and wear discretely.

Brands to Know

Goorin Bros.: Goorin Bros. was founded in Pittsburgh in 1895. The brand began with making classic styles of hats with an outdoorsy influence. They eventually expanded into sportswear hats, and they were the official head-wear of the VIII Winter Olympics. The company remains a family-owned operation focused on not only creating quality products but on building community with small hat shops across the United States and Canada.

Lock & Co.: Lock & Co. was founded in London in 1676 and is believed to be both the world's oldest hat shop and one of the oldest known family-owned businesses still in existence. They are known for creating the bowler/coke hat, widely recognized as the type of hat worn by Charlie Chaplin on the silent screen. The brand is very passionate about hats and believes in using the best fabrics to create hats with precision and personalization while also providing exceptional services to its customers.

Musto: Musto began in 1980 as a technical manufacturer of sailing knits created by a British Olympic sailor. The brand expanded to included products for equestrian and shooting sports. Musto is dedicated to creating products that are high quality, comfortable, and help improve the performance function of its wearers.

Porkpie

The porkpie has a narrow brim that is always turned up and a flat top with a circular indent. As with the trilby, the porkpie is a cool-looking hat and has been appropriated by hipsters who wear it with jeans and a black T-shirt at a pool hall.[2] Given its trendy association and turned up front (which in my opinion makes most wearers look less intelligent), I can't really recommend this hat for the Professional Gentleman. It is mentioned here merely as a caution and for fulsomeness. If you are committed to wearing it, Goorin Bros. makes a serviceable one.

Boater

The boater is a men's summer formal hat made of stiff straw. It's characterized by its inflexible brim, flat top, and wide grosgrain band (which is often striped).[3] The boater is quite formal and is worn most correctly with a blazer or a formal suit. This is a dandy's hat. As with the porkpie, I can't recommend this hat to the Professional Gentleman.

---

2. A notable porkpie in recent television history is worn by Bryan Cranston's character Walter White in *Breaking Bad*, appearing as his alter ego "Heisenberg."
3. This band should actually be solid black for a traditional summer formal occasion.

The Panama

This is the traditional brimmed straw hat of Ecuadorian (not Panamanian) origin. Traditionally, Panama hats were made from the plaited leaves of the Carludovica palmata, a palm-like plant, rather than a true palm. It is angled down in the front and angled up in the back with proportions similar to a classic fedora. The rarest and most expensive Panama hats can have many weaves per square inch (up to 2500). Known as *Montecristis* after the town of Montecristi, where they are produced. The best Panama hats can, purportedly, hold water, and when rolled for storage pass through a wedding ring. For the Professional Gentleman working in warm climates, the Panama hat is aces. Wear it with pride and comfort.

The Driving Cap

The driving cap traces its history from Southern Italy, Northern England, and parts of Scotland, and goes by way too many names.[4] Materials used to make the driving cap include tweed, wool, and cotton. The inside of the driving cap is commonly lined for comfort as well as for warmth. I wear wool versions of the driving cap from Lock & Co. and Musto Shooting, which make traditional English versions for the Professional Gentleman.

Umbrellas

The umbrella is an easy opportunity to look capable and elegant, or quite the opposite. Most men do not invest in the umbrella but rather purchase cheap versions, which never work well and end up collapsing during a downpour or in high winds. These cheap versions never add to the Professional Gentleman's style and often significantly detract from it. So invest in at least one good, properly constructed umbrella, and don't lose it.

---

4. It is also referred to as the ivy cap, cabbie cap, longshoreman's cap, cloth cap, scally cap, Wigens cap, golf cap, duffer cap, driving cap, bicycle cap, Jeff cap, Steve cap, Irish cap, and Paddy cap.

Law #46

~

*The Professional Gentleman shall invest in
at least one well-made umbrella.*

~

If you only have one good umbrella, it should be black. But once you see the wisdom of this Law and enjoy the efficiency and verve of your proper full-size umbrella, you'll want a navy blue version to better pair with brown shoes. From there you may stray into other colors, and assuming the umbrella is a well-made version, you'll still look capable and elegant. I have an orange London Undercover umbrella that I take out from time to time, and it never looks bad—even if there is no other orange in my ensemble.

The umbrella actually derived from the parasol, which was designed to shade the user from the sun, rather than to keep rain off the head. The parasol dates back to numerous ancient civilizations, but the useful umbrellas that the parasol gave birth to were articles for women only. Men stoically slogged around in large capes and wax overcoats for centuries with the umbrella being considered effeminate. Around 1750, a confident man named Jonas Hanway started using an umbrella. While he was initially met with ridicule, the inherent advantages in carrying such a useful article eventually held sway.

The full-sized umbrella is regal. It harkens back to a time when gentlemen had a cane or umbrella with them rain or shine. These were essential daily carry in the eighteenth century. Beyond use as a walking stick, there is the very real use of a sturdy hand weapon if you find yourself in an unwanted melee with thugs confronting you in the street or at the ATM. Granted, a black belt in jiu-jitsu[5] or a can of mace will serve you better. But for style points, it's hard to beat a well-crafted manual umbrella with a good, solid wooden hook handle for hanging over your arm when you need both hands. With its horizontal reach and dome, the full-sized umbrella provides proper coverage—not too little, not too much. It also performs well in the wind. The longer stems that form the spine of the machine keep

---

5. The IBJJF requires a practitioner remain a black and red belt for a minimum of 7 years. When a Brazilian jiu-jitsu black belt reaches the seventh degree, he or she is awarded an alternating red-and-black belt, similar to the one earned at the sixth degree in Judo. This belt is commonly known as the coral belt.

it sturdy in high winds and allow this type of umbrella to last longer than collapsible versions.

Brands to Know

London Undercover: Established in 2008 by designer Jamie Milestone, the brand treats the umbrella as a potential canvas for personal expression and has done brand collaborations with such un-British brands as Vans and Billionaire Boys Club. Nevertheless, London Undercover still puts out a high-quality product with subtle touches most Professional Gentlemen will appreciate.

Fox: Founded by Thomas Fox in 1868 on Fore Street in London, by the 1930s, Fox Umbrellas were being sold around the world. During World War II, the brand began making parachutes for British service members. From this experience, Fox Umbrellas introduced the first nylon canopy, effectively transforming the umbrella market. Fox is the genuine article, and for the Professional Gentleman who cares about such things, it will have him covered.

Francesco Maglia: This Italian craftsman produces umbrellas for many prestigious luxury brands but also puts out a select few handmade umbrellas from their small Milanese workshop. These beauties are works of art, and the price tag reflects it. For the discerning Service Professional for whom money is no object, bespoke umbrellas can be made to order.

Collapsible umbrellas are not preferred but sometimes are a necessity. They don't have the panache or the capabilities of full-sized versions, but they're compact, convenient, and tuck neatly into your briefcase. Most versions are cheap, which has given the collapsible umbrella a bad rep. In the case of well-crafted models, they are feats of engineering and will open effortlessly with the touch of a button. Capable and, if not as elegant as their full-sized cousins, pragmatic.

A note on using golf umbrellas. They are fine for golf. They are also serviceable in the back of your car for use in urban settings that are not pedestrian metropolises (e.g., Los Angeles, Melbourne, Frankfurt, Houston) where you might be going from your car into a parking garage complex attached to your firm's office building and during that time likely not encountering others nor the elements. However, the use of the golf umbrella in an urban center people commute by mass transit to and walk on the city streets of is detestable, repugnant, and loathsome. There are rules of umbrella etiquette on a city sidewalk, and one of the most fundamental of them is that your umbrella shall not be so large as to require others to remove theirs from covering themselves. To our shame, this is a rule that Professional Gentlemen breach a lot. Listen, I realize many of us play golf. I do too.[6] It's an important social lubricant for many of us and a reprieve from stress for others. We go to golf outings and get these decently made but absurdly massive golf umbrellas that could cover a family of refugees. Where some of us stray is to think those umbrellas should be permitted on city sidewalks. Forcing others to part in the wake of your Trump National oversized golf umbrella while you, safe and dry, strut down the sidewalk, talking into a mobile phone, is far from stylish. It's boorish and gives us all a bad name.

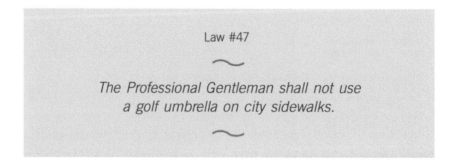

Law #47

~

*The Professional Gentleman shall not use
a golf umbrella on city sidewalks.*

~

Scarves

Scarves are *way* underrated. They are like a functional tie that can be removed. Since almost any scarf the Professional Gentleman will wear will be taken off once indoors, its transient nature gives you a wonderful and yet non-committal, temporary style opportunity. They can also punch up your outerwear, which unless you have more than six overcoats, is typically bland. Brands like Andrea's 1947, Drake's, and Colombo put out quality versions.

---

6. Poorly, to be sure. I'm about a 18 handicap.

Brands to Know

Drake's: This English brand was founded in 1977 by Michael Drake, Jeremy Hull, and Isabel Dickson. The Drake's collection focuses on quality men's scarves, neckties, and silk-printed handkerchiefs. Drake's products are completely handmade in a small workshop in the northeast section of London. Patterns are tasteful and elegant. Construction and quality are top-notch. From the ancient madder prints to modern wool ties, Drake's works closely with silk mills and printers to come up with timeless, yet continually renewed, collections.

Andrea's 1947: This brand has been manufacturing textiles the old-fashioned way, by hand on vintage shuttle looms, for over 50 years. The fineness of the cashmere and silk used is exceptionally high quality for the softest of neck accompaniment for the Professional Gentleman.

Colombo: This Italian company is the world leader in the field of cashmere weaving and specializes in the production of fabrics in noble fibers such as vicuna and guanac. They make exquisite scarves and knits with a flair all their own.

Regarding function—scarves are surprisingly versatile and can do an excellent job of protecting your neck from cold or sun. A thick wool scarf can keep your neck warm on a cold morning in Berlin, while a linen scarf can protect your neck from the sun and sand in Abu Dhabi. In addition, scarves add flair, especially when they introduce color to an otherwise mild outfit. As long as it doesn't compromise functionality, few will question even a brightly colored piece of cashmere that brightens up a Professional Gentleman's black Brioni overcoat or tan Burberry raincoat. So you get a bit of sartorial license with the appropriately worn scarf. Use it!

There are multiple ways to wear the scarf. Simply throwing one end or both ends of the scarf around the neck is the simplest configuration, which I probably do most of the time I wear a scarf. There are also various knots. The overhand knot (or Ascot) or the fake knot, in either case, should be done loosely. The French knot can be done a little tighter, and I usually opt for this when it's quite cold out and I want to get the scarf right up on my neck.

The scarf should be worn underneath your overcoat or, if you are only wearing a jacket, underneath the jacket lapel. It does not do much good sitting on top of your garments and makes you look like you are simply wearing the scarf for show or have no idea how to wear it properly. Not capable. Not elegant.

The Overcoat

If you live in a seasonal city or if it just gets cold outside on occasion, an overcoat—greatcoat or topcoat—is the only acceptable outerwear to pair with a suit or smart business casual odd-jacket ensemble.[7] The overcoat is made for either cold or specifically for rain and, if the former, is typically made of wool or cashmere (or a blend of the two)[8] or, if the latter, of cotton gabardine, Gore-Tex or some rubberized material. Wearing a parka or some other modern jacket, however functional, with business attire is simply not appropriate.

Law #48

~

When the weather requires it, the Professional Gentleman shall wear an overcoat over his suit or odd jacket.

~

---

7. While these terms are often used interchangeably, *overcoat* is most general (basically, it just means any long coat worn on top of something else) and top coat versus great coat pertain to the weight of the overcoat and how it will be worn. To wit: a topcoat is a lightweight overcoat, and a greatcoat is a heavy, double-breasted overcoat with some military history.

8. While way more luxurious, cashmere will show more wear, particularly on the collar, cuffs, and elbows. For my money, I think a traditional black cashmere overcoat to be worn for formal occasions is essential. After that, any additional cashmere overcoat is subject to personal preference.

I'm reminded of an M&A closing that took place at year end (to come in under the wire for certain tax regulations that were to take effect January 1). As the final documents came in and the wires were confirmed (and on my strong suggestion to the senior partner on the deal that it was the right thing to do), we announced our firm would be feting the client and their merger partners, and our bankers, and our banker's lawyers, and the merger partner's bankers, and the merger partner's banker's lawyers, and the merger partner's lawyer's, as well as the information agent and few other consultants who were hanging around, to a celebratory dinner and drinks at Sparks (a local expensive steakhouse that was about five blocks away from our offices in midtown Manhattan). Outside, it was 20 degrees Fahrenheit and lightly snowing. Thrilled with the successful closing of the deal and with my own pluck in helping to put together a well-deserved if relatively impromptu cabal, I rushed up a few floors to my office to get my overcoat. As I slid on my simple but tasteful, single-breasted, notch collar, wool, black Lord & Taylor private label overcoat,[9] the partner on the deal came in with a red puffer jacket from Izod or Land's End. He thanked me for my hard work on the deal and for suggesting this opportunity for some genuine and celebratory client interaction. If only I could have given him some candid and on the spot sartorial advice. As we all gingerly yet merrily walked over to the gathering—the bankers in DB overcoats of English or Italian provenance, the client representatives in proper overcoats, and even a paralegal in an inoffensive, some might even say sporty, camel duffle coat with wooden toggles and hemp loops, in each case, over their suits—the partner who had poured months of his life into the deal looked like an ersatz Professional Gentleman.[10] When the maître d' refused to look at him while we were sorting out our table and the coat check girl snottily accepted his pathetic jacket (all of this in front of the client), the vigor of the night as an opportunity to highlight his—and our firm's—accomplishments was diminished. It was a sad moment, easily avoided.

---

9. This was 1999, and a single black overcoat was all I could reasonably afford on my junior associate salary while still budgeting to pay off student loans. It helped that my girlfriend at the time was a buyer at L&T, and I got a massive discount. Nevertheless, this single coat, I recognized, was a significant purchase.

10. The New York Giants knit cap didn't help his sartorial cause either.

Brands to Know

J&J Crombie: Founded in 1805, the British company J&J Crombie produces top-notch overcoats in most styles. They are so synonymous with quality coats that the word *Crombie* is sometimes used by other companies to refer to their own coats produced in the style of Crombie's most famous three-quarter length (usually wool) overcoat (as any good IP lawyer would advise them to, J&J Crombie has been known to take legal action to prevent this trademark word from being used generically). Crombie has manufactured from several different mills in Scotland and England for over two centuries, initially at Cothal Mills in Aberdeen, and most famously from 1859 at Grandholm Mill, also in Aberdeen.

Private White V.C.: Private Jack White V.C. was awarded the Victoria Cross, the UK's highest military honor, during WWI. He also founded a clothing factory in Manchester, England, which has endured over the years and now produces a men's line focused on outerwear. The clothing line has a subtle nod to Jack's military legacy, with many items based on classic wartime pieces, updated with added functionality and detail for the modern man.

Mackintosh: Ubiquitous with the raincoat itself, in the mid-1990s the Mackintosh brand owner, Traditional Weatherwear, was on the verge of closing its factory in Cumbernauld near Glasgow. In a cheeky MBO, management acquired the company and established the traditional rubberized Mackintosh coat as an upmarket English brand in its own right. In 2007, Mackintosh was bought by Tokyo firm Yagi Tsusho. With the backing of its parent company, Mackintosh has continued to expand its reputation and marketing operations.

As the name implies, the overcoat needs to fit *over* your sport coat or suit jacket—comfortably.[11] A looser fit ensures the overcoat will fit over all

---

11. When purchasing an overcoat, wear a jacket because the coat has to fit on top of it. At sample sales, I've failed to follow this rule and had to endure lovely coats in my closet that I can wear only infrequently because they do not properly fit over most of my jackets. Closet space, at least in my apartment, is far too precious to make this mistake multiple times.

of your jackets and be comfortable. A trimmer fit will be more challenging to fit over your heavier jackets, but will look more stylish. An overcoat's sleeves need to fully cover your jacket's sleeve as well, obviously, as the shirt cuff, and ideally reach a little farther down.[12] I've seen men who do not understand this and have coats that show jacket cuff (which are properly fitted and hence show shirt cuff). That makes for challenging tailoring and pretty cold wrists unless you are wearing hockey gloves or you are planning on keeping your hands in your pockets.[13]

Overcoats can be rather long, with the full-length coat extending to just above the cuff of one's trousers, which provides the body full warmth. More typical is the knee-length version. Like with suits, the best coats have a sewn canvas, whereas less-expensive versions will have a fused canvas. A sewn canvas is unquestionably more enduring and long-lasting, whereas a cheaply glued interlining is likely to come loose after a few years, destroying the overcoat.

There are many styles to choose from, many with great legacies. Greatcoats feature quasi-functional military embellishment like epaulets, through storm pockets, sleeve straps, gun flaps, external belts, and D-rings. Other overcoats feature massive collars, sometimes contrasting with black velvet, hook and eye closures at the neck, and deep back yokes. After length, one fundamental stylistic choice is single versus double breasted. Double breasted reads more formal and more military. Single breasted, while certainly not casual, can more easily be worn unbuttoned, and is, as a result, more functional for the Professional Gentleman. Some iconic overcoat designs follow, but the Professional Gentleman must have at least two of these coats and, if the weather he lives in or travel frequently to demands it, he should have several more.

---

12. The sleeve of the overcoat should reach to the base of your thumb. Such that the sleeves underneath are covered completely.
13. In which case, no one would see your cuffs anyway.

Law #49

~

The Professional Gentleman shall have at least a serviceable Chesterfield coat and a trench coat.

~

The Polo Coat

The polo coat is not exclusive to Ralph Lauren (though they do make a fine version). This is a casual wool overcoat that is somewhat evocative of a bathrobe that is made out of camel hair.[14] Indeed, originally, the polo coat was designed as a wrap coat. Instead of buttons, it just had a belt. It's very preppy.

Not to be confused with the polo shirt, the origins of the coat are nevertheless the same. Originally a similar coat was worn by polo players in between chukkers[15] to keep warm. In the 1920s, the polo coat became particularly popular with Ivy League students, many of whom, as we know, went on to careers as Professional Gentlemen—taking their adoration of this garment with them.

As the polo coat became democratized, a button closure was added (the 6x3 double-breasted polo coat with a half belt, patch pockets, and an Ulster collar is the most common polo coat around today. But you can certainly find single-breasted versions, old-school ones with a full belt, more modern versions with no belt, eight buttons instead of six, and even peaked lapels.

---

14. Camel hair usually is used in its natural tan patina, but occasionally it comes in black, charcoal, or navy.
15. A polo match is 1.5 hours long and is divided into seven-minute time periods called chukkers. There are six chukkers in a high-goal match.

Brands to Know

Ralph Lauren: This eponymous brand began in 1967 with ties but has become *the* American mega lifestyle brand. Spanning apparel, home, accessories, and fragrances—the menswear offerings have always been core. Their lines, or "labels," are often a source of confusion. Purple Label is the top and the most expensive. Most of these items are tailored versions of classic styles. Quality materials, excellent construction. Black label is the most progressive of the menswear lines, with a slimmer "modern" cut and silhouette. Polo Ralph Lauren is the basic menswear offering.

Ermenegildo Zegna: This Italian menswear designer, founded in 1910, is world renowned for its elegant and finely made clothing and accessories. The largest menswear producer in the world as measured by revenue, Zegna sells fabrics, suits, neckties, and other accessories. Not only do they manufacture suits for their own labels, they also produce suits for luxury brands such as Gucci, Yves Saint Laurent, and Tom Ford. Its outerwear and overcoats are also sublime. This Italian design house maintains its tradition through family ownership and is currently being run by the fourth generation of the Zegna family.

The Chesterfield

The Chesterfield coat is a menswear standard that has been around since the mid 1800s. Arguably, the first true overcoat meant to be worn over tailored clothing outside and taken off when inside, the coat got its name from none other than the Earl of Chesterfield (big surprise).[16] Philip Stanhope, the fourth Earl of Chesterfield, purportedly wore an early version of this functional coat in the early 1800s, but it is his raffish grandson George Stanhope, sixth Earl of Chesterfield, who really put his stamp on it

---

16. Prior to the advent of the Chesterfield, most men wore coats that were cut close to the body and tailored to be worn both inside and outside. Taking one's coat off in public, even inside, before then would have been a gaffe.

in the mid-nineteenth century.[17] Typically found in sober colors like black, charcoal, and navy, the Chesterfield is a very versatile piece of outerwear suitable for everything from business casual to formal events. Unlike many military-inspired coats, the Chesterfield lacks waist seams or darts in the front. It has a single-breasted stance with fly front (which means the buttons are hidden under an additional extension of the coat's fabric. The lapel is notched and rather short. The waist pockets are straight and often flapped (though jetted pockets appear commonly, as well), and the chest pocket is usually jetted but sometimes even absent. The back of the coat is similarly minimal with a single vent and no other adornment. Given how long it has been around, it is a surprisingly modern-looking garment. One of my first overcoat investments was a navy blue cashmere Chesterfield from Ermenegildo Zegna which was on sale at Bergdorf Goodman. It wore so well, I followed it up before the next winter with a black version of the exact same coat and this time bought it full price (do black coats ever go on sale?). I've had both coats for two decades now. If your suiting preferences tilt towards the minimalistic, the Chesterfield is a good coat for you.

The Covert coat is the countrified dashing cousin to the Chesterfield. It was originally designed on the same basic structure but to be made out of distinctive tan-green Covert cloth for hunting and other outdoor activities.[18] To the basic Chesterfield design, the Covert coat adds lines of stitching at the cuffs and the hem (and sometimes on the flapped chest pocket).[19] It also adds a center vent and what's referred to as a poacher's pocket, which is a large pocket inside that the professional gentleman can use to store a small computer or the Wall Street Journal (instead of the small game it was originally designed for—much more civilized).

---

17. Grandfather Phillip cast a long shadow to be sure (erudite and well regarded by all—he's responsible for such quotes as, "Whatever is worth doing at all, is worth doing well," and "I recommend you to take care of the minutes, for the hours will take care of themselves.") Good grandson that he was, apparently George ran with a group of serious style mavericks (chaps like Count d'Orsay and, ahem, Lord Byron) who followed the great Beau Brummel's sartorial views on trading fussy Regency era norms for the more minimalistic Victorian style.

18. The name is apparently derived from the word for a thicket which provides cover for game—a "covert." Traditionally a very thick fabric of up to 30 ounces, it is now more commonly used in weights about half that amount, unless it's actually being used for riding through cold brambles.

19. This feature is said to be a vestige of the coat's sporting origins as the stitching prevented the Covert cloth from being pulled out from these exposed margins of the coat when caught by brambles while riding. Not sure if that will work for the Professional Gentleman in a taxicab door, but it does look smart and distinctive

The Trench Coat

It's hard to think of a coat with more of a hardcore functional legacy than the trench coat. The ubiquitous khaki raincoat we know as the trench coat today came about as an invention of Thomas Burberry in the 1870s. Burberry employed gabardine (a sturdy textile of woven long cotton yarn) as a novel fabric for his coat, which was both lightweight and breathable and yet waterproof when necessary (because the fibers shrink once exposed to water). The iconic belted Tielocken model of Burberry's coat with its thick notched collar gained prominence in the trenches of World War I, as modeled by the intrepid English Field Marshal Lord Kitchener.[20] As its military associations grew, so did its functional components, with elements like D rings,[21] gun flaps across the right shoulder,[22] raglan sleeves,[23] sleeve straps,[24] epaulettes,[25] and a double-breasted 5x2 button stance, completing the battle-ready look. Not so soldierly is the now common plaid lining.[26] But it does look nifty about town.

The trench coat is a three-season coat in many climates as it is breathable enough to be worn on warmer wet days but can also be layered (if one does not have a proper wool overcoat) to be serviceable in winter as well.[27] Obviously, on cold, rainy days it should be the Professional Gentleman's coat of choice. There are not many other acceptable garments that make you look like a capable and elegant professional as well as a soldier of fortune. It travels well and does not show creases if well hung (ahem) after a voyage. It is an essential and should be one of your first coat purchases.

---

20. Of English war propaganda poster "Your country needs you!" fame, Kitchener had a storied military career spanning several continents (such was the British empire at its height) as well as a fabulous mustache.

21. You can attach grenades to these. Really.

22. To help absorb a rifle's recoil, provided you are shooting right handed. For us lefties we are just SOL unless we go bespoke.

23. A raglan sleeve extends in a single piece up to the collar which makes it very easy to slip on.

24. To restrict the entry of water or keep the arteries in a soldier's wrists bound.

25. To hold your beret, gloves, or, if you are really in the trenches (or just working in Bejing or New Delhi), your gas mask.

26. A registered trademark for Burberry no less, the tan, black, white, and red plaid appears on everything from scarves, to tote bags, to underwear. But most trench coats have adopted this general mode of lining, if not in the same (or even similar) plaid lest they get served with a cease and desist notice.

27. Many trench coats come with a detachable liner.

Brands to Know

Burberry: This British fashion house was established in 1856. Burberry is most famous for its trench coat. Its coats were worn in the trenches of World War I by British soldiers, and for decades thereafter, Burberry became so much a part of British culture that Queen Elizabeth II and the Prince of Wales have granted the company Royal Warrants. Its main fashion house focuses on and distributes ready-to-wear outerwear, accessories, and even fragrances, sunglasses, and cosmetics. Its distinctive check pattern has become one of its most widely recognized trademarks.

Baracuta: This English brand began in 1937 by John and Isaac Miller in Manchester in rainwear. The Miller brothers were scratch golfers, and this played a large role in the design of the iconic short Harrington jacket, with angled flap pockets (ideal for keeping golf balls), and elasticized waist and wrists allowing for a free swing of the arms. Baracuta also makes snappy trench coats with a mod edge. Price points are reasonable.

Herno: This Italian brand was founded in 1948, in Lesa, on the shores of Lake Maggiore, by Giuseppe Marenzi and his wife Alessandra Diana. Raincoats are first and foremost in the Herno line, but cashmere coats are offered as well with a focus on double-faced items. Trench coats, field coats, and car coats are all well made.

The Paletot Coat and the Guards Coat

This French style of coat features a large, wide collar and lapels. It is double breasted and more form-fitting like a military coat. It features flapped hip pockets and an open breast coat pocket. The Guards Coat is similar to the Paletot but has welted pockets and a belted back. In charcoal or navy blue, either the Paletot or the Guards Coat is a handsome companion and works well for Professional Gentlemen who favor slim-fitting suits.

The Ulster Coat

This is typically a Donegal tweed, large, long, double-breasted overcoat, which sometimes, in old school versions, has a cape over its sleeves and even a hood (though these features were much more popular in the Victorian era in which the coat originated than they are today).[28] In keeping its country origins, the Ulster has patch pockets and contrast stitching along the cuffs and edges. Its notched lapels are rather large and can be folded over when buttoned up all the way. As a final functional touch, the Ulster has a belted back with adjustable buttons so you can change the amount of suppression around the midsection.

The Professional Gentleman opting for this overcoat will wear it with similarly countrified suits in tweed and heavy wool as it may look slightly out of place with more formal business attire.

The Pea Coat and the Duffle Coat

These short coats are rather casual, and Professional Gentlemen wears either of them best on business casual days as their abbreviated length makes them look and wear informal.

The pea coat was originated by sailors who needed their legs exposed to more adroitly climb the rigging of sailing ships. The coat ends just below the wearer's bottom, is double breasted, and made of a heavy melton wool. The pea coat features notch lapels and a large collar that should be worn popped up for stylish charm and a more arresting presence (as well as more warmth). The slash pockets sit high on the torso—for warming active hands. Very naval. Black and dark navy are the best colors for the pea coat.

The duffle coat is another informal coat with military origins. Purportedly, the coat was originally made from fabric from the Belgian town of Duffle.[29] The coat was associated with the Polish military frock coat developed in the 1820s, but was later adopted by the British and became popularized by its military officers in World War II. The duffle coat's characteristics include the large hood (sized to fit over a hat), yoked collar (constructed like a football jersey), and its toggle closures (made of wood, or in some more stylish versions, horn with twine or leather loops). Patch pockets complete

---

28. Indeed, the hooded caped version is most associated with Sherlock Holmes, the famous detective character of British author Sir Arthur Conan Doyle.
29. The same coarse black fabric the duffle bag was originally made of.

this short coat, which today is made of melton wool, usually less heavy than the pea coat. In camel, it's a great casual option, but it comes in all colors.

Brands to Know

Moncler: An Italian outerwear manufacturer founded in 1952 by René Ramillon, most known for its down jackets and sportswear. Moncler took its name from the abbreviation of Monestier-de-Clermont, an alpine town near Grenoble. In 2003, the brand was bought by the Italian entrepreneur Remo Ruffini. Moncler's flagship store is on the Rue du Faubourg Saint-Honoré in Paris. For the professional gentleman on a casual day.

Aspesi: Mr. Alberto Aspesi founded his eponymous label in 1969, which has become renowned for stylish wardrobe staples—particularly outerwear—all carefully constructed with a strong emphasis on fabric research and development. These items are for the modern Professional Gentleman looking for sleek outerwear with a non-traditional edge.

The British Warm Coat

A British warm coat is used to refer to a greatcoat that is double breasted, made of 100% melton wool and is, generally, taupe colored. The British warm first appeared around 1914 as a military coat for British officers, but Winston Churchill made it famous. The British warm should have peak lapels and leather buttons and usually, in keeping with its military heritage, epaulettes. It is also sometimes belted. It falls just above the knee. It is a fine-looking addition to any Professional Gentleman's wardrobe.

Ignorantia juris non excusat.

—14—

More Accessorizing: Timepieces/"Jewelry"

"Men are like Geneva watches with crystal faces,
which expose the whole movement."
—Ralph Waldo Emerson[1]

Most Professional Gentlemen are trained to avoid risk, and choice of accessories often reflects that propensity. Hence, as far as jewelry goes, most Professional Gentlemen go no further than a watch and (if they get married) a wedding band. However, throwing a random but inoffensive accessory into a conservative dress mix is a safe challenge I encourage you to take. This is particularly so when that item is small.

There was a corporate tax specialist I used to work with—a very senior partner at a major international firm—let's call him Robert Price III. He used to wear a little medal with tassels, which he kept in the fob pocket of his waistcoat and was attached to a chain as if it was a pocket watch. Now it *was* a bit odd, but it was also oddly cool. The medal was purportedly Robert Price II's from WWI, and when deep in his tax code ruminations, Robert

---

1. American poet born in 1803, Emerson was a champion of individualism and led the transcendentalist movement of the mid-nineteenth century.

would look out the window thoughtfully and stroke the tassels (which, I'll admit, was a bit unsettlingly odd).

Yet to some degree I've appropriated this predilection for secreted and unusual accessories. I have a silver keychain fashioned in the shape of an enigmatic and skeletal hand (please note my last name). The fingers of the hand extend over my trouser pocket and expose the Goth-like fingers to infrequent view. Now I realize that a little piece of peculiar jewelry like my key chain is a little outside of a typical lawyer's uniform. But it's been described in terms ranging from "very interesting" to "magnificently quirky" to me by people who matter (not only in the legal industry but also the fashion industry). And listen, in practice, the thing is actually quite functional.[2]

There are certainly other objects one can carry that are useful, even if rarely so. Amongst those with a preparedness bent (or obsession), everyday carry ("EDC") has become pretty mainstream.[3] A lighter, a tourniquet, a small high-powered flashlight, a Swiss Army knife, or other multi-tool are all easily ensconced within what you wear, but serve as talismans of your virility and preparedness. These items announce your readiness for anything. Clients like that in a Professional Gentleman.[4]

A vintage fountain pen peeking out of the breast coat pocket? Nice. Even better if there's a credible story behind it, like, "My grandfather used this pen for the bar exam," or "I used this pen to sign my marriage certificate." Arguably the most elegant and defining writing instrument, the fountain pen is a retro touch with pens from Montblanc, Visconti, and S.T. Dupont being the best. But they are a bit impractical and difficult to use. For most Professional Gentlemen, ballpoint pens present a better option. Constructed of high-quality materials such as precious resin, platinum, rhodium, silver, or even gold, they are often made by hand. A good ballpoint pen (one that you'd consider an accessory) can be had for

---

2. The hand keychain keeps not only my keys from bunching at the bottom of my pants (allowing the trousers to retain their line), but it also keeps my keys more accessible (for those quick dives into the locked file drawer).
3. See Rafil Kroll-Zaidi, "The Politics of Preparedness," *New York Times Magazine*, March 6, 2016.
4. I did this once with an "EveryTool" I was given prior to a trip to Africa. I didn't realize there was a blade in it, and, while I flew from Tanzania to Amsterdam with the thing in my carry-on, I was stopped from boarding a flight from Amsterdam to New York. Good thing I was articulate and dressed, even while traveling so far, according to the Laws as I was allowed to proceed (without my EveryTool, of course.)

few hundred dollars, but you could certainly spend in the thousands for limited editions. There are many well-crafted ballpoint pens produced by companies like Pelikan, Graf von Faber-Castell, Parker, Lamy, Waterman, Pilot, and Cross.

Brands to Know

Montblanc: In 1906, a German banker and engineer recognized the need in the market for well-made pens for the Professional Gentleman. Since then, the brand has been committed to producing high-quality and well-crafted fountain pens. The Montblanc star emblem became the brand logo in 1913, and it is still how the pens are often identified today. In the mid-1920s, Montblac began producing small luxury leather items and then entered into jewelry and watch market in 1996. The brand's philosophy is based on tradition, storytelling, elegance, and preservation.

Visconti: Visconti was founded in 1988 in Florence, Italy. Its craftsmanship is focused on passion, art, and technology. The inspiration for the Visconti pen clip was the Ponte Vecchio Bridge in Florence. The brand has remained true to its Italian roots, is proud to support the culture, and believes that their pens are the bridge connecting the heart to paper. Visconti is also the creator of the traveling ink pot, which makes refilling ink simpler and quicker.

S.T. Dupont: S.T. Dupont was founded in Paris in 1872. The brand aims to create products that stand the test of time. S.T. Dupont has always had many notable clients from world leaders, movie stars, and artists. Jackie Kennedy Onassis inspired the brand's first luxury ballpoint pen when she requested a pen to match her personalized lighter. The brand believes in the art of living well with quality products that are designed to last.

Pelikan: In the early 1830s, a chemist in Hanover, Germany founded his own color and ink factory, and in 1838, Pelikan was officially founded and began sales. The company logo was one of the first German trademarks ever recorded in 1878; the use of the pelican transpired because it was part of the current chemist's family emblem. Over the years, the brand grew to sell many different products and expanded to sell them all over the world. Pelikan remains committed to creating products that are solutions to its customers' needs.

Graf von Faber-Castell: Faber-Castell was founded in Germany in 1761 when Kaspar Faber began producing pencils. The luxury brand Graf von Faber-Castell launched in 1993, making pencils, pens, and select accessories, all crafted with high-end materials. Since 2003, the brand has been known for their extravagant Pen of the Year edition. The brand continues to create unique items by using premium woods and precious metals.

Parker: The Parker Pen Company was founded in 1888 in the United States with the determination to create a pen without ink leakage. Parker received a patent on the "Lucky Curve" feed pen, which drew excess ink back into the pen body when the pen was not in use. Beginning with this innovation, the company has remained committed to using technology to improve its products.

Lamy: Lamy was founded in 1930 in Heidelberg, Germany. The iconic Lamy design was created in 1966, named LAMY 2000. Lamy also created the "twin pen," which had the ability to convert with a twist into a propelling pencil. Lamy products embody their German design and engineering with a commitment to the ideal that form follows function.

Waterman: The Ideal Pen Company (now known as Waterman Paris) was created in 1883 in France. L.E. Waterman patented what was known as the first reliable fountain pen in NYC, named the Regular. The brand continues to pull inspiration from its Parisian roots and prides itself on creating unique pen designs that are both high quality and personal.

Pilot: Pilot is a Japanese pen company based in Tokyo founded in 1918. The company expanded around the globe in the late 1920s. Pilot remains the oldest and largest writing instrument manufacturer in Japan. The brand has continued to focus on making writing a pleasure to its customers by offering a range of products to suit all of the various writing needs.

Cross: Cross was established in 1846 in Providence, Rhode Island. In the 1940s, Cross became known for their custom personalization services. Founded by artists and jewelry makers, the brand has remained committed to design and aesthetic. Under President Bill Clinton, the Cross Townsend pen became the official pen of US presidents, and a Cross–White House program was established.

So are there boundaries here? Sure. Similar to the Law on patterns, I wouldn't advocate having more than one whimsical accessory going at once. Also importantly, I wouldn't ever make the accessory a focal point. I'd also encourage you to have it be actually useful in some practical, even if improbable, way or to have some personal connection to the item. But within those limits, I think you can show some real character. There is a Law here:

Law #50

~

The Professional Gentleman shall not have more than a single whimsical accessory or EDC on his person at one time, and such item should (i) have a personal connection to him and/or (ii) be notionally a useful item.

~

Watch Me Now

Of course wrist watches are by far the most acceptable piece of male jewelry (beyond the wedding ring) that a Professional Gentleman can wear. To most people, your wrist looks bare without a watch. I know this because as a left-handed gent, I wear my watch, unlike most people, on my left wrist. I've seen more than a few people gaze at my right wrist with a puzzled stare at the lack of a watch there. Now part of this is due to the fact that many Professional Gentlemen, indeed, many people, size you up by assessing the quality of the watch on your wrist. I don't want you to fall into this trap, but I do want you to recognize it and pay heed to its impact on the Laws. Particularly the affluence ceiling.

Purchasing a good watch is an investment, and certain watches seem to denote membership to a club of good taste.[5] No matter what your views on the subject, a proper watch is an almost universal indicator of status and power. Admittedly, there is something profound about having a piece

---

5. Indeed, watch collecting—*horology*, to give its proper name.

of almost ancient technology on your wrist dedicated to the weighty task of telling us the time. Some might even say it shows a respect for time itself—a sentiment those of us who bill hourly can certainly relate to.

Brands to Know

Longines: One of the oldest Swiss watch-making companies, this brand was founded by Auguste Agassiz in 1832 and is currently owned by the Swatch Group. Its winged hourglass logo is the oldest registered trademark for a watchmaker. Known for classic elegance and technical impeccability offered at price points more accessible than Rolex, Omega, and their ilk. A good entry-level statement watch for the Professional Gentleman.

Timex: The Timex brand debuted in 1950, beginning the emergence of high-quality mass-produced watches. Their innovative spirit led to the creation of the Timex Ironman, the first sports watch, and the Indiglo night light, which allowed the watch wearer to view the time in the dark. Today, Timex sells a variety of affordable timepieces for men, women, and children, ranging from dress watches, to more casual timepieces, to sports watches. The brand aims to produce watches that are timeless, durable, simple, and on-trend while keeping their accessories modestly priced.

I think a few notes on what makes watches tick are in order here. The mechanism inside the watch that powers it is called the movement (also called a calibre). In modern watches there are a couple of types of movement. The first type is called quartz, which makes use of an oscillator, regulated by a piece of quartz and powered by a battery. Quartz movements are inexpensive to make and really the most accurate.

The second type of movement is called mechanical and for most Professional Gentlemen, this is the only acceptable way of powering a "proper" watch. Mechanical watches require the winding of a mainspring, which in turn delivers power to the watch. The mainspring can be manually wound (like the Omega Speedmaster) or by using the movement of your wrist—so called "automatics."[6] Several of the best watch brands produce in-house calibres, which are painstakingly hand crafted and exhaustively tested. They are truly marvelous feats of both engineering and workmanship technique.[7]

Watch snobs prefer mechanical watches because, let's face it, the watch is jewelry and in the case of the watch, it's not just about telling the time but *how* it tells the time. The process. The craftsmanship and detail inherent in that process. Consider that while a 1969 Ferrari Dino is not going to be as safe, reliable, or even comfortable as a brand-new Chevrolet Malibu, you will get from A to B in much more style in the Dino. The Professional Gentlemen following the Laws understand this distinction.

Law #51

~

The Professional Gentleman shall, when within budget, obtain a nice mechanical watch he is proud to wear.

~

Styles of watches vary pretty widely. I encourage you to collect a nice selection of watches within your budget. Minimalist timepieces are simplistic in nature and design. They are a popular choice since many of them are quite affordable. Referencing minimal Bauhaus design, these watches tend to be powered by quartz movements. They often have faces with no numbers at all but simply points of demarcation. Wear these with more modern suits and casual options as they will pair nicely.

---

6. Bear in mind if you take off your automatic watch, it'll eventually stop. Many will work for 36–48 hours before they need rewinding, while some models can go on for a full five days.

7. Other watch companies buy in ready-made movements from specialist manufacturers, which are used in many different, more moderately priced automatics.

Brands to Know

Larsson & Jennings: A new brand of affordable Swiss-made but English-designed watches with a minimalistic approach to design aesthetic and a vertically integrated business plan that is compelling. Great for the junior Professional Gentleman on a budget for an unassailable look. DISCLOSURE: my firm, HBA, represents Larsson & Jennings.

Mondaine: This Swiss brand has always been influenced by the simple precision of railway clocks. They offer several options for the Professional Gentleman; one of the best is the Mondaine Helvetica, which has minimalistic design with a bit of whimsy. Mondaine timepieces are affordable.

IWC: International Watch Co., also known as IWC, is a luxury Swiss watch manufacturer founded in 1868. IWC Schaffhausen is notable for being the only major Swiss watch factory located in eastern Switzerland, as the majority of the well-known Swiss watch manufacturers are located in western Switzerland. Not surprisingly, the lingua franca of IWC is German. The price points are *sehr teuer*.[8]

Now gentlemen start your engines. Sports watches are the most popular and come in three types: motorsport, aviator, and diving. Each "sport" has a manly and technical association—perfect for watch manufacturers to display often useless but exciting elements of technology and craftsmanship. Motorsport (or driving) watches have a chronograph complication—the stopwatch feature takes its provenance from motor-racing. Aviator watches can be similar but with more going on. The aviator watch conveys vast amounts of time-related information, which was essential for pilots before electronic navigation became a reality. Most aviation timepieces have a black face with glowing numerals and dials allowing them to be read in the dark. Diving watches also feature luminous dials and hands, as well as a unidirectional bezel. This device sits on top of the case and can be used to tell a diver how much time he has left—to breathe. All sports watches fea-

---

8. "Very expensive"—in German.

ture robust construction, usually of metal, and can come in steel to precious metals. Given their origins in masculine pursuits, they look like they mean business but are decidedly less formal than the dress watch.

Brands to Know

Omega: Founded in 1848 by Louis Brandt and based in Biel, Switzerland, the Omega brand has a long association with aviators, including the British Royal Flying Corps who chose Omega watches for combat units in 1917 (as did the American army one year later). NASA chose the Omega Speedmaster Professional Chronograph for astronauts for the first moon mission and all Apollo missions. Marketing gold. I own this watch and it's an envied possession amongst watchheads. In 1995, the brand formed a bond with 007, starting with the Pierce Brosnan Bond films and continuing today with Daniel Craig's Bond films. 007 has worn Seamaster versions from Omega.

Breitling: A Swiss brand associated with watches for aviators (the brand sponsors a "jet team" of aerobatic performers), Breitling has played a crucial role in the advancement of the wrist chronograph since 1884 and fits certified chronometers in all models. These are typically bold watches. They now have an affiliation with Bentley (the Bentley Supersport B55) and have become a tad too "high-octane" for my tastes, but Breitling's are quite noticeable, and given their luxury price point, many men prefer that.

Tudor: Considered the ugly stepchild of the Rolex by watch snobs and insecure people, Tudor is actually a sub-brand of Rolex—a diffusion brand at a lower price point. The Swiss Montres Tudor SA has designed, manufactured, and marketed Tudor watches since 1946. Since 2015, however, Tudor has begun to manufacture watches with in-house movements. Tudor discontinued sales of Tudor-branded watches in the United States in 2004 but returned in 2013.

Dressing up the most jewelry-like of timepieces, a dress watch is the most likely to be made from a precious metal. This timepiece tends to be understated. The typical dress watch will have a simple face with Roman numerals and a lack of technical adornments. In most cases, the dress watch is attached to a leather strap with a slim profile to better fit under a French cuff. Note that if you want your leathers to match, you should consider getting both black and brown removable leather straps. Many Professional Gentlemen find this to be a convenient excuse to simply get another dress watch so they don't have to swap out the straps.

Brands to Know

Patek Phillipe: A Swiss watch manufacturer founded in 1851. It designs and manufactures timepieces and movements, including some of the most complicated mechanical watches. It is considered by many experts and aficionados to be one of the most prestigious watch manufactures. Watch snobs will notice this on your wrist if you can afford it. Goals AF.

Blancpain: Since 1735, Blancpain has been contributing to the development of mechanical watchmaking, while conserving the traditional skills of its founder. Blancpain is now the world's oldest watchmaking brand. To weather the pricing pressures of industrialization Jules-Emile Blancpain had the idea to specialize in high-end watches. Blancpain, to this day, produces fewer than 30 watches per day and each watch is produced by a single watchmaker from start to finish.

A.Lange & Söhne: This German brand established in 1845 makes exceptional dress watches with their highest quality pieces receiving their "1A" designation. Mechanical movements, distinctive asymmetrical face layout, and sumptuous styling add high price point.

Mix and match watchbands on occasion to zing your color possibilities up. While extra metal and leather straps can be obtained, there can often be quite a process involved in swapping them out.[9] Canvas NATO varieties are way easier to switch and colorful striped versions can present a diverting seasonal alteration.

Cufflinks

Cufflinks are another obvious accessory choice for the Professional Gentleman. Please note, however, that because they are worn with a French cuff shirt (and always with a tie), there is an inherent degree of rank and formality implied by such a presentation. Cufflinks are a power indicator. Wear with caution and pay heed to the Laws if you are still rising up within the firm.

No matter what your standing is, avoid the large (nothing larger than a US nickel, please), the obnoxious (e.g., dollar signs, skull and crossbones), and the obvious (e.g., sharks, scales of justice). Also steer clear of wearing cufflinks with business casual garb, with more casual suits, or odd jacket combinations. Cufflinks and a French cuff shirt may look peculiar with these less formal outfits. Beyond that, you the Professional Gentleman can find a degree of self-expression in these small embellishments.

Silk knots in muted colors (not shinny) are my preferred cufflinks. They are also quite cheap and easy to store. Silk knots come in a wide variety of colors, which allow you to pick up on a color theme present in your shirt, tie, or hankie.

Brands to Know

Codis Maya: This English brand produces cufflinks with an understated elegance, designed for Professional Gentlemen who want to express a touch of individuality discreetly. Codis Maya has distinctive and definitive designs that take on geometric or floral forms, all enhanced by the patina of richly colored enamels.

---

9. This can be an arduous process, taking valuable time in the morning hours while getting dressed. It also can, over time, do damage to the exterior of the timepiece where the straps are affixed.

Deakin & Francis: For the Professional Gentleman who misses his toys, this storied English brand is like Christmas morning. The highly original designs of things like airplanes, cars, and dogs are carefully executed and beautifully delivered. As England's oldest family jeweler, Deakin & Francis has been manufacturing the luxury cufflinks since 1786.

Udeshi: Founded in 1999, this brand evinces the high design and thoughtfulness of its founder, Oscar Udeshi, who became the youngest elected chairman of the British Menswear Guild in 2008. The mother-of-pearl cufflinks in subtle natural configurations are a perfect pairing for the cerebral Professional Gentleman.

Jan Leslie: This eponymous American brand knows the Professional Gentleman as its founder is a former "Big Eight" accounting firm consultant. Best known for her vibrant hand-painted enamels and stunning semi-precious stone collections, her thrilling designs appeal to the partner/MD—unafraid to have Monopoly game pieces on his wrists.

Metal cufflinks can also look rakish, but unless the rest of your outfit can support shiny gold or silver details, go with more subdued metal tones. Gunmetal and brass work well. Please avoid precious gems. You will look like a fight promoter, not a Professional Gentleman. When wearing metal cufflinks, try to match them with your other metals. So don't wear silver cufflinks with a blue blazer with brass buttons or a gold belt buckle unless you have a Bridge item with both gold and silver in it. Storing and maintaining true silver or gold cufflinks can be a drag as they do need to be polished. But if you are into them, I imagine this process can be a satisfying pastime. Keep your cufflinks safe in a padded box for that purpose. The metals can be scuffed and the posts harmed by just dumping them in a bowl or ashtray. Proper storage is padded and allows each cufflink to be kept separate and safe.

Other Jewelry

Jewelry on men can be somewhat vexing. On Professional Gentlemen it can be downright disturbing. A term like *mewellery* is not in my style lexicon. Like most things, wearing jewelry is only appropriate with decorum and in moderation. In general, but let's make it a Law, the Professional Gentleman should not be found in business attire with more than three pieces of jewelry on his person (and this is including a watch and/or cufflinks):

Law #52

~

The Professional Gentleman shall not wear more than three items of jewelry at the same time.

~

So let's break down what is acceptable.

A ring is evident and gets noticed. It is on your hand, which, after your face, is probably the part of your body most people look at. Unless you are wearing "the one ring to rule them all" on a chain around your neck like Frodo, a ring will not hide under your shirt. When worn in abundance, rings can make the wearer look like he's part of a crime family. A wedding band is, of course, totally acceptable. This shows you are a serious person. You've made a commitment, a legally binding one no less, to a partner. It's a sign of adulthood and assurance. These are all positive traits to display for the Professional Gentleman. Also, considering that your spouse may have issues if you don't wear your wedding ring, best to wear it.[10] A class ring, okay . . . okay if you must, but honestly, to me this looks a bit lame. You are a Professional Gentleman for chrissakes; everyone knows you've been to college and grad school. Wearing a ring that displays this fact seems like unnecessary overkill. Don't be an amateur. Any other rings (other than some ring that serves as badass and unique evidence of being a *legitimate* sports champion, like a Collegiate Bowl ring, not some ring your intramural softball team all wore) are not advisable.[11]

---

10. A happy wife is a happy life.
11. Even then, I'd not advise wearing anything with a lower level of prestige than, say, the Sun Bowl or even the Cotton Bowl. The TaxSlayer Bowl or the Famous Idaho Potato Bowl could just serve as someone's punchline rather than cast you as a stylish former athlete.

Brands to Know

Miansai: Founded by Michael Saiger, who started his artfully discreet collection in 2008. One of his earliest pieces, a multiple-band bracelet that secures with an unpretentious hook closure, became his brand's signature. Crafted in the USA of fine Italian leather, precious metals, and custom-made marine-grade ropes, Miansai's designs transform raw materials into distinguished pieces suitable for the Professional Gentleman.

Paolo Penko: Master goldsmith, designer, and sculptor Paolo Penko creates unique pieces of jewelery entirely by hand at his Italian workshop. Penko draws his inspiration from the jeweler depicted in works by Florentine masters, while the fine craftsmanship of his pieces is reminiscent of the vaults, spirals, friezes, geometric patterns, and marquetry found in the city's architecture. Penko's methods are sourced from the Florentine goldsmith tradition, such as fretwork and engraving. He has worked with the Pope, yes *the* Pope. Divine stuff indeed.

Viola Milano: Known for their bracelets of stone beads, which pair surprisingly well with sport watches, Viola Milano also produces an extremely well curated offering of rep and printed ties. An Italian brand with a niche view, Viola Milano is not cheap, but is certainly distinguished.

A bracelet? Sure, fine, but be careful with wearing several, as this is perilous ground and a slippery slope. Subtlety is paramount; so nothing that could be described, even by an 85-year-old Episcopal priest, as "bling" should ever be on your arm. Those leather cuffs favored by the early Conan the Barbarian—no. A large gold ID bracelet—no. Small beaded, woven leather or understated ID bracelets are best.

A necklace? This is possible if kept tucked away and out of sight. Many men wear pendants for religious reasons. To this, I say, "God bless." Or if recently out of military service, wearing your dog tags would certainly seem appropriate and give you a certain swagger few Professional Gentlemen can muster. I'm not sure the door is open to much else, though. I pity the fool who does not heed this.[12]

---

12. In 2006, Lawrence Tureaud (aka, Mr. T) hosted a reality show "Pity the Fool," which lasted six episodes.

Brands to Know

Le Gramme: This French jewelry brand founded by Adrien Messié and Erwan Le Louër produces ethically minded simple pieces. Using recycled 925 sterling silver pieces, it secured a reputation for minimalist luxury. Continuing to embrace simplicity, the brand now also uses red gold to produce its clean-lined collection of bracelets. This jewelry is discrete and will not compete with anything in your wardrobe. For the Professional Gentleman who is not sure he can pull off jewelry, this is a good place to start.

Alexander McQueen: For you closeted (or hopefully open) Joy Division or Bauhaus fans, McQueen's men's jewelry offers a subtle and well-produced nod to Goth culture. Wearing a bracelet with understated skull embellishments made by such a well-respected fashion house gives you a viable excuse and presents a better product than you are likely to find at a Renaissance fair. Reasonably priced, if you've lost control again.[13]

Luis Morais: Founded in 2001, Brazilian jeweler Luis Morais is revered for his stylish beaded men's jewelry. Another brand with an edge thanks to the designer's signature skulls, but given the Brazilian bent and colors, this is more carnival than Goth inspired. Each piece is immaculately constructed from fine materials, including ebony, sandalwood, and gold.

Mikia: This Japanese brand was established in 1998 by Aki Mitsubayashi. Mikia produces unique pieces inspired by traveling. Their colorful beaded bracelets and necklaces bring a hit of flair to the Professional Gentleman's wardrobe.

I've no useful advice to offer you on ear or nose rings other than just—no.

---

13. Joy Division, "She's Lost Control Again," *Unknown* Pleasures (Factory Records, 1979).

There is, however, a wonderful carve-out from these general prohibitions which is:

Law #53

~

The Professional Gentleman may wear any jewelry actually made by his children or that supports some laudable social cause that the Professional Gentleman is actively involved in and can articulate the mission statement of.

~

I've used this proviso many times, permitting a number of colorful bracelets made by my son at camp or on vacation to become a whimsical, colorful, and meaningful part of my look from time to time.

Regarding materials, you may have noticed somewhat ironically that I did not mention any actual jewels in this section on jewelry. Precious stones are ostentatious and a brazen breach of elegance for a man. They look like you are trying to tell the world how rich you are, which is tasteless. Subject to the Client Inversion Qualification, please don't wear them. As with leathers (shoes and belts matching), metals should also match (with the exception of the wedding band). So, if you have a silver divers watch on, do not add a copper bracelet or necklace. In fact, if you can coordinate it, best to have a silver belt buckle as well.

Ignorantia juris non excusat.

— 15 —

Feeling Good Means Looking Good and Breaking the Laws

"Beauty is power; a smile is its sword."
—Charles Reade[1]

Being comfortable in one's skin (and clothing) only helps one look better and feel more stylish. This final chapter explores the apotheosis of your sartorial style—the general sense of well-being that comes from confidence in your presentation and the self-fulfilling cycle of affirmative self-image and personal style. Positive reaction from others and the feedback this provides helps boost confidence further. This confidence further enhances appearance. Fernando was wrong, darling.[2] It's not "better to look good than to feel good." You look good when you feel good, and the better you look the better you'll feel.

---

1. Reade was a nineteenth century English novelist and dramatist.
2. See Billy Crystal's *SNL* "Fernando's Hideaway" skits (debuted November 3, 1984—God, I am old) in which he parodied Fernando Lamas, who would interview various celebrities.

The Comfort Imperative

No man can be truly stylish if he is uncomfortable in his clothing. As we discussed *supra*, you should feel only marginally more restricted and uneasy in your business wear than you do in a pair of proper pajamas.[3]

Law #54

~

The Professional Gentleman shall feel comfortable and confident in his clothing if he is to succeed.

~

Honestly, gentlemen, this is paramount. It's hard to be confident when you are uncomfortable. If a man is not comfortable, his habits and bearing will show it, and his confidence will suffer. Far from looking stylish, he will look weak, his manner will be irritable, and his motion laconic, bordering on odd. This is not elegance. This does not convey capability. It is not style.

So fit, as discussed *supra*, is a foremost concern and requirement in your garments. I'm reminded of an embarrassing episode from my own early career. It took place in a parking lot near downtown Los Angeles—the City of Commerce (perhaps not so aptly named) to be precise.

Now this is not a typical backdrop for a junior corporate associate of a top New York law firm on an assignment in a hostile M&A transaction. But there I was. Our client was a significant stockholder in the target, which itself was a public company with corporate headquarters in the City of Commerce[4] and significant operations there. In order to disseminate information to all other stockholders to promote our client's unsolicited deal and the virtuous transformation it heralded (which involved the removal of several members of the Board of Directors and other changes to the status quo), I had been tasked with showing up at the target's headquarters in person and demanding the stockholder list.

---

3. Like the kind you might see in a bedroom scene from a movie from the '50s. Think Ward Cleaver in the morning.
4. An ironic name, to be sure, as not much commerce goes on there.

I knew the law on this subject.[5] I knew it cold. We were entitled to the stockholder list, but the particulars of when and how it had to be provided where not clear. In other words, the target's executives could make the list available to me in a potentially unusable form. So I prepared. I had another associate and a couple of support staff with me as well as, believe it or not, a large (certainly by today's standards—this was the late '90s) photocopy machine with which to copy the stockholders list in the event the company did not make a copy, nor made a photocopier available to me. It was approaching 100 degrees on a bright and blistering day in downtown Los Angeles.

I was young, complete in my self-assurance, full of righteous indignation, fully prepared and buoyant in the justification of my client's cause. I was also in an ill-fitting Hugo Boss fused suit with the armholes cut too high. Completing this ill-advised look was a too-jaunty Etro tie and Vaurnet sunglasses.

Brands to Know

Hugo Boss: This one is in here as a warning. Founded in 1924, this German eponymous brand originally focused on uniforms for Nazi Party organizations both before and during World War II. After the war and the founder's death in 1948, it turned its focus from uniforms to men's suits. Most Hugo Boss suits are fused and overpriced. The Professional Gentleman should avoid them.

Etro: Established in 1968 as a textile design company, Etro remains an Italian family business now producing a menswear line in addition to accessories. The company is best known for its unconventional "swirling" paisley-patterned designs. Too peculiar for many Professional Gentleman, Etro has always maintained its own odd perspective, yet their products are fine examples of Italian craftsmanship.

Vuarnet: This French eyewear brand is named after the alpine ski racer Jean Vuarnet, who won a gold medal at the 1960 Winter Olympics. Recently, the brand did a sunglasses collaboration with Rag & Bone.

---

5. Delaware General Corporation Law Section 220(b) provides that "Any stockholder, in person or by attorney or other agent, shall, upon written demand under oath stating the purpose thereof, have the right during the usual hours for business to inspect for any proper purpose, and to make copies and extracts from . . . [t]he corporation's stock ledger, a list of its stockholders, and its other books and records . . ."

Everything was, more or less, going according to plan as I was ushered into the target's waiting room to be provided with the stockholders list after a 30-minute wait in the parking lot and some terse words for everyone from the security guards to the CFO. But my body temperature, coupled with the uncomfortable fabrication and stance of my jacket (which I was dutifully wearing), was wreaking aesthetic havoc. I could tell I was sweating profusely, but what I could not tell was that I had actually perspired to such a degree that there were visible underarm stains on my suit. I was not comfortable, and my irritation only grew as the CFO and his finance and communications team stalled . . . and stalled.

I eventually got the stockholders list, but I did not cover myself in sartorial glory with my colleagues. My sorry condition actually gave the poorly dressed but nevertheless glib CFO of the target the opportunity to hit me with a parting shot of, "Mr. Hand, we are very happy to have accommodated your request without recourse to your photocopier. Please do your best to keep those documents dry."

Granted, this is a fairly extreme example. But my point is that without comfort, confidence is lacking. And if confidence is lacking, appearance necessarily suffers. Moreover, as we've seen, your garments, even the most formal of them, can be made to be comfortable. They can be worn with great comfort—and therefore confidence.

Confidence!

Caring about how you look isn't self-importance or narcissism. It is not some vapid pastime for dilettantes. Looking good is a basic form self-respect, and how you dress affords you a degree of creativity and self-expression. Your personal style is how you choose to put yourself out in the world. It is a wonderful opportunity, when done well and in accordance with the Laws, to give you confidence. Looking better and being more stylish helps one feel more comfortable in one's skin (and in life). Confidence is infectious and charismatic.

We know this intrinsically, but so few of us are able to put it into practice. There's generally so much in life and in ourselves to doubt. There is so much in our jobs as Professional Gentlemen to question. We are intrinsically prone not to trust we've arrived at the right answer—at the best answer—without dogged analysis. But in matters of dress, this can be folly. Certainly, you should take care in your sartorial selections and purchases; do your retail diligence. But once that all is done, you should trust what you've purchased and therefore what you end up selecting from your closet to put on for any particular day. Then leave for work and revel in your insouciance.

"Walk like you have three men walking behind you."

—Oscar de la Renta[6]

You've come this far (this is the final chapter, my good man). You know the Laws, you recognize their inherent wisdom, you'll implement them, and you'll look good. As we've discussed at length now, the Laws are anodyne. I'm not guiding you into self-embarrassment or career suicide. I hope and expect that by now you can very clearly see that. I'm guiding you to the safe mean. The sartorial Eudaimonia. You should be secure in the fact that by following the Laws, you'll look your best, you'll be dressed properly for the occasion, and that you'll be a man of style.

Positive Feedback Loop

My dear friend, menswear designer Luis Fernandez, once told me that style "is an enabler . . . both mentally and physically." I've never forgotten that. When you are confident, you walk tall, your head is held high, your posture is erect, your chin is out, your senses are vital—you look good. Your confidence is thereby additionally enhanced. As a result, you look even better, further fueling your confidence. Your assurance in how great you look is self-fulfilling.

How simple! How easy! How lovely and wonderful for the fellow in the advertisement who seems to be doing it "right." But we are smart. We are educated. We are Professional Gentlemen. We can't trick ourselves into this

---

6. *Que rico!* Oscar the Dominican-American fashion designer, who passed away in 2014, became internationally known in the 1960s for dressing Jacqueline Kennedy, and his eponymous fashion house continues to this day.

feedback loop of confidence/handsomeness. And one can't just fake it. It needs to be authentic to be so, and authenticity is enigmatic. It does not just spring out of nowhere. That handsomeness does not just fall over us like some warm blanket from the Gods. It has to be real.

So make it real! Christ, my lad, nothing of value was obtained without hard work. We know this from grad school. Get to it! Follow the Laws. Exhibit the best style your body, budget, and circumstances allow. As the inimitable designer Dianne von Furstenberg said, "The most important relationship you have in life is the one you have with yourself. And then after that, I'd say once you have that, it may be hard work, but you can actually design your life."

A man's sartorial choices represent a subtle vernacular about who he is as a human being. One's style is embedded in his appearance and how he holds himself out to the world. Clothing, then, is a coded delivery device for communicating one's self. For the Professional Gentlemen who unduly limits his sartorial choices, the semiotics of the observer become that much easier and uninteresting. In other words, a banal style communicates a prosaic self to the world. But now you have a map, you have a guidebook, you have the Laws.

I promise you that following the Laws is a worthy investment as it is an investment in yourself. Yes, it's an investment of time to absorb the Laws and to study and learn a small amount about the designers you prefer, the tailors you trust, the clothing you choose to put on, and the accessories you choose to use. Yes, it's an investment of money when purchasing clothing and accessories—particularly the quality pieces—and paying the tailors and handlers of it to keep it all in good shape. But listen, my good mates, my best chums—this is an investment in YOU. Don't short yourself, man. Go triple long on YOU. It will pay dividends over and over again in your career and in your measure of who you are as a man.

Creativity: Breaking the Laws

By now, I hope you've come to realize that there is still an immense degree of creativity that goes into the sartorial choices you make. There is the reality of the function of the garments you select to the task at hand, the weather and circumstances you will find yourself in for that day. And then there are the selections of color and pattern and texture and accessories that go to make up the elegant and capable and [insert other elements that are YOU] presentation you will make that day. It's actually quite instinctual. But it is also a glorious and thought-provoking equation to solve over and over again. Each day can be something new. Isn't that important? Sort of the very essence of life in a lot of ways? Variety being the spice and all of that.[7]

My hope and expectation is that confidence will eventually give you the ability, if not the outright desire, to flout some of the very Laws set forth herein.[8] Granted, this is best done later in your career, when you are more advanced and more grounded in your potency and standing at your craft and within your firm. As we've discussed, the Laws give you more leeway with more seniority. But done every so often, breaking the rules for a stylish Professional Gentleman is a true signal of confidence. It is the stylish gentleman's way of showing how confident he is. Again, confidence is paramount. If the critical tension between panache and ridiculousness is a narrow tightrope, then confidence is your balance bar. The more confidence you go out on that thin line with, the better chance you have of not plummeting to sartorial ruin.

Take for instance my real estate partner, Casper. He's a seasoned and very well-credentialed Professional Gentleman; an expert in the field of retail lease negotiation for fashion brands. It's a focused area, and he's one of the best I know at it. Knowing Casper as well as I do, I'm sure he would loudly agree with me. Almost as loudly as some of the trousers he chooses to wear when he's not suited up, which is actually pretty often. His services come at a high price, and he's worth it. He also dresses well, has a good tailor, knows fit, pattern, texture and, importantly, the Laws.

His station secure and his style in form, he's taken some liberties, again, particularly with his choice of pants: bright yellow, red pinstripes, plaids, Madras. And this is not while he's on vacation, but coming into the office or onsite at a store site. The odd jacket he pairs with these wild trousers are always muted as are, generally, the other elements of his ensemble. So while he's exhibiting sophistication in recognizing the balance necessary for these eccentric pants to work, he's also showing personality. He's colorful, and he's confident enough to know he's pulling it off or brazen enough to not care if someone thinks he's dressed like an ass.

---

7. Famous idiom attributed to William Cowper, an English poet with a bent toward reflecting everyday life and scenes of the English countryside.
8. Oh Oedipus! He who unwittingly (?) kills his father, Laius, and marries his mother, Jocasta. Based on the myth of *Oedipus Rex*, and later written as a play by Sophocles, circa 429 B.C.

Again, gentlemen, this kind of dressing is not advisable, it is merely *possible*. It should be a lesson in what you can do with confidence, and I've no doubt Casper feels great being himself. Who doesn't?

Listen, menswear *is* moving forward. Like many things cultural, the pace has been glacial. And as Professional Gentlemen, we are NOT on the forefront of this change. I'm not advising that you become a sartorial peacock. After all, while regal in bearing and objectively beautiful, the peacock can barely fly. But we can be on the periphery of this movement and thereby indulge in a few of the advances, in a bit of the chaos. The tectonic shift may be overdue. As GQ style editor Will Welch put it, "The fact that there was this really influential community, throwing Molotov cocktails into what was, for so long, such a stiff discussion [about menswear] just felt necessary. When you see a guy who looks like trends exploded on him, you can't help but mock him a little bit. But we all need that guy to pull the culture forward."[9]

Now you won't be *that* guy. You likely won't even be that guy's drinking buddy. But you *can* be a small and puissant part of the vanguard. We are Professional Gentlemen, after all. In many arenas, we help pull the strings that dictate global affairs, capital markets, and geopolitical events. I don't mean to get Orwellian on you at this late stage, but my point here is that we are influential, and our style will be heard. You are influential and your style, if you chose to create one, will be heard.

As I've said, caring about how you present yourself stems from a very natural place: pride. Moreover, it can be an extremely gratifying and creative endeavor to apply personal philosophy and aesthetics to yourself. As we reach our end and I take my leave of you, you should now have a sense that there is way of dressing that is secure and stylish. A way of dressing that can become an external expression of your inner refinement. "Vivid and in your prime, you will leave me behind."[10] I hope it gives you satisfaction, my brothers, as well as advances your career and enhances your earning capabilities. This is a noble, ever-evolving and lifelong project. Enjoy it!

---

9. Lauren Sherman, "Do Men Need GQ Style?" *Business of Fashion*, May 10, 2016, https://www.businessoffashion.com/articles/intelligence/do-men-need-gq-style.
10. The Smiths, "These Things Take Time," *The Smiths* (Rough Trade, 1980).

The Laws

1. The Professional Gentleman shall dress in a manner that is elegant and capable.

2. The Professional Gentleman shall always dress more formally than his clients.

3. The Professional Gentleman shall not dress more affluently than his clients.

4. The Professional Gentleman may have certain articles of clothing and/or accessories that are expensive relative to his clients'; provided, however, that these articles are subtle or hidden from view.

5. The Professional Gentleman shall dress less affluently than his clients; provided, however, that if his clients lack sophistication, he may dress more affluently.

6. The Professional Gentleman shall dress according to rank and seniority within the firm.

7. The intelligent and wise Professional Gentleman shall dress better than his peers.

8. The Professional Gentleman shall not be recognized as "fashionable."

9. The Professional Gentleman shall dress better than the professional he is opposing.

10. The Professional Gentleman shall appear confident about his clothing and personal appearance. Ideally, he shall actually be so.

11. The Professional Gentleman shall allocate the bulk of his footwear budget on the purchase of the Foundational Five.

12. Non-dress shoes shall not be worn as formal business attire by the Professional Gentleman.

13. The Professional Gentleman shall properly maintain his shoes.

14. The Professional Gentleman shall not wear black socks with brown shoes, nor brown socks with black shoes, nor white socks with dress shoes, ever.

15. The Professional Gentleman shall wear socks that cover all of his legs that might be exposed by his pant cuff lifting.

16. The Professional Gentleman shall not wear socks with "pop" too often.

17. The Professional Gentleman shall not wear certain garish pairs of socks, ever.

18. The first four suits of the Professional Gentleman shall be the Fundamental Four.

19. The four suits of the highest quality in the Professional Gentleman's wardrobe shall be the Fundamental Four.

20. The Professional Gentleman shall know the name of their tailor and treat them as a trusted advisor.

21. The Professional Gentleman shall maintain his suits in good working condition and treat them with care.

22. White dress shirts shall constitute the bulk of the Professional Gentleman's shirting inventory.

23. The Professional Gentleman shall have and maintain a good relationship with his cleaners.

24. The Professional Gentleman shall always wear his dress shirt tucked into his trousers.

25. The Professional Gentleman shall not wear a rep tie if it represents a university or club he did not attend or does not belong to.

26. The Professional Gentleman shall have many ties to choose from and shall mix them into his wardrobe.

27. The Professional Gentleman shall not wear a business suit without a tie.

28. The Professional Gentleman shall not exactly match his tie and pocket square.

29. Only after obtaining a blue blazer, tweed sport coat, and modest unstructured blazer shall the Professional Gentleman purchase more esoteric odd jackets.

30. The Professional Gentleman shall not wear deep-necked knits without a shirt underneath.

31. The Professional Gentleman shall own a pair of gray flannel trousers.

32. The Professional Gentleman shall not take "business casual" casually.

33. The polo shirt shall be worn to the office infrequently and under specific guidelines of business appropriateness.

34. The Professional Gentleman shall not wear black shoes with blue denim.

35. The Professional Gentleman shall not wear sportswear/gym clothing into the office.

36. The Professional Gentleman need not mix and match patterns and textures, but in doing so properly, he shall attain degrees of style.

37. The Professional Gentleman shall not wear just a single item with a pattern or texture that monopolizes his sartorial presentation.

38. The Professional Gentleman shall not attempt to integrate more than three patterns in the same outfit.

39. The Professional Gentleman shall not wear fabrics that are suitable for fall/winter together with fabrics that are suitable for spring/summer in the same outfit.

40. The Professional Gentleman shall have his leathers and his metals in his ensemble match or be bridged with matching colors/patterns.

41. The Professional Gentleman shall carry a briefcase.

42. The Professional Gentleman shall not overload his wallet.

43. The Professional Gentleman shall not carry a sports wallet with a Velcro closure.

44. The Professional Gentleman shall have the Three Requisites and a belt to match any other pairs of shoes he regularly wears.

45. The Professional Gentleman shall wear subdued suspenders to enhance the rest of his ensemble.

46. The Professional Gentleman shall only wear sunglasses outside in bright environments or while operating a vehicle.

47. The Professional Gentleman shall invest in at least on well-made umbrella.

48. The Professional Gentleman shall not use a golf umbrella on city sidewalks.

49. When the weather requires it, the Professional Gentleman shall wear an overcoat over his suit or odd jacket.

50. The Professional Gentleman shall have at least a serviceable Chester-field coat and a trench coat.

51. The Professional Gentleman shall not have more than a single whimsical accessory item on his person at one time, and such item should (i) have a personal connection to him and/or (ii) be notionally a useful item.

52. The Professional Gentleman shall, when within budget, obtain a nice mechanical watch he is proud to wear.

53. The Professional Gentleman shall not wear more than three items of jewelry at the same time.

54. The Professional Gentleman may wear any jewelry actually made by his children or that supports some laudable social cause that the Professional Gentleman is actively involved in and can articulate the mission statement of.

55. The Professional Gentleman shall feel comfortable and confident in his clothing if he is to succeed.

Playlist

- Yes, "Roundabout," on *Fragile* (Atlantic Records, 1971).
- Gang of Four, "Not Great Men," on *Entertainment* (EMI, 1979).
- The Four Seasons, "Walk Like a Man," on *Big Girls Don't Cry and Twelve Others* (Vee-Jay Records, 1963).
- Gerardo, "Rico Suave," on *Mo' Ritmo* (Interscope, 1991).
- Roxy Music, "Avalon," on *Avalon* (E.G. Records/Polydor, 1982).
- The Beatles, "Love Me Do," on *Please Please Me* (Parlophone, 1962).
- Arcade Fire, "Neon Bible," on *Neon Bible* (Merge, 2007).
- Modest Mouse, "Broke," on *Building Nothing Out of Something* (Up Records, 1999).
- The National, "All the Wine," on *Cherry Tree* (Brassland, 2004).
- The Talking Heads, "Warning Sign," on *More Songs About Buildings and Food* (Sire, 1978).
- Timbuk3, "The Future's So Bright, I Gotta Wear Shades," on *Greetings from Timbuk3* (I.R.S., 1986).
- Corey Hart, "Sunglasses at Night," on *First Offense* (EMI America, 1984).
- The Pixies, "Here Comes Your Man," on *Doolittle* (Elektra, 1989).
- Radiohead, "Everything in Its Right Place," on *Kid A* (Capitol, 2000).
- The Smiths, Johnny Marr and Steven Morrissey, "These Things Take Time," on *The Smiths* (Rough Trade, 1982).

- David Bowie, "Rebel Rebel," on *Diamond Dogs* (RCA Victor, 1973).
- Joe Jackson, "Look Sharp," on *Look Sharp* (A&M, 1979).
- Daft Punk, "Doin' It Right," on *Random Access Memories* (Columbia Records, 2013).
- Big In Japan, "Alphaville," on *Forever Young* (WEA, 1984).
- Joy Division, "She's Lost Control," on *Unknown Pleasures* (Factory Records, 1979).

Subject Index

Name Index

Brand Index

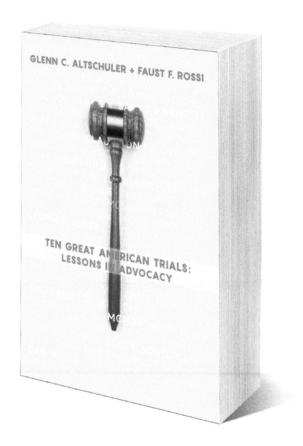

From the
American Bar Association

The Introverted Lawyer:
A Seven-Step Journey Toward
Authentically Empowered Advocacy
Lili A. Vasileff

To order 🌐 visit **www.ShopABA.org**
or call 📞 **(800) 285-2221.**

From the
American Bar Association

 ABA Publishing

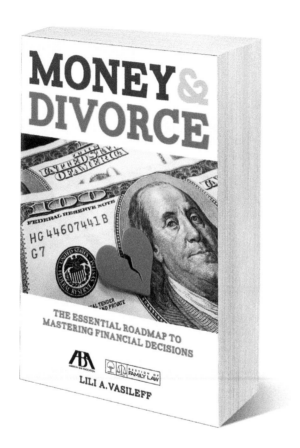

Money and Divorce:
The Essential Roadmap to
Mastering Financial Decisions

Lili A. Vasileff

To order 🌐 visit **www.ShopABA.org**
or call 📞 **(800) 285-2221.**

From the American Bar Association

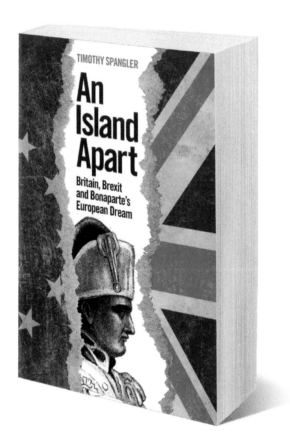